But CAN YOU TAKE IT?? MUFON beware:

Oh, the mockery, oh, the size of those rectal probes! And what about THIS: Chris Ryall knows the biggest secret of all—the fact that aliens smoke... a lot.

Now, back to the rectal business. I had a problem with his probes. He has erroneously used a design that is intended not for humans or even cattle, but for things like hippos and baleen whales. No human being could survive a probe the size of the ones depicted in this story.

I know they tried, Chris and Ben Templesmith. Of course they tried. They got all kinds of blueprints and information from Area 51—including some REAL inside information, and CAN YOU FIND IT??!

But those cats over there, you just have to watch them. Bunch of jerks, always trying to make their big-eyed friends look good. Here, the aliens only smoke two cigarettes at once. Try six, folks, and be warned, there is no non-smoking section aboard a UFO. (Of course, if you're a smoker, abduction is heaven. You can do a pack an hour, just on the blowby.)

Another thing, if you get abducted, don't be a moron. Bring beer! Right away, you're off the probe table and into the DRUG ROOM. Uh-oh! Bad! Uh, except John Law is about fifty light-years away, yes? You figure it out.

The secret of the little gray guys is that they are real devils. Or—oops, I'm not allowed to say that! Oh, no, fellas I'm sorry, my mind control was out of synch! Now, calm down. NO! NO! That thing only works on baleen whales! Gaaaaa....

Whitley Strieber
Summer 2009

Whitley Strieber's Website is UnknownCountry.com.

GROOM LAKE

CHRIS RYALL

BEN TEMPLESMITH

GROOM LAKE

Written by Chris Ryall

Art by Ben Templesmith

Letters by Robbie Robbins

Foreword by Whitley Strieber

Collection Edits by Justin Eisinger

Collection Design by Neil Uyetake

www.idwpublishing.com

ISBN: 1-978-160010-536-4   12 11 10 09   1 2 3 4

Groom Lake created by Chris Ryall and Ben Templesmith

IDW Publishing is: Operations: Ted Adams, Chief Executive Officer • Greg Goldstein, Chi Operating Officer • Matthew Ruzicka, CPA, Chief Financial Officer • Alan Payne, VP of Sale • Lorelei Bunjes, Dir. of Digital Services • AnnaMaria White, Marketing & PR Manager Marci Hubbard, Executive Assistant • Alonzo Simon, Shipping Manager • Angela Loggir Staff Accountant • Editorial: Chris Ryall, Publisher/Editor-in-Chief • Scott Dunbier, Edit Special Projects • Andy Schmidt, Senior Editor • Justin Eisinger, Editor • Kris Opriske Editor/Foreign Lic. • Denton J. Tipton, Editor • Tom Waltz, Editor • Mariah Huehne Associate Editor • Carlos Guzman, Editorial Assistant • Design: Robbie Robbins, EVP/S Graphic Artist • Neil Uyetake, Art Director • Chris Mowry, Graphic Artist • Amauri Osori Graphic Artist • Gilberto Lazcano, Production Assistant

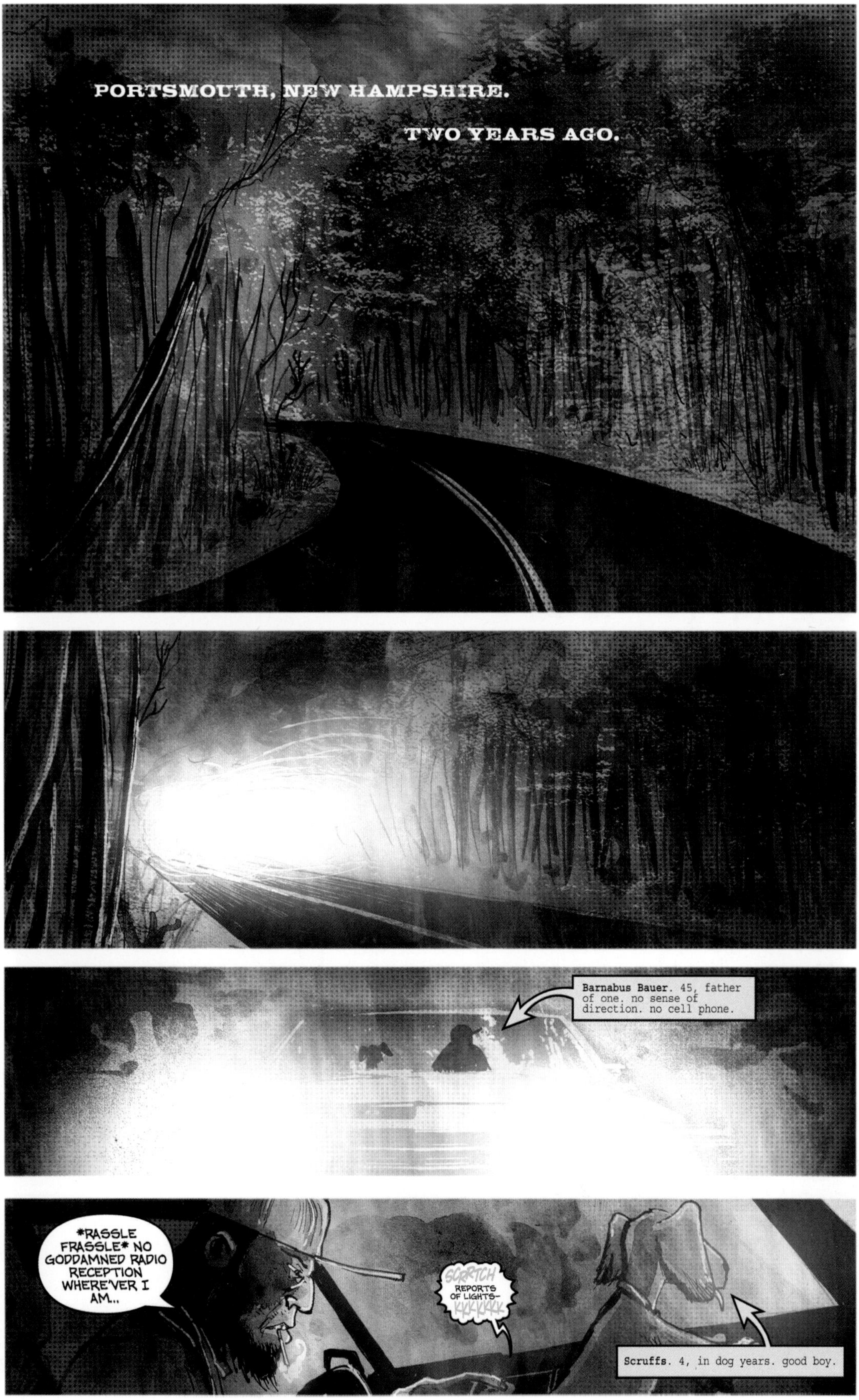

CHAPTER 1

PORTSMOUTH, NEW HAMPSHIRE.
TWO YEARS AGO.
Barnabus Bauer. 45, father of one. no sense of direction. no cell phone.
RASSLE FRASSLE NO GODDAMNED RADIO RECEPTION WHERE'VER I AM...
SCRRTCH REPORTS OF LIGHTS- KKKKKKK
Scruffs. 4, in dog years. good boy.

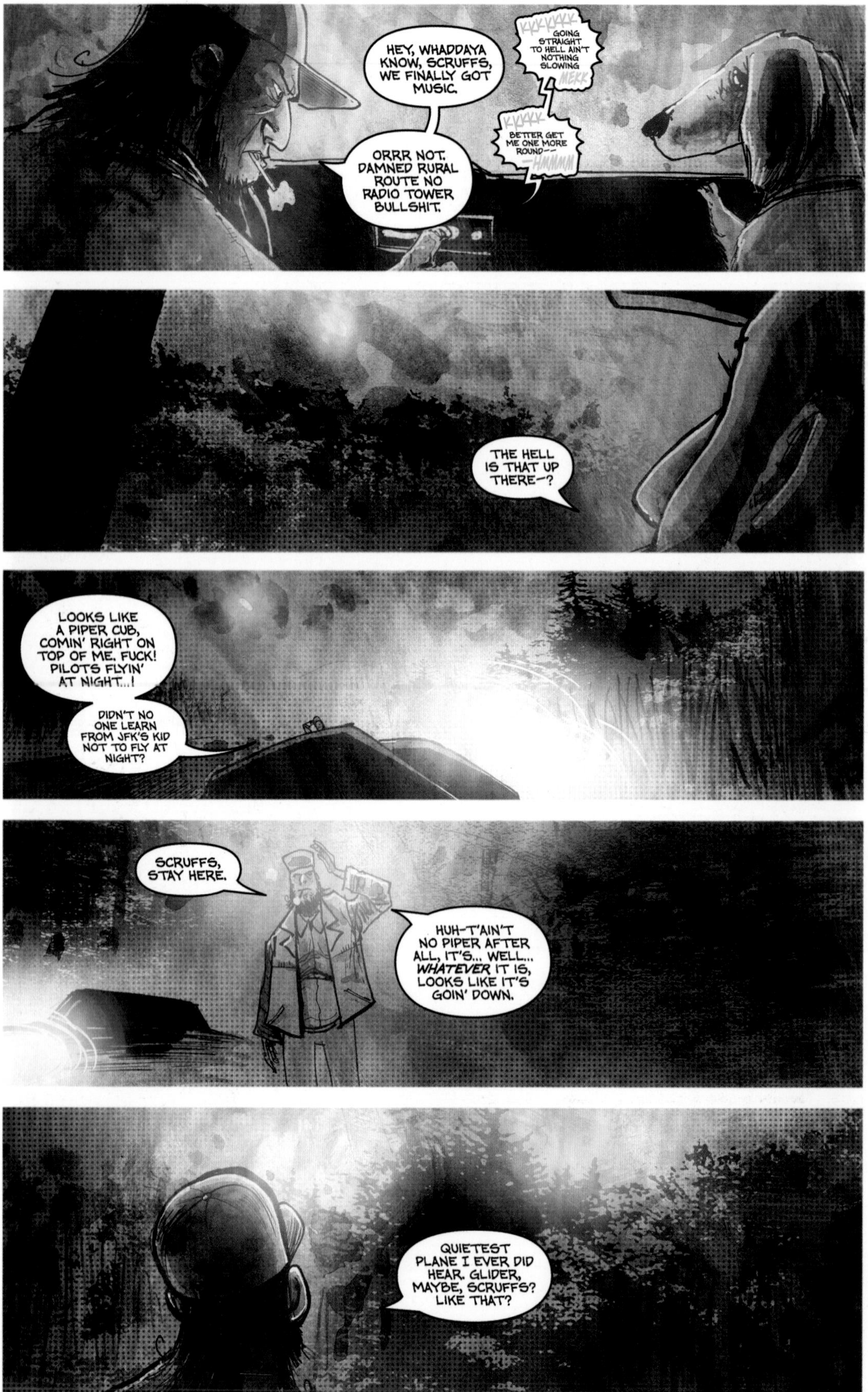
HEY, WHADDAYA KNOW, SCRUFFS, WE FINALLY GOT MUSIC.
KKKKKKK GOING STRAIGHT TO HELL AIN'T NOTHING SLOWING MERK
ORRR NOT. DAMNED RURAL ROUTE NO RADIO TOWER BULLSHIT.
KKKKK BETTER GET ME ONE MORE ROUND-- HMMMM
THE HELL IS THAT UP THERE--?
LOOKS LIKE A PIPER CUB, COMIN' RIGHT ON TOP OF ME. FUCK! PILOTS FLYIN' AT NIGHT...!
DIDN'T NO ONE LEARN FROM JFK'S KID NOT TO FLY AT NIGHT?
SCRUFFS, STAY HERE.
HUH-T'AIN'T NO PIPER AFTER ALL, IT'S... WELL... WHATEVER IT IS, LOOKS LIKE IT'S GOIN' DOWN.
QUIETEST PLANE I EVER DID HEAR. GLIDER, MAYBE, SCRUFFS? LIKE THAT?

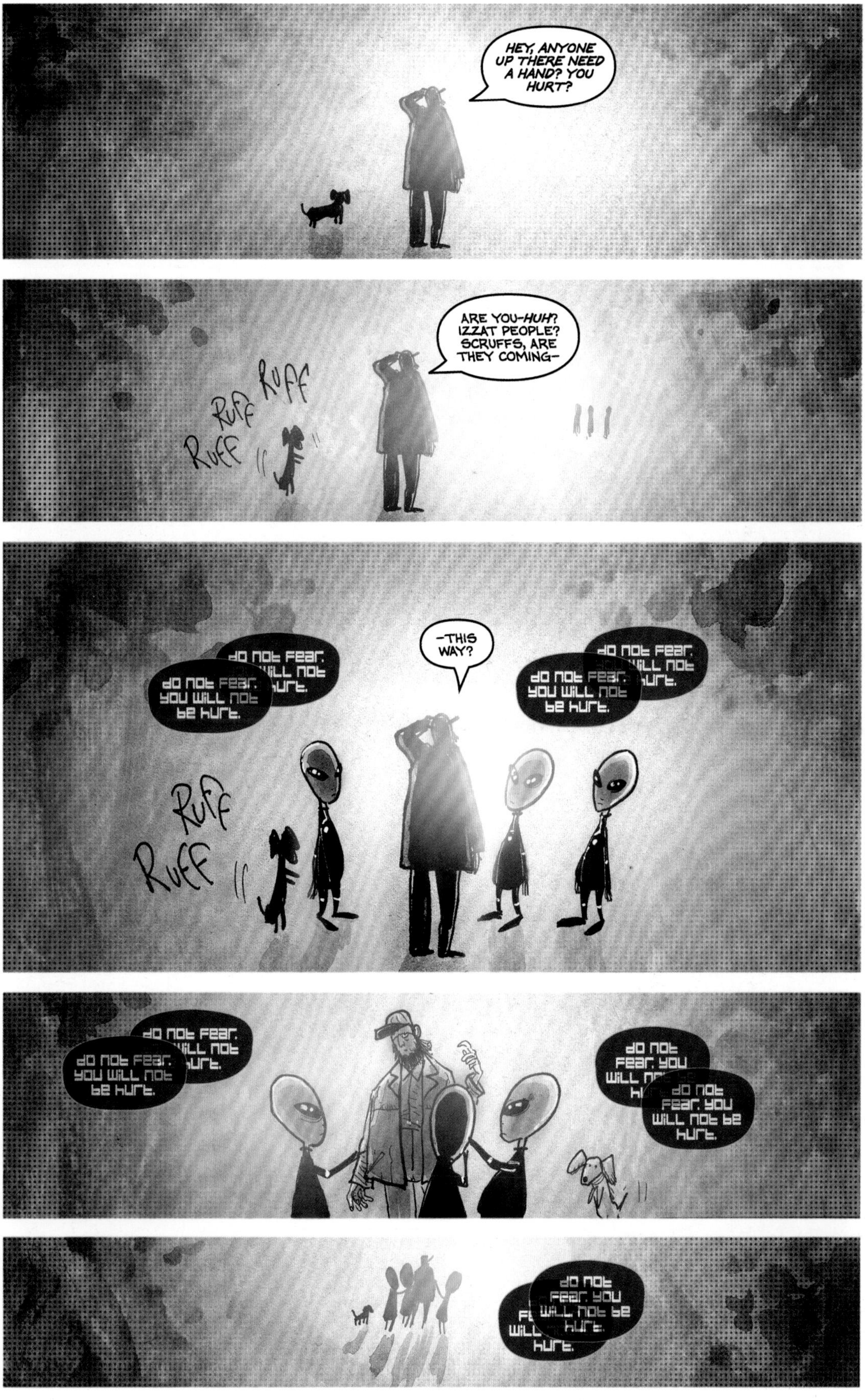

HEY, ANYONE UP THERE NEED A HAND? YOU HURT?
ARE YOU-HUH? IZZAT PEOPLE? SCRUFFS, ARE THEY COMING-
RUFF RUFF RUFF
-THIS WAY?
do not fear.
do not fear. you will not be hurt.
do not fear.
do not fear. you will not be hurt.
RUFF RUFF
do not fear.
do not fear. you will not be hurt.
do not fear. you
do not fear. you will not be hurt.
do not fear. you will not be hurt.

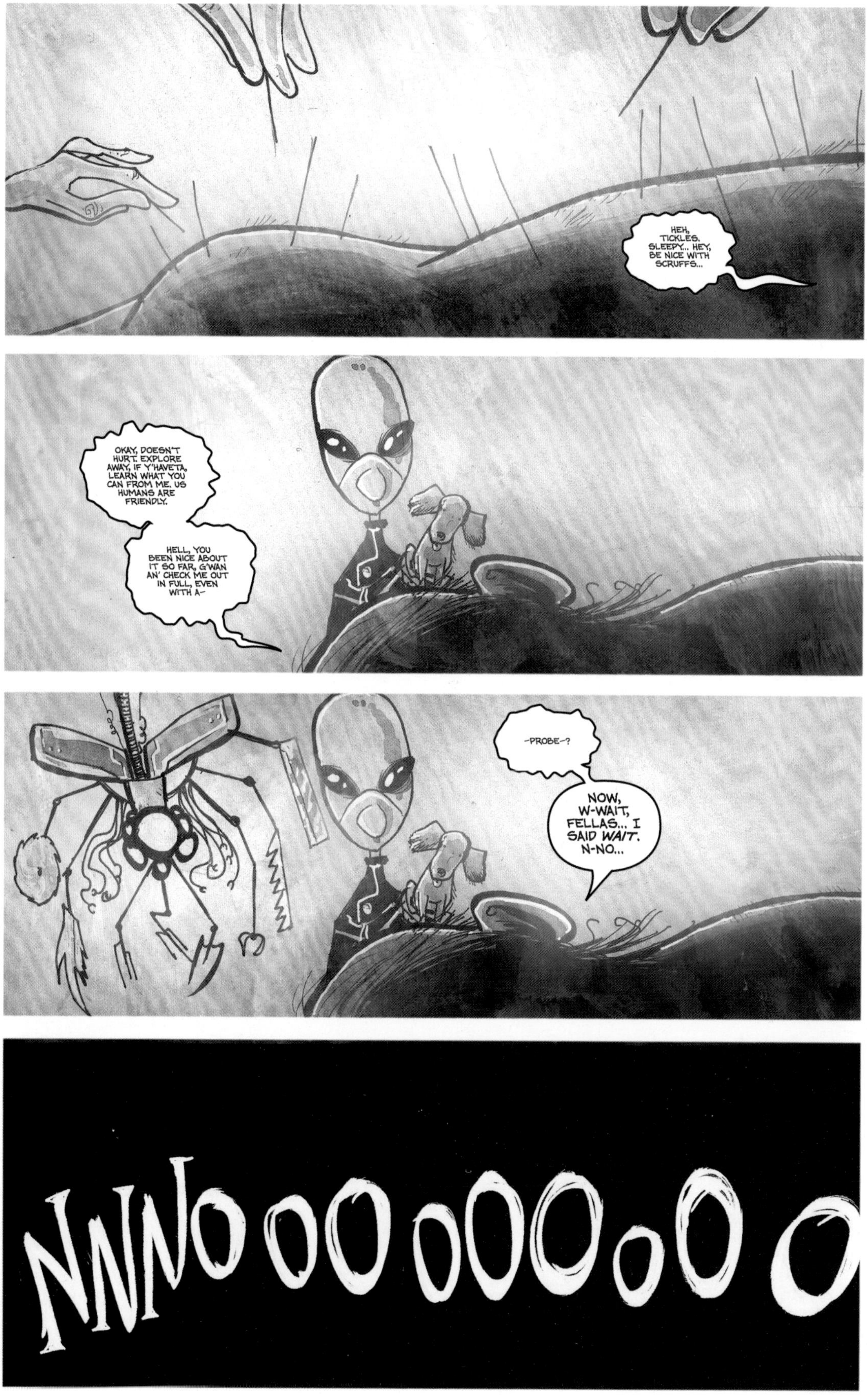
HEH, TICKLES. SLEEPY... HEY, BE NICE WITH SCRUFFS...
OKAY, DOESN'T HURT. EXPLORE AWAY, IF Y'HAVETA, LEARN WHAT YOU CAN FROM ME. US HUMANS ARE FRIENDLY.
HELL, YOU BEEN NICE ABOUT IT SO FAR, G'WAN AN' CHECK ME OUT IN FULL, EVEN WITH A-
-PROBE-?
NOW, W-WAIT, FELLAS... I SAID *WAIT*. N-NO...
NNNOOOOOOOOOO

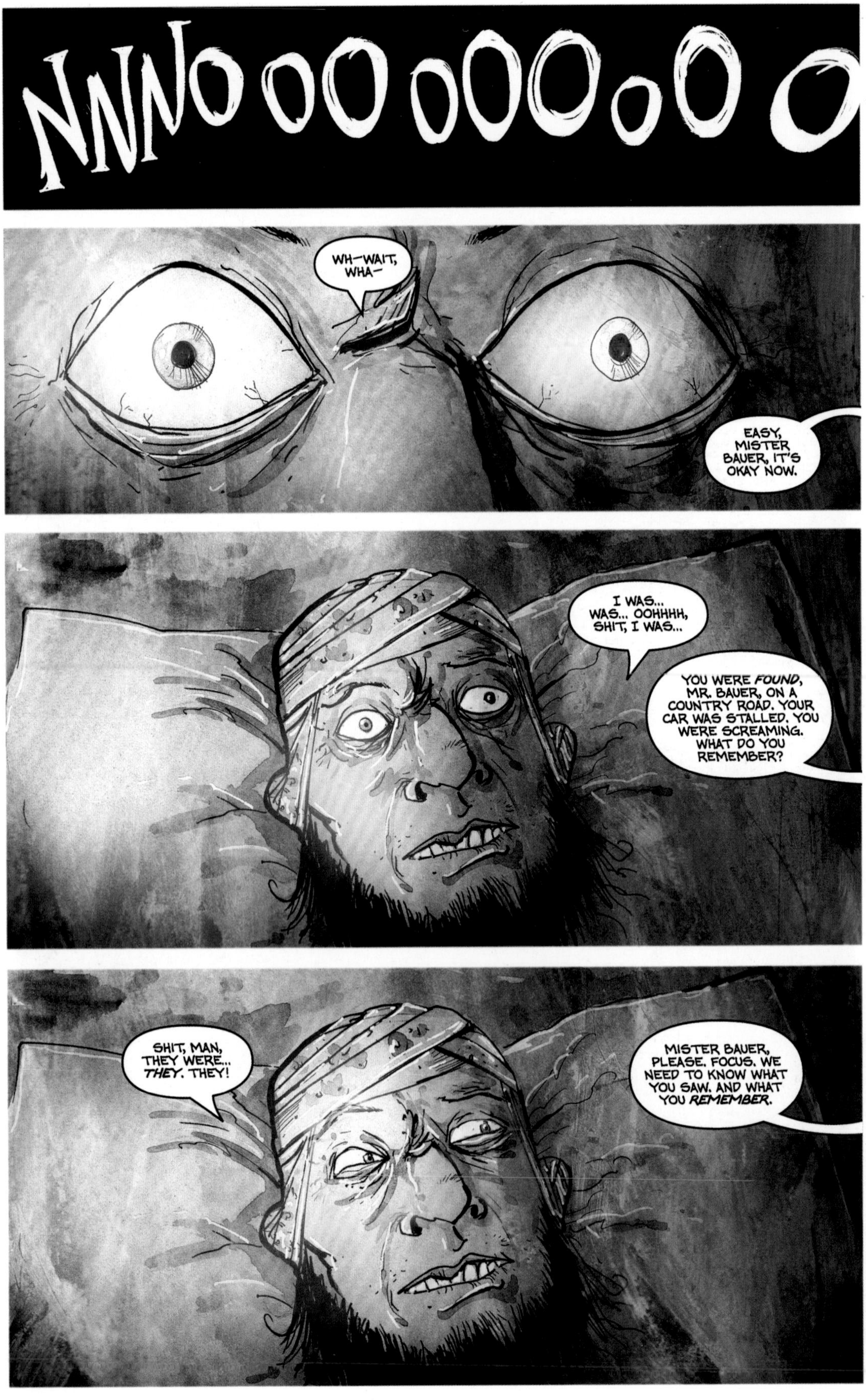
NNNOOOOOOOOOOO
WH—WAIT, WHA—
EASY, MISTER BAUER, IT'S OKAY NOW.
I WAS... WAS... OOHHHH, SHIT, I WAS...
YOU WERE FOUND, MR. BAUER, ON A COUNTRY ROAD. YOUR CAR WAS STALLED. YOU WERE SCREAMING. WHAT DO YOU REMEMBER?
SHIT, MAN, THEY WERE... THEY. THEY!
MISTER BAUER, PLEASE. FOCUS. WE NEED TO KNOW WHAT YOU SAW. AND WHAT YOU REMEMBER.

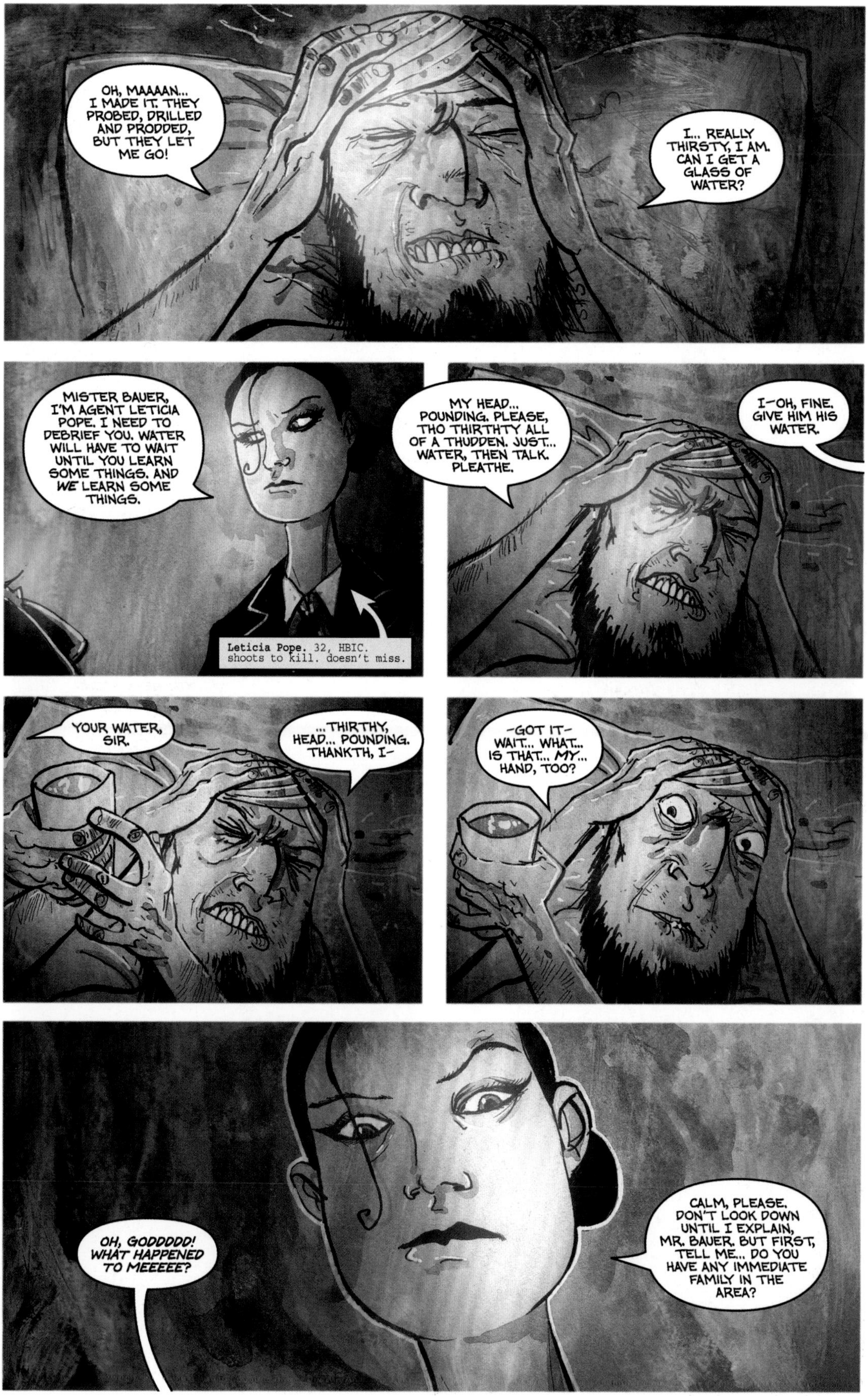
OH, MAAAAN... I MADE IT. THEY PROBED, DRILLED AND PRODDED, BUT THEY LET ME GO!
I... REALLY THIRSTY, I AM. CAN I GET A GLASS OF WATER?
MISTER BAUER, I'M AGENT LETICIA POPE. I NEED TO DEBRIEF YOU. WATER WILL HAVE TO WAIT UNTIL YOU LEARN SOME THINGS. AND *WE* LEARN SOME THINGS.
Leticia Pope. 32, HBIC. shoots to kill. doesn't miss.
MY HEAD... POUNDING. PLEASE, THO THIRTHTY ALL OF A THUDDEN. JUST... WATER, THEN TALK. PLEATHE.
I—OH, FINE. GIVE HIM HIS WATER.
YOUR WATER, SIR.
...THIRTHY, HEAD... POUNDING. THANKTH, I-
-GOT IT- WAIT... WHAT... IS THAT... *MY*... HAND, TOO?
OH, GODDDDD! WHAT HAPPENED TO MEEEEE?
CALM, PLEASE. DON'T LOOK DOWN UNTIL I EXPLAIN, MR. BAUER. BUT FIRST, TELL ME... DO YOU HAVE ANY IMMEDIATE FAMILY IN THE AREA?

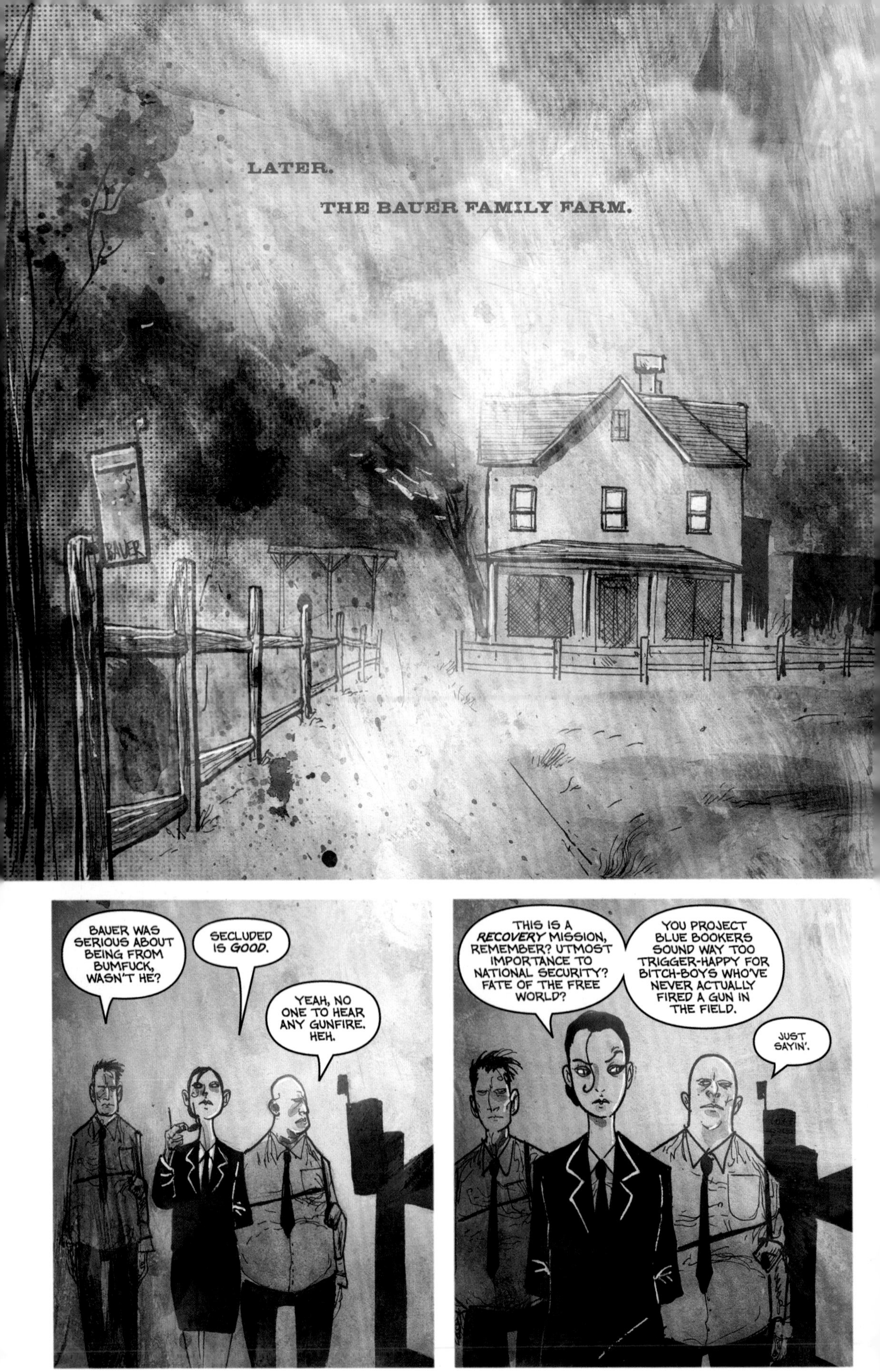
LATER.
THE BAUER FAMILY FARM.
BAUER
BAUER WAS SERIOUS ABOUT BEING FROM BUMFUCK, WASN'T HE?
SECLUDED IS *GOOD*.
YEAH, NO ONE TO HEAR ANY GUNFIRE. HEH.
THIS IS A *RECOVERY* MISSION, REMEMBER? UTMOST IMPORTANCE TO NATIONAL SECURITY? FATE OF THE FREE WORLD?
YOU PROJECT BLUE BOOKERS SOUND WAY TOO TRIGGER-HAPPY FOR BITCH-BOYS WHO'VE NEVER ACTUALLY FIRED A GUN IN THE FIELD.
JUST SAYIN'.

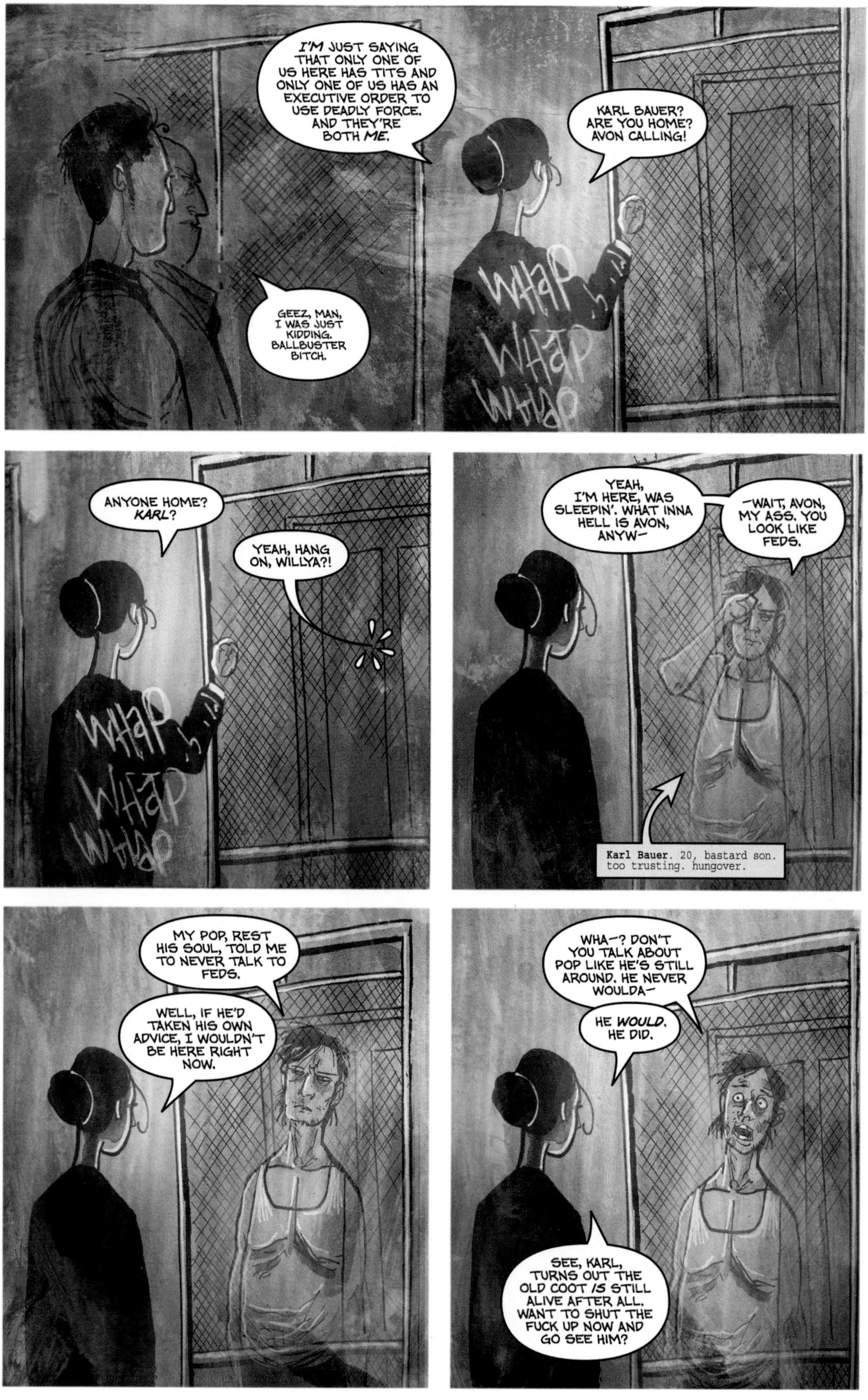

I'M JUST SAYING THAT ONLY ONE OF US HERE HAS TITS AND ONLY ONE OF US HAS AN EXECUTIVE ORDER TO USE DEADLY FORCE. AND THEY'RE BOTH ME.
KARL BAUER? ARE YOU HOME? AVON CALLING!
GEEZ, MAN, I WAS JUST KIDDING. BALLBUSTER BITCH.
WHAP WHAP WHAP
ANYONE HOME? KARL?
YEAH, HANG ON, WILLYA?!
WHAP WHAP WHAP
YEAH, I'M HERE, WAS SLEEPIN'. WHAT INNA HELL IS AVON, ANYW—
—WAIT, AVON, MY ASS. YOU LOOK LIKE FEDS.
Karl Bauer. 20, bastard son. too trusting. hungover.
MY POP, REST HIS SOUL, TOLD ME TO NEVER TALK TO FEDS.
WELL, IF HE'D TAKEN HIS OWN ADVICE, I WOULDN'T BE HERE RIGHT NOW.
WHA—? DON'T YOU TALK ABOUT POP LIKE HE'S STILL AROUND. HE NEVER WOULDA—
HE WOULD. HE DID.
SEE, KARL, TURNS OUT THE OLD COOT IS STILL ALIVE AFTER ALL. WANT TO SHUT THE FUCK UP NOW AND GO SEE HIM?

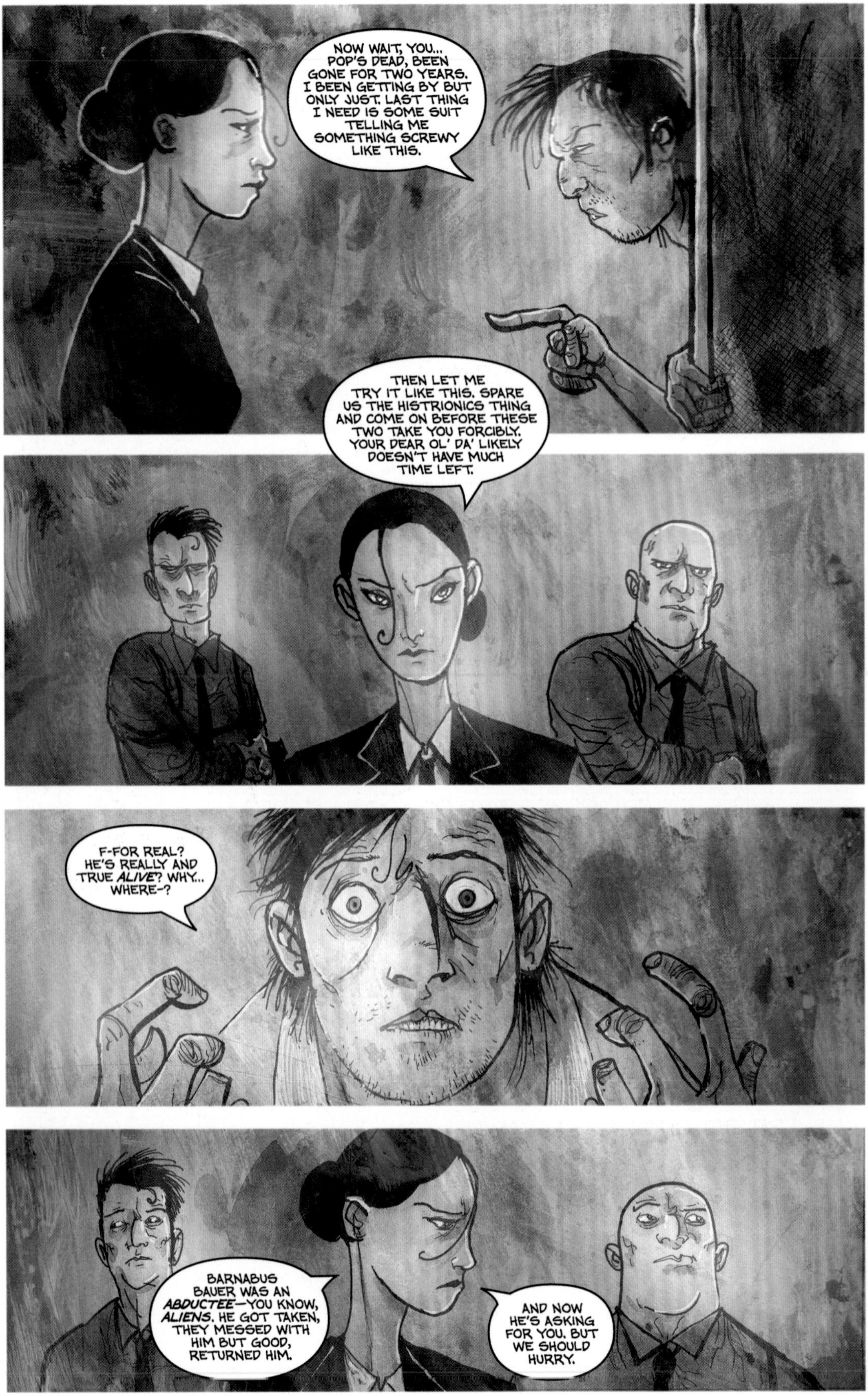
NOW WAIT, YOU... POP'S DEAD, BEEN GONE FOR TWO YEARS. I BEEN GETTING BY BUT ONLY JUST. LAST THING I NEED IS SOME SUIT TELLING ME SOMETHING SCREWY LIKE THIS.
THEN LET ME TRY IT LIKE THIS. SPARE US THE HISTRIONICS THING AND COME ON BEFORE THESE TWO TAKE YOU FORCIBLY. YOUR DEAR OL' DA' LIKELY DOESN'T HAVE MUCH TIME LEFT.
F-FOR REAL? HE'S REALLY AND TRUE *ALIVE*? WHY... WHERE-?
BARNABUS BAUER WAS AN ***ABDUCTEE***—YOU KNOW, ***ALIENS***. HE GOT TAKEN, THEY MESSED WITH HIM BUT GOOD, RETURNED HIM.
AND NOW HE'S ASKING FOR YOU, BUT WE SHOULD HURRY.

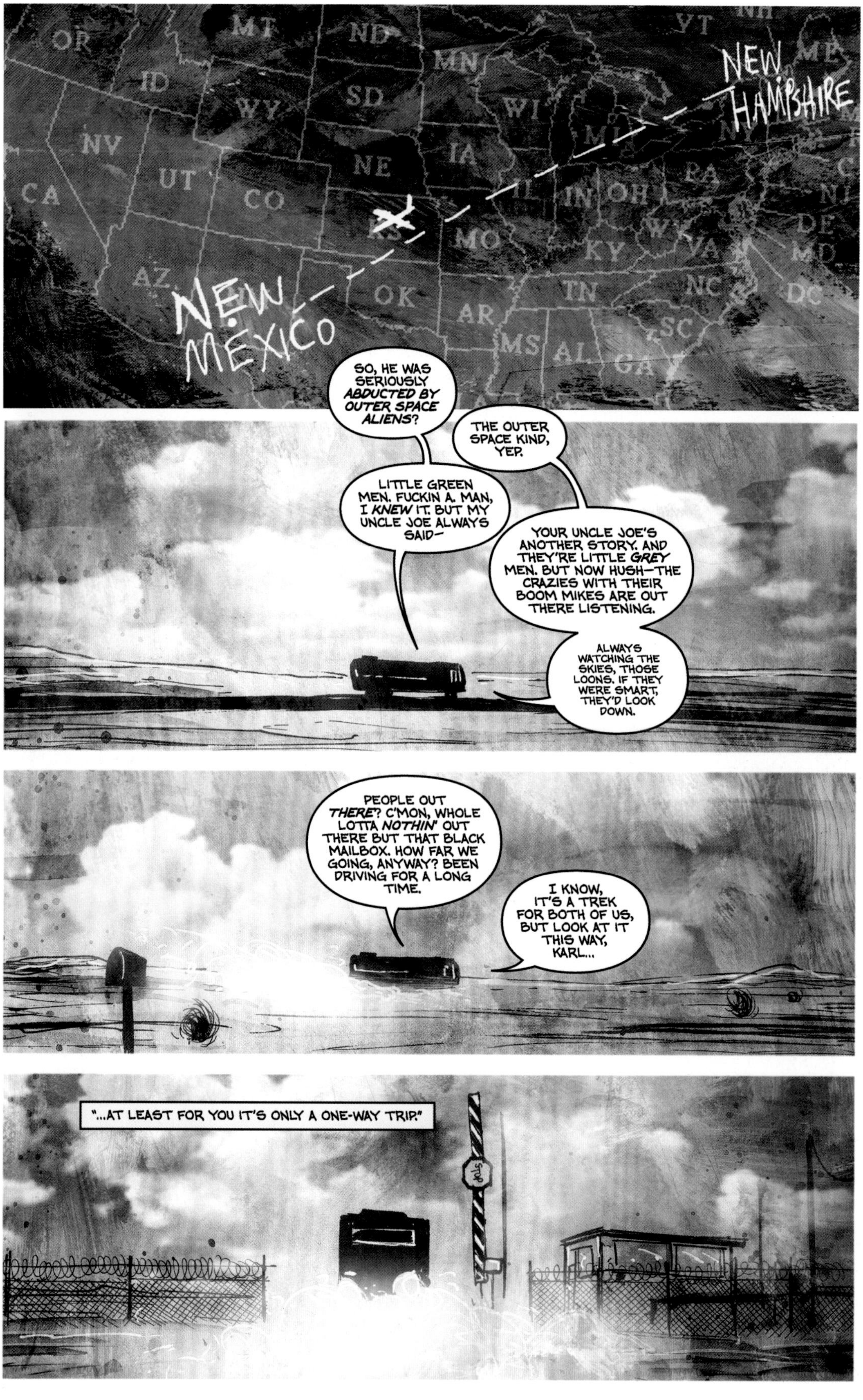
NEW HAMPSHIRE
NEW MEXICO
SO, HE WAS SERIOUSLY *ABDUCTED BY OUTER SPACE ALIENS*?
THE OUTER SPACE KIND, YEP.
LITTLE GREEN MEN. FUCKIN A. MAN, I *KNEW* IT. BUT MY UNCLE JOE ALWAYS SAID–
YOUR UNCLE JOE'S ANOTHER STORY. AND THEY'RE LITTLE *GREY* MEN. BUT NOW HUSH—THE CRAZIES WITH THEIR BOOM MIKES ARE OUT THERE LISTENING.
ALWAYS WATCHING THE SKIES, THOSE LOONS. IF THEY WERE SMART, THEY'D LOOK DOWN.
PEOPLE OUT *THERE*? C'MON, WHOLE LOTTA *NOTHIN'* OUT THERE BUT THAT BLACK MAILBOX. HOW FAR WE GOING, ANYWAY? BEEN DRIVING FOR A LONG TIME.
I KNOW, IT'S A TREK FOR BOTH OF US, BUT LOOK AT IT THIS WAY, KARL...
"...AT LEAST FOR YOU IT'S ONLY A ONE-WAY TRIP."
STOP

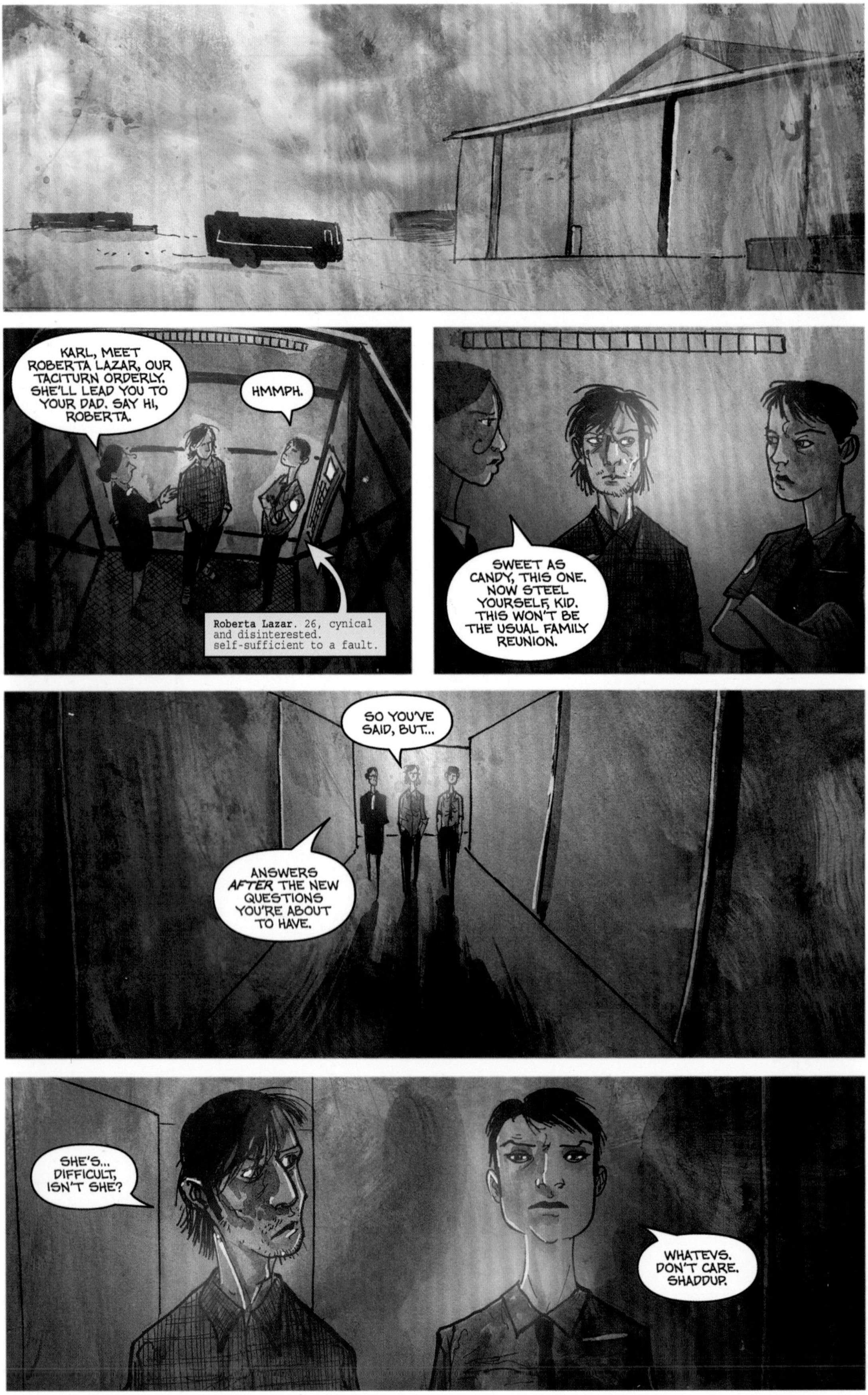
KARL, MEET ROBERTA LAZAR, OUR TACITURN ORDERLY. SHE'LL LEAD YOU TO YOUR DAD. SAY HI, ROBERTA.
HMMPH.
Roberta Lazar. 26, cynical and disinterested. self-sufficient to a fault.
SWEET AS CANDY, THIS ONE. NOW STEEL YOURSELF, KID. THIS WON'T BE THE USUAL FAMILY REUNION.
SO YOU'VE SAID, BUT...
ANSWERS *AFTER* THE NEW QUESTIONS YOU'RE ABOUT TO HAVE.
SHE'S... DIFFICULT, ISN'T SHE?
WHATEVS. DON'T CARE. SHADDUP.

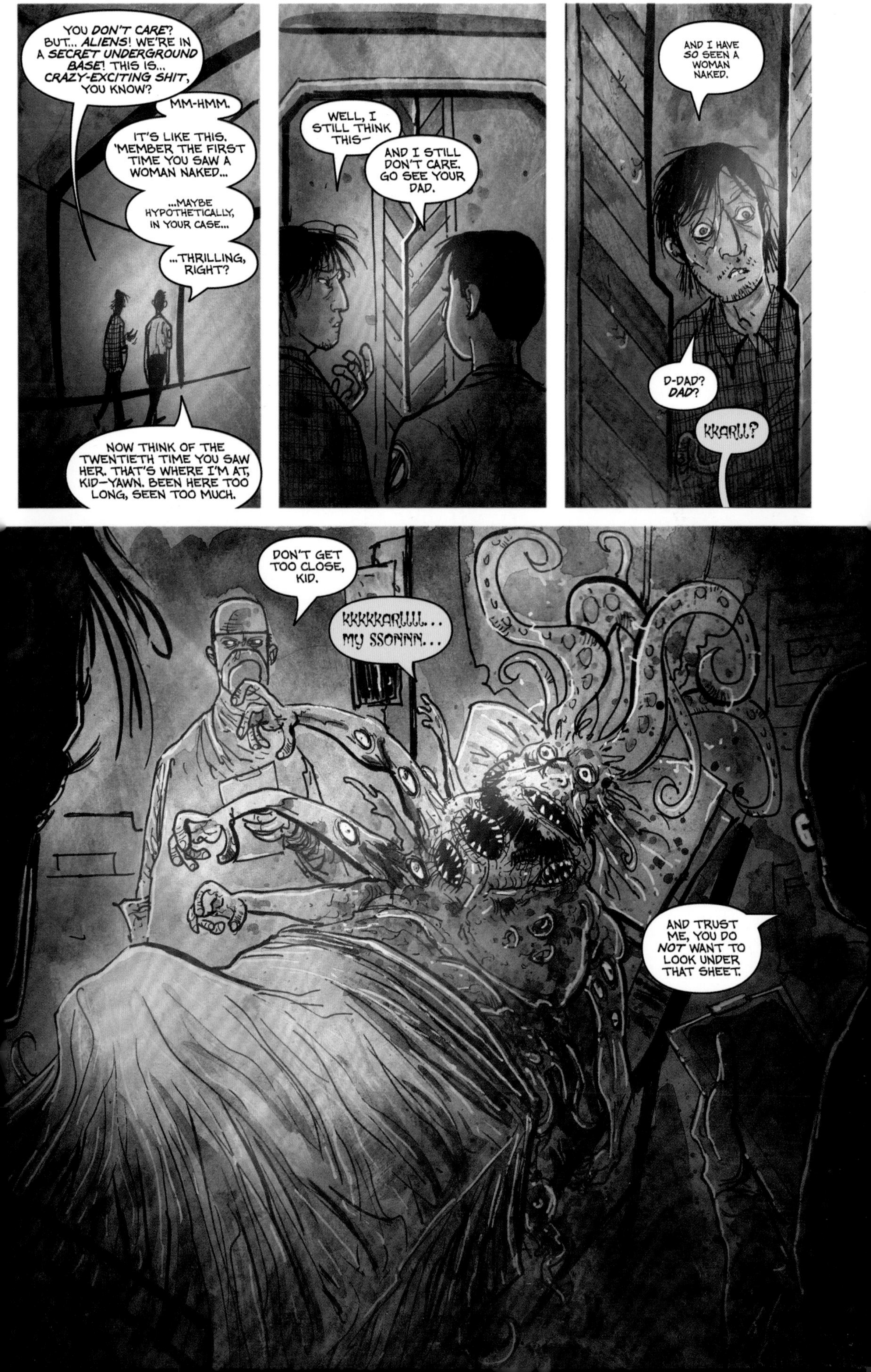
YOU DON'T CARE? BUT... ALIENS! WE'RE IN A SECRET UNDERGROUND BASE! THIS IS... CRAZY-EXCITING SHIT, YOU KNOW?
MM-HMM.
IT'S LIKE THIS. 'MEMBER THE FIRST TIME YOU SAW A WOMAN NAKED...
...MAYBE HYPOTHETICALLY, IN YOUR CASE...
...THRILLING, RIGHT?
NOW THINK OF THE TWENTIETH TIME YOU SAW HER. THAT'S WHERE I'M AT, KID—YAWN. BEEN HERE TOO LONG, SEEN TOO MUCH.
WELL, I STILL THINK THIS—
AND I STILL DON'T CARE. GO SEE YOUR DAD.
AND I HAVE SO SEEN A WOMAN NAKED.
D-DAD? DAD?
KKARLL?
DON'T GET TOO CLOSE, KID.
KKKKKARLLLL... MY SSONNN...
AND TRUST ME, YOU DO NOT WANT TO LOOK UNDER THAT SHEET.

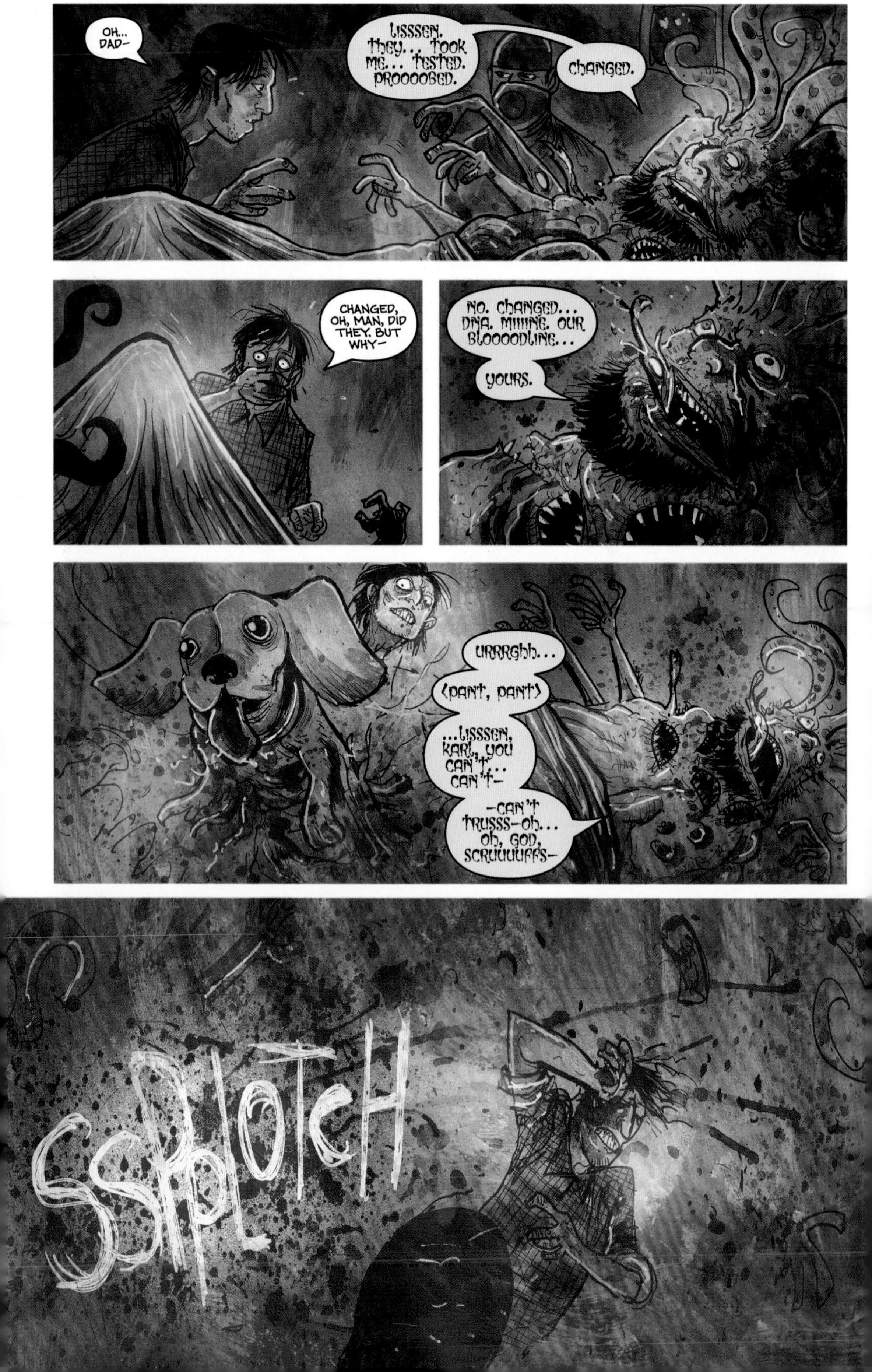
OH... DAD—
LISSSEN. THEY... TOOK ME... TESTED. PROOOOBED.
CHANGED.
CHANGED, OH, MAN, DID THEY. BUT WHY—
NO. CHANGED... DNA. MIIIINE. OUR BLOOOODLINE...
YOURS.
URRRGHH...
(PANT, PANT)
...LISSSEN, KARL, YOU CAN'T... CAN'T—
—CAN'T TRUSSS—OH... OH, GOD, SCRUUUUFFS—
SSPPLOTCH

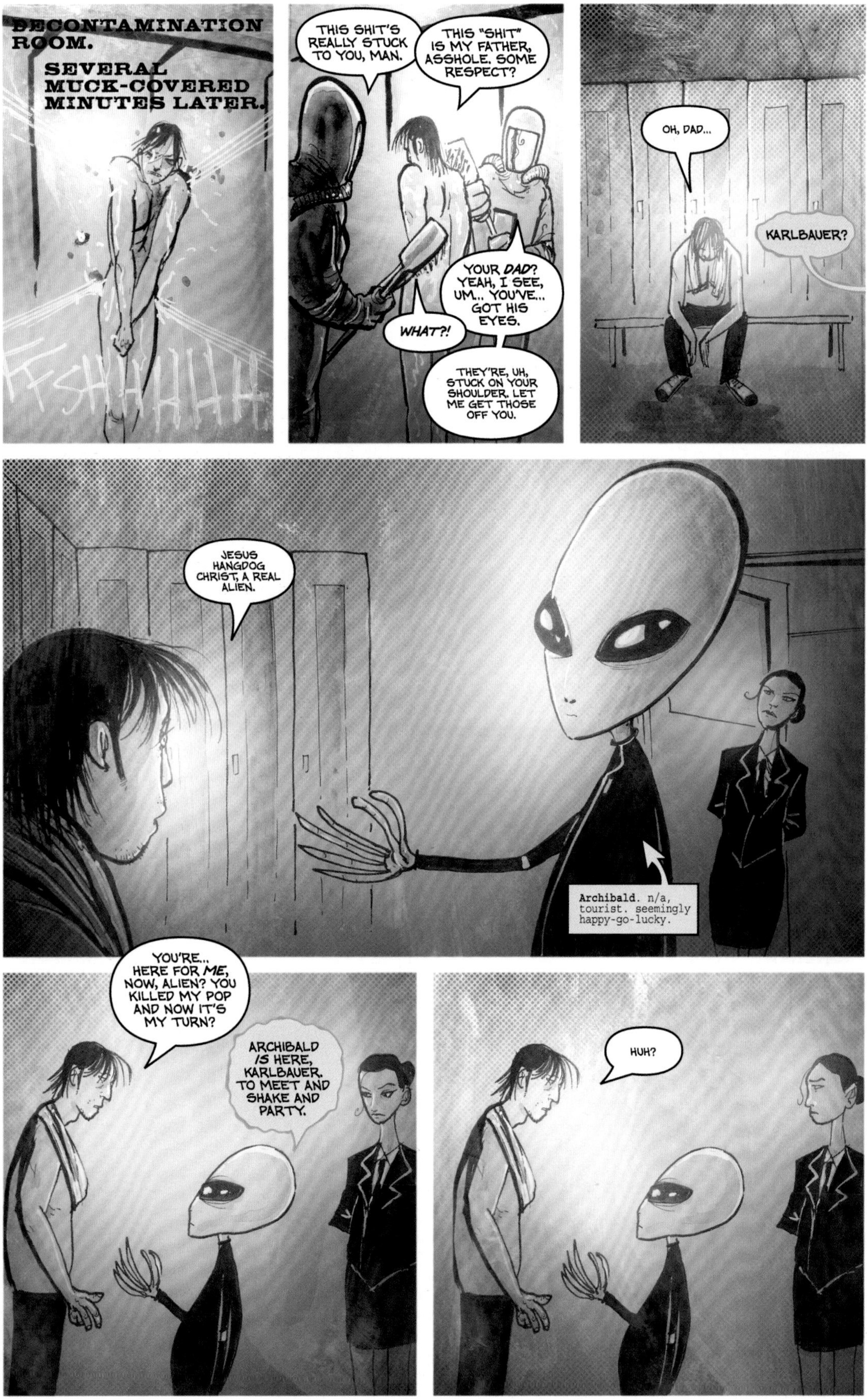
DECONTAMINATION ROOM.
SEVERAL MUCK-COVERED MINUTES LATER.
FFSHHHHH
THIS SHIT'S REALLY STUCK TO YOU, MAN.
THIS "SHIT" IS MY FATHER, ASSHOLE. SOME RESPECT?
YOUR DAD? YEAH, I SEE, UM... YOU'VE... GOT HIS EYES.
WHAT?!
THEY'RE, UH, STUCK ON YOUR SHOULDER. LET ME GET THOSE OFF YOU.
OH, DAD...
KARLBAUER?
JESUS HANGDOG CHRIST, A REAL ALIEN.
Archibald. n/a, tourist. seemingly happy-go-lucky.
YOU'RE... HERE FOR ME, NOW, ALIEN? YOU KILLED MY POP AND NOW IT'S MY TURN?
ARCHIBALD IS HERE, KARLBAUER. TO MEET AND SHAKE AND PARTY.
HUH?

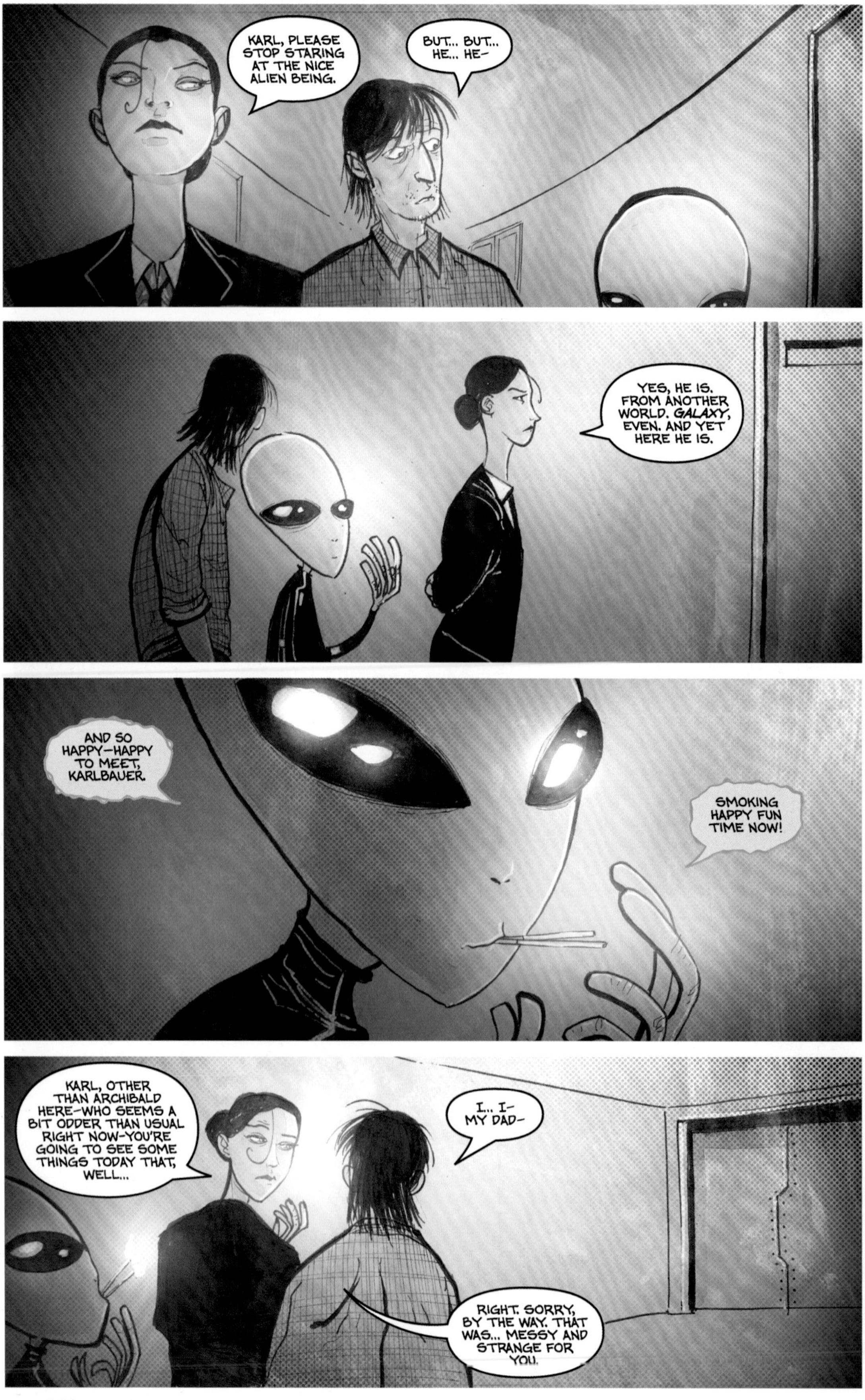
KARL, PLEASE STOP STARING AT THE NICE ALIEN BEING.
BUT... BUT... HE... HE-
YES, HE IS. FROM ANOTHER WORLD. *GALAXY*, EVEN. AND YET HERE HE IS.
AND SO HAPPY-HAPPY TO MEET, KARLBAUER.
SMOKING HAPPY FUN TIME NOW!
KARL, OTHER THAN ARCHIBALD HERE-WHO SEEMS A BIT ODDER THAN USUAL RIGHT NOW-YOU'RE GOING TO SEE SOME THINGS TODAY THAT, WELL...
I... I- MY DAD-
RIGHT. SORRY, BY THE WAY. THAT WAS... MESSY AND STRANGE FOR YOU.

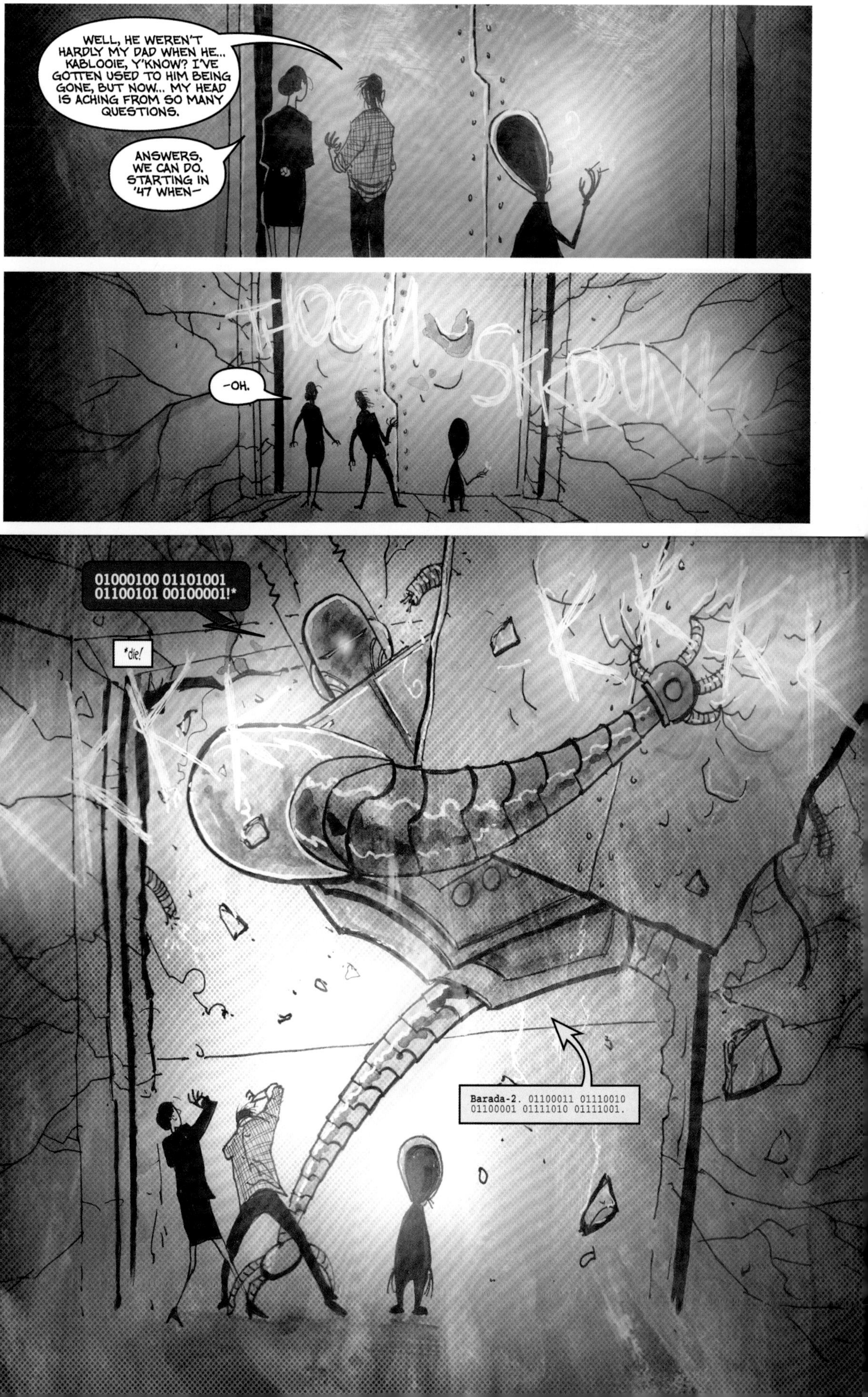
WELL, HE WEREN'T HARDLY MY DAD WHEN HE... KABLOOIE, Y'KNOW? I'VE GOTTEN USED TO HIM BEING GONE, BUT NOW... MY HEAD IS ACHING FROM SO MANY QUESTIONS.
ANSWERS, WE CAN DO. STARTING IN '47 WHEN—
THOOM
SKKRUNK
—OH.
01000100 01101001 01100101 00100001!*
*die!
Barada-2. 01100011 01110010 01100001 01111010 01111001.

KILLER ROBOT FROM OUTER SPACE!
BARADA TIME!
HEY. IT'S ME. GODDAMNED 'BOT IS FREE AGAIN.
BARADA-BADA-FOFADA!
MOVE IT, KID!
SHIIIIT!
01001011 01101010 01101100 00100001!*
*kill!
MS. POPE? WANT TOTAL SHUTDOWN?

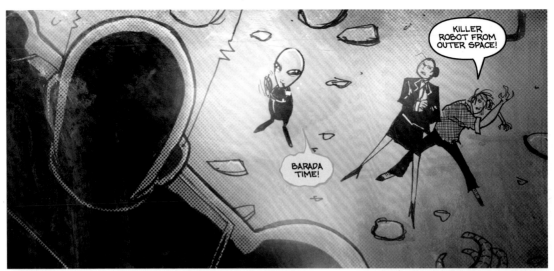

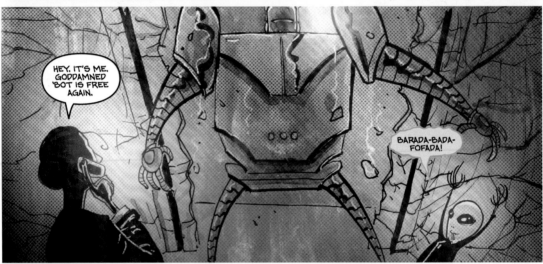

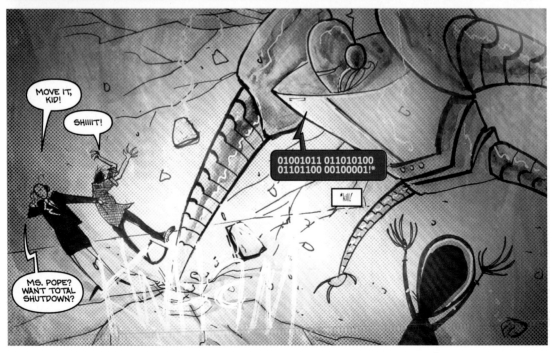

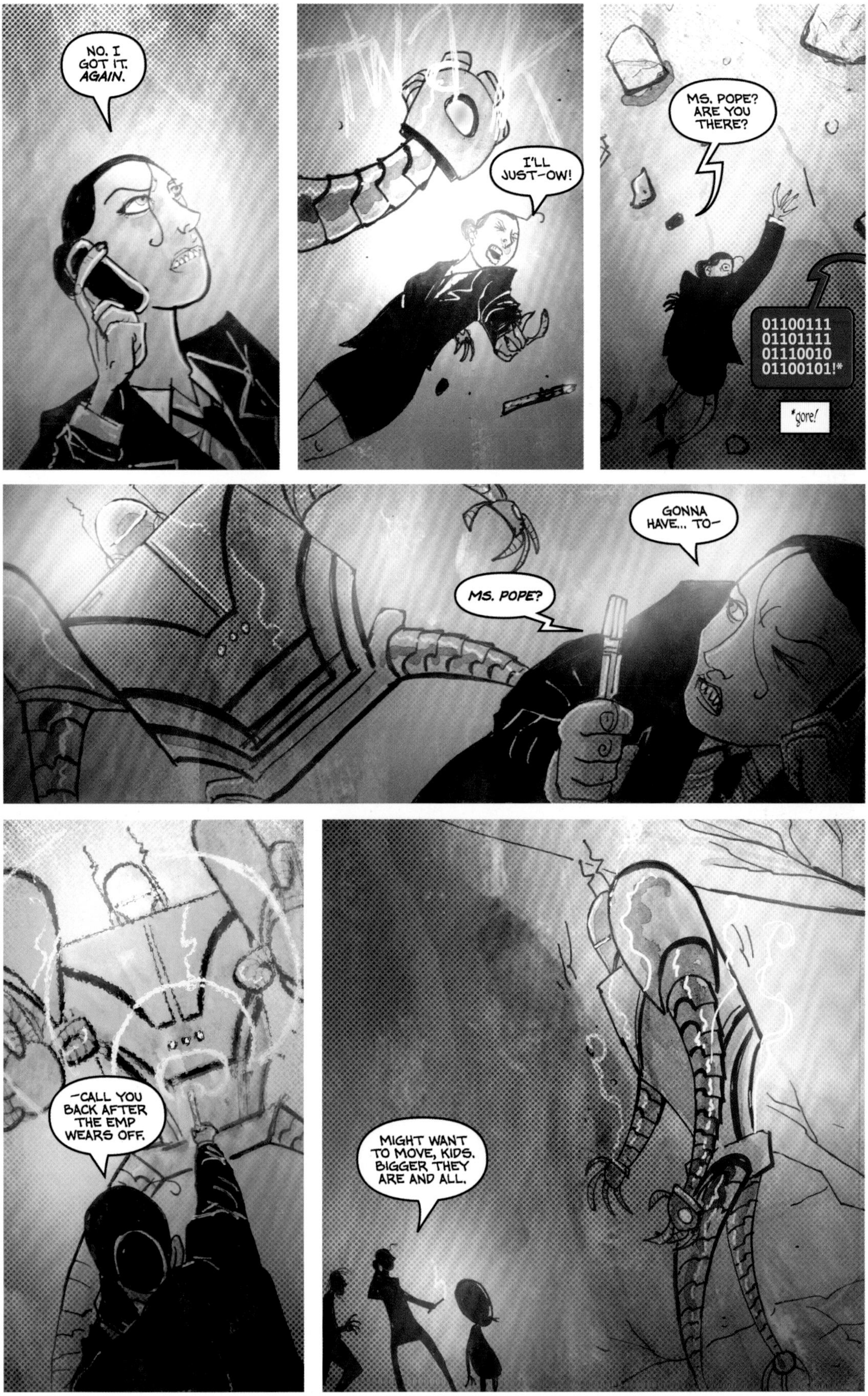
NO. I GOT IT. AGAIN.
I'LL JUST-OW!
MS. POPE? ARE YOU THERE?
01100111 01101111 01110010 01100101!*
*gore!
GONNA HAVE... TO-
MS. POPE?
-CALL YOU BACK AFTER THE EMP WEARS OFF.
MIGHT WANT TO MOVE, KIDS. BIGGER THEY ARE AND ALL.

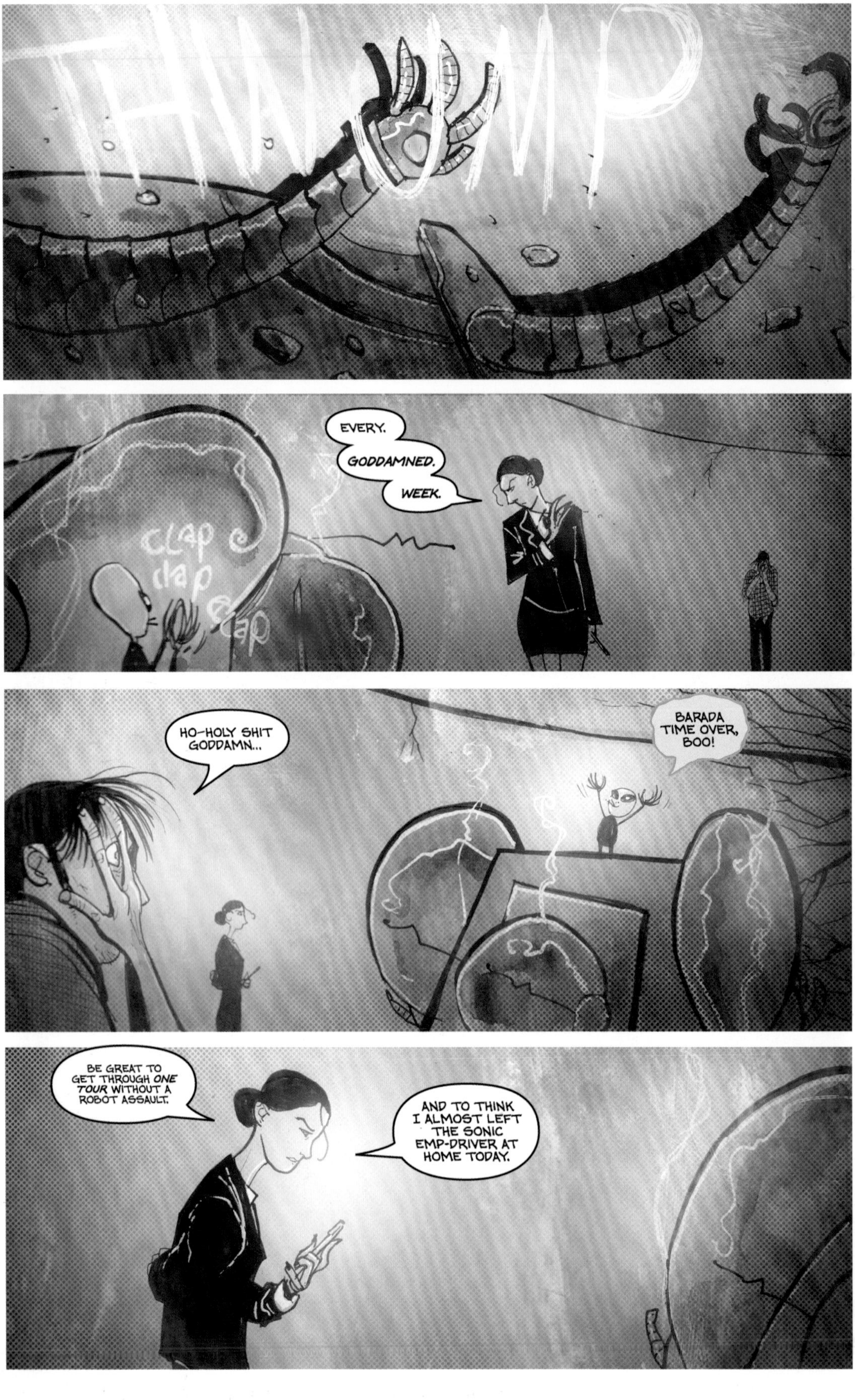
EVERY.
GODDAMNED.
WEEK.
clap clap clap
HO–HOLY SHIT GODDAMN...
BARADA TIME OVER, BOO!
BE GREAT TO GET THROUGH *ONE TOUR* WITHOUT A ROBOT ASSAULT.
AND TO THINK I ALMOST LEFT THE SONIC EMP-DRIVER AT HOME TODAY.

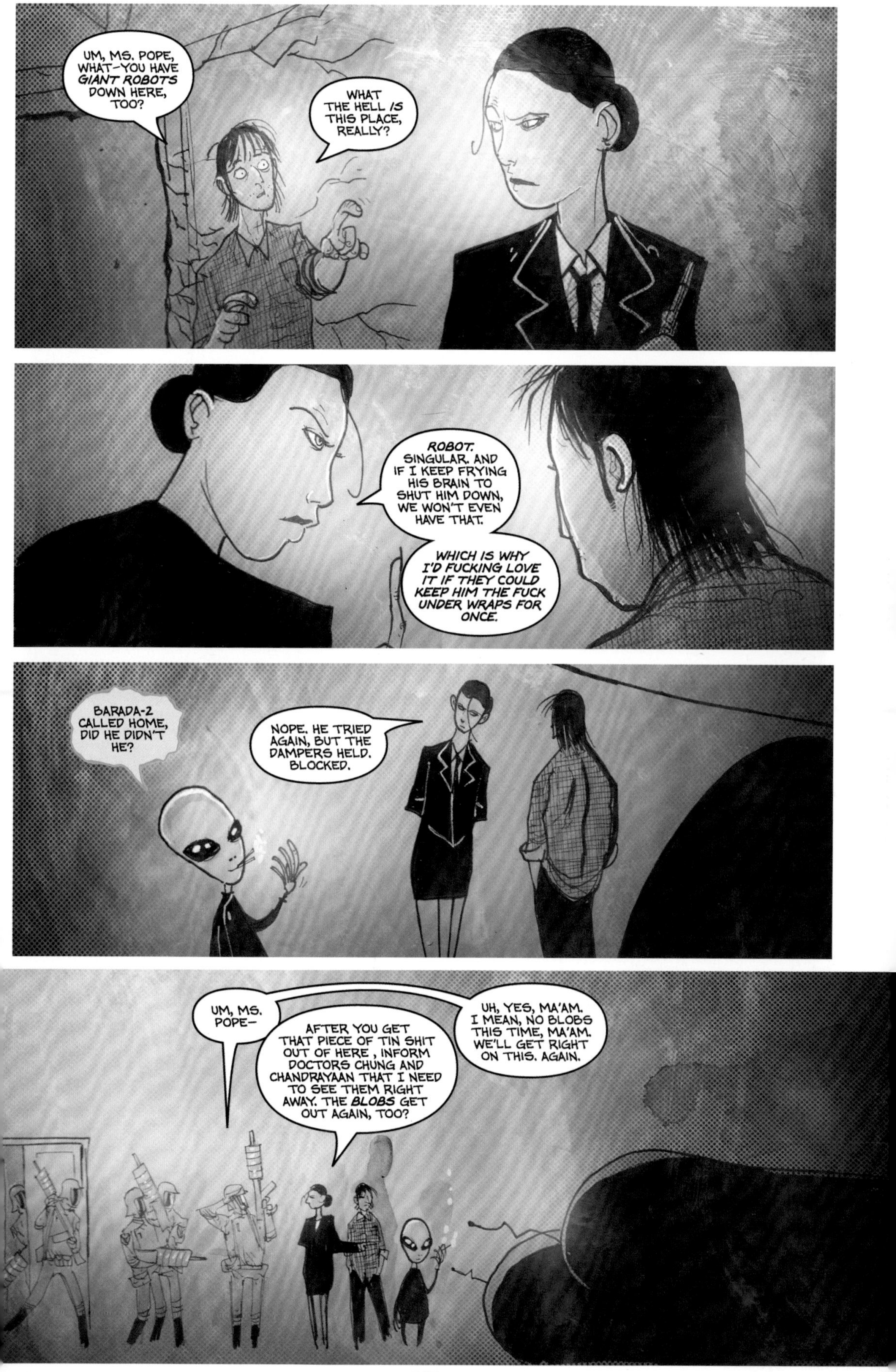
UM, MS. POPE, WHAT-YOU HAVE GIANT ROBOTS DOWN HERE, TOO?
WHAT THE HELL IS THIS PLACE, REALLY?
ROBOT. SINGULAR. AND IF I KEEP FRYING HIS BRAIN TO SHUT HIM DOWN, WE WON'T EVEN HAVE THAT.
WHICH IS WHY I'D FUCKING LOVE IT IF THEY COULD KEEP HIM THE FUCK UNDER WRAPS FOR ONCE.
BARADA-2 CALLED HOME, DID HE DIDN'T HE?
NOPE. HE TRIED AGAIN, BUT THE DAMPERS HELD. BLOCKED.
UM, MS. POPE-
AFTER YOU GET THAT PIECE OF TIN SHIT OUT OF HERE , INFORM DOCTORS CHUNG AND CHANDRAYAAN THAT I NEED TO SEE THEM RIGHT AWAY. THE BLOBS GET OUT AGAIN, TOO?
UH, YES, MA'AM. I MEAN, NO BLOBS THIS TIME, MA'AM. WE'LL GET RIGHT ON THIS. AGAIN.

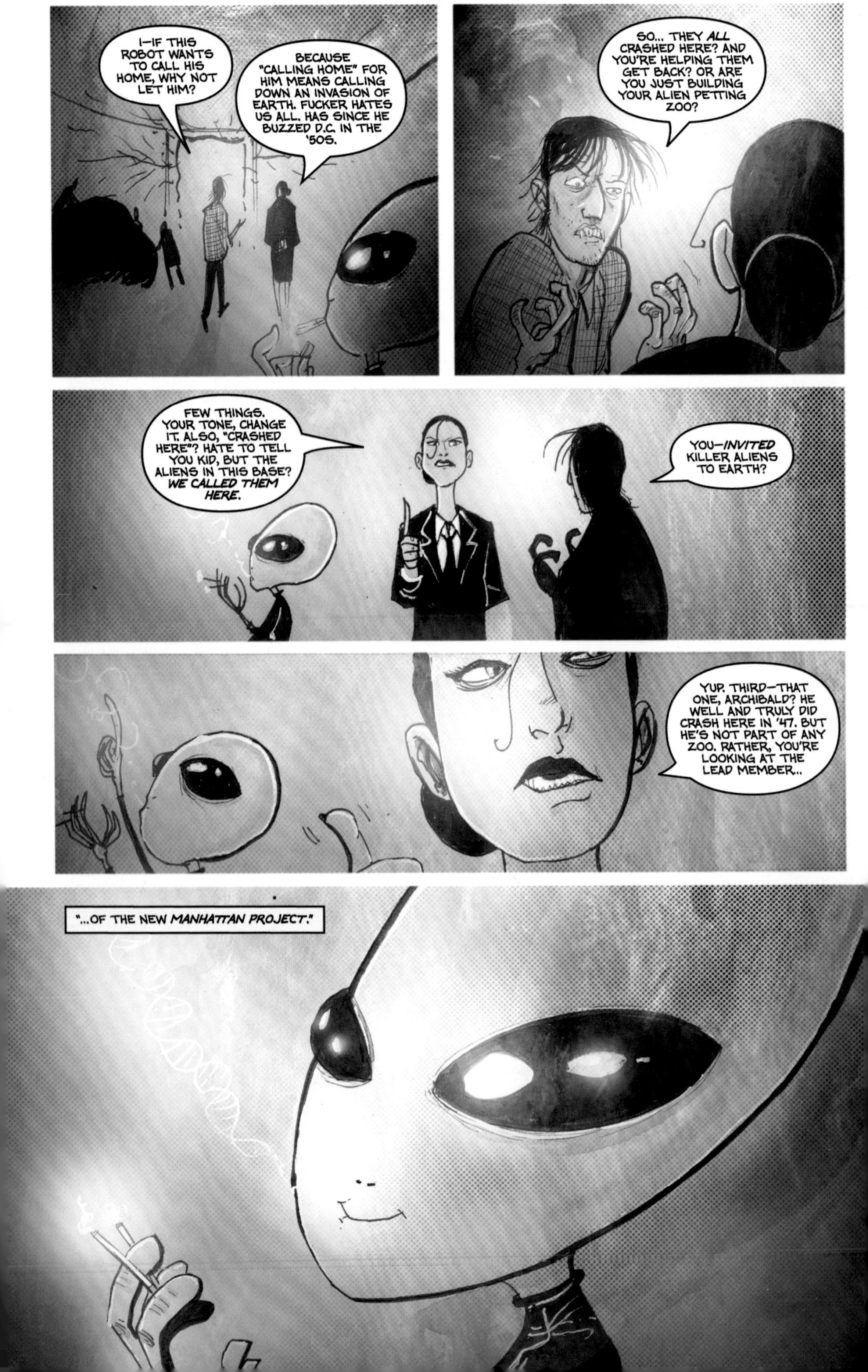

I—IF THIS ROBOT WANTS TO CALL HIS HOME, WHY NOT LET HIM?
BECAUSE "CALLING HOME" FOR HIM MEANS CALLING DOWN AN INVASION OF EARTH. FUCKER HATES US ALL. HAS SINCE HE BUZZED D.C. IN THE '50S.
SO... THEY ALL CRASHED HERE? AND YOU'RE HELPING THEM GET BACK? OR ARE YOU JUST BUILDING YOUR ALIEN PETTING ZOO?
FEW THINGS. YOUR TONE, CHANGE IT. ALSO, "CRASHED HERE"? HATE TO TELL YOU KID, BUT THE ALIENS IN THIS BASE? WE CALLED THEM HERE.
YOU—INVITED KILLER ALIENS TO EARTH?
YUP. THIRD—THAT ONE, ARCHIBALD? HE WELL AND TRULY DID CRASH HERE IN '47. BUT HE'S NOT PART OF ANY ZOO. RATHER, YOU'RE LOOKING AT THE LEAD MEMBER...
"...OF THE NEW MANHATTAN PROJECT."

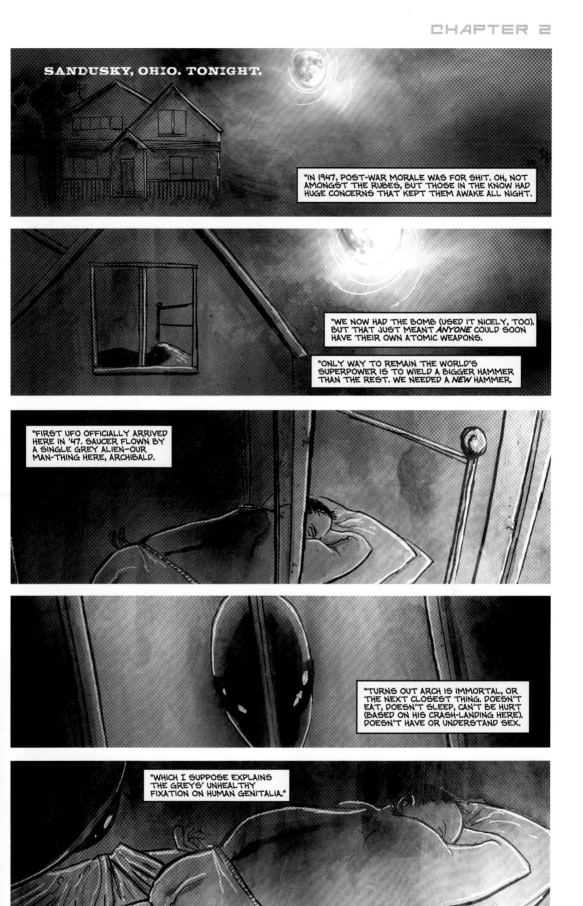

CHAPTER 2

SANDUSKY, OHIO. TONIGHT.

"IN 1947, POST-WAR MORALE WAS FOR SHIT. OH, NOT AMONGST THE RUBES, BUT THOSE IN THE KNOW HAD HUGE CONCERNS THAT KEPT THEM AWAKE ALL NIGHT.

"WE NOW HAD THE BOMB (USED IT NICELY, TOO), BUT THAT JUST MEANT *ANYONE* COULD SOON HAVE THEIR OWN ATOMIC WEAPONS.

"ONLY WAY TO REMAIN THE WORLD'S SUPERPOWER IS TO WIELD A BIGGER HAMMER THAN THE REST. WE NEEDED A *NEW* HAMMER.

"FIRST UFO OFFICIALLY ARRIVED HERE IN '47. SAUCER FLOWN BY A SINGLE GREY ALIEN—OUR MAN-THING HERE, ARCHIBALD.

"TURNS OUT ARCH IS IMMORTAL, OR THE NEXT CLOSEST THING. DOESN'T EAT, DOESN'T SLEEP, CAN'T BE HURT (BASED ON HIS CRASH-LANDING HERE). DOESN'T HAVE OR UNDERSTAND SEX.

"WHICH I SUPPOSE EXPLAINS THE GREYS' UNHEALTHY FIXATION ON HUMAN GENITALIA."

"ANYWAY, ARCHIBALD PROVED TO BE A GREAT, IF SECRET, AMBASSADOR ON OUR PLANET. WE'VE BEEN TRADING WITH HIS PEOPLE FOR YEARS."

"TRADING? TRADING *WHAT?*"

"SECRETS OF THE UNIVERSE, KARL, IN EXCHANGE FOR A FEW HILLBILLIES TO EXPERIMENT ON. I'D SAY WE GOT THE BETTER END OF THE DEAL."

"..."

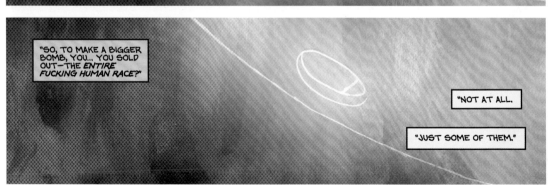

"SO, TO MAKE A BIGGER BOMB, YOU... YOU SOLD OUT—THE *ENTIRE FUCKING HUMAN RACE?*"

"NOT AT ALL.

"JUST SOME OF THEM."

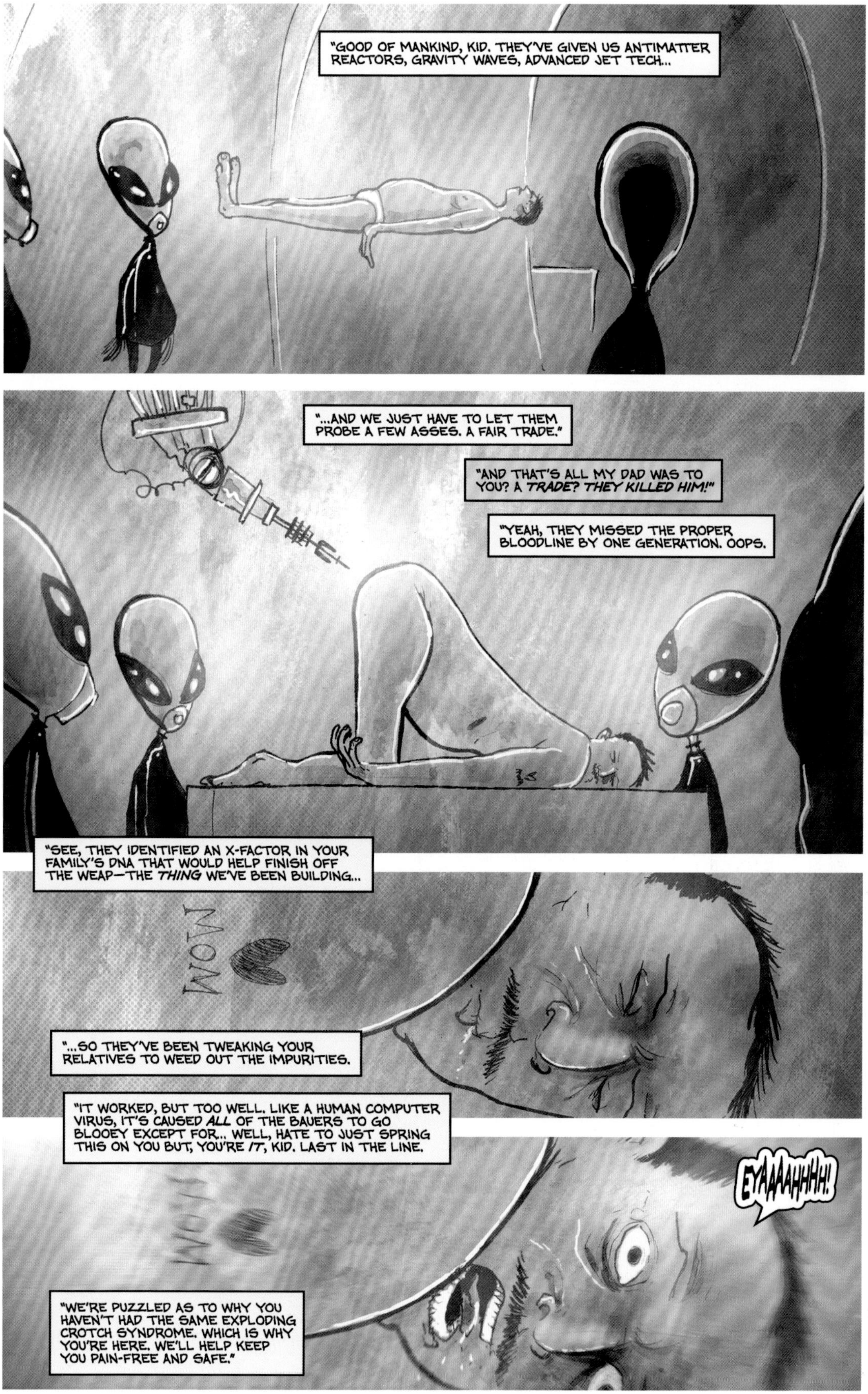
"GOOD OF MANKIND, KID. THEY'VE GIVEN US ANTIMATTER REACTORS, GRAVITY WAVES, ADVANCED JET TECH...
"...AND WE JUST HAVE TO LET THEM PROBE A FEW ASSES. A FAIR TRADE."
"AND THAT'S ALL MY DAD WAS TO YOU? A *TRADE? THEY KILLED HIM!*"
"YEAH, THEY MISSED THE PROPER BLOODLINE BY ONE GENERATION. OOPS.
"SEE, THEY IDENTIFIED AN X-FACTOR IN YOUR FAMILY'S DNA THAT WOULD HELP FINISH OFF THE WEAP—THE *THING* WE'VE BEEN BUILDING...
MOM
"...SO THEY'VE BEEN TWEAKING YOUR RELATIVES TO WEED OUT THE IMPURITIES.
"IT WORKED, BUT TOO WELL. LIKE A HUMAN COMPUTER VIRUS, IT'S CAUSED *ALL* OF THE BAUERS TO GO BLOOEY EXCEPT FOR... WELL, HATE TO JUST SPRING THIS ON YOU BUT, YOU'RE *IT*, KID. LAST IN THE LINE.
EYAAAAHHHH!
"WE'RE PUZZLED AS TO WHY YOU HAVEN'T HAD THE SAME EXPLODING CROTCH SYNDROME. WHICH IS WHY YOU'RE HERE. WE'LL HELP KEEP YOU PAIN-FREE AND SAFE."

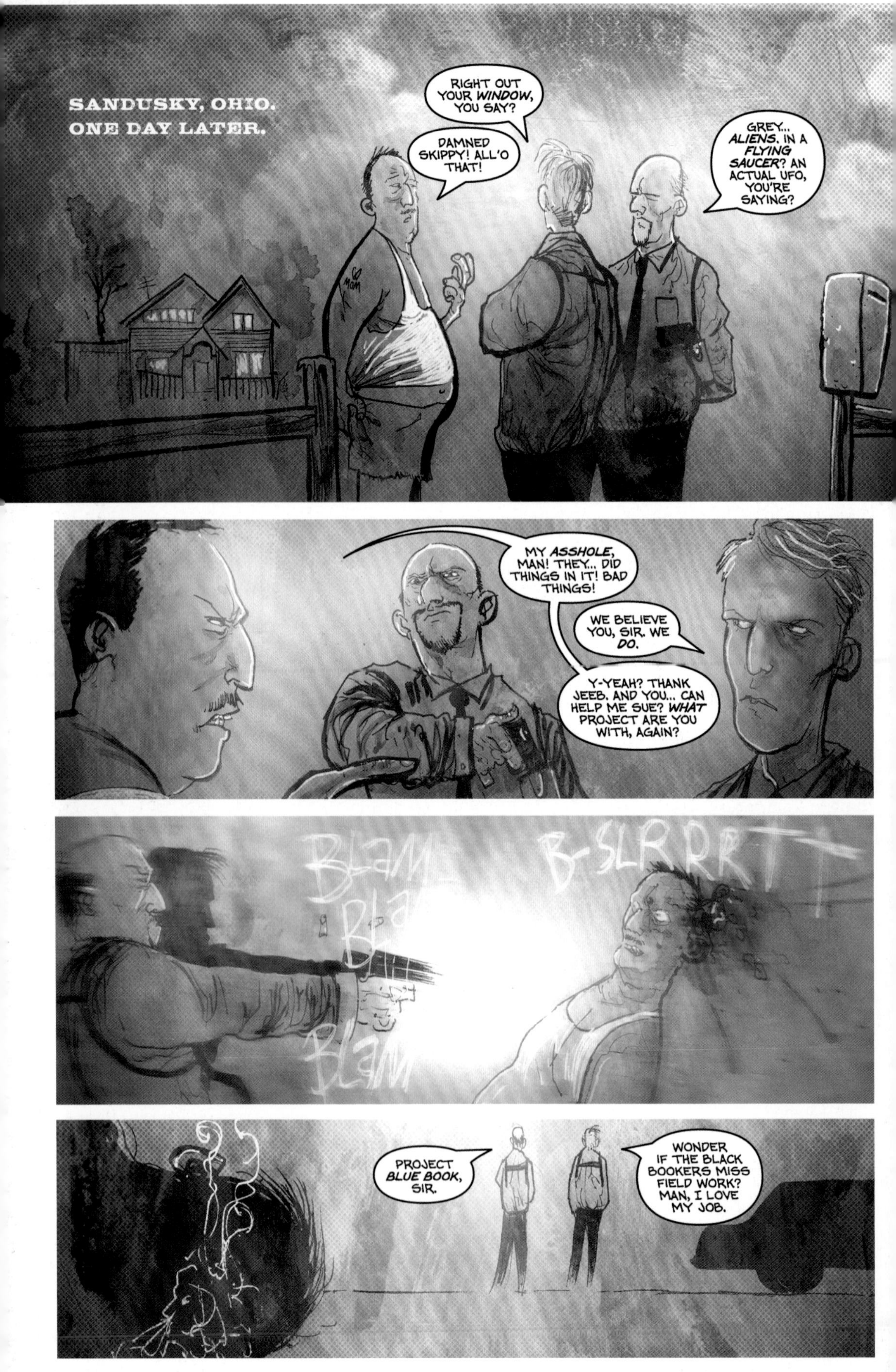
SANDUSKY, OHIO.
ONE DAY LATER.
RIGHT OUT YOUR WINDOW, YOU SAY?
DAMNED SKIPPY! ALL'O THAT!
GREY... ALIENS. IN A FLYING SAUCER? AN ACTUAL UFO, YOU'RE SAYING?
MOM
MY ASSHOLE, MAN! THEY... DID THINGS IN IT! BAD THINGS!
WE BELIEVE YOU, SIR. WE DO.
Y-YEAH? THANK JEEB. AND YOU... CAN HELP ME SUE? WHAT PROJECT ARE YOU WITH, AGAIN?
Blam
B-SLRRRTT
Blam
PROJECT BLUE BOOK, SIR.
WONDER IF THE BLACK BOOKERS MISS FIELD WORK? MAN, I LOVE MY JOB.

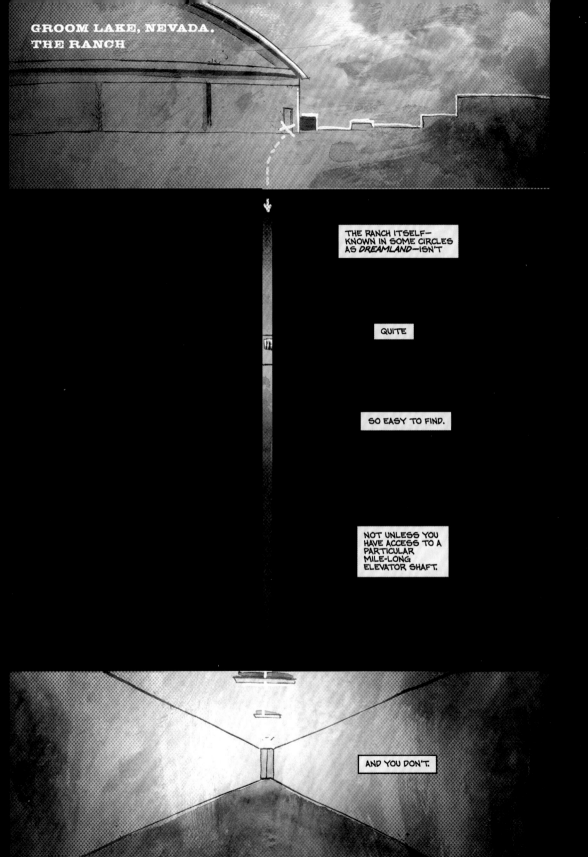

GROOM LAKE, NEVADA,
THE RANCH

THE RANCH ITSELF—
KNOWN IN SOME CIRCLES
AS *DREAMLAND*—ISN'T

QUITE

SO EASY TO FIND.

NOT UNLESS YOU
HAVE ACCESS TO A
PARTICULAR
MILE-LONG
ELEVATOR SHAFT.

AND YOU DON'T.

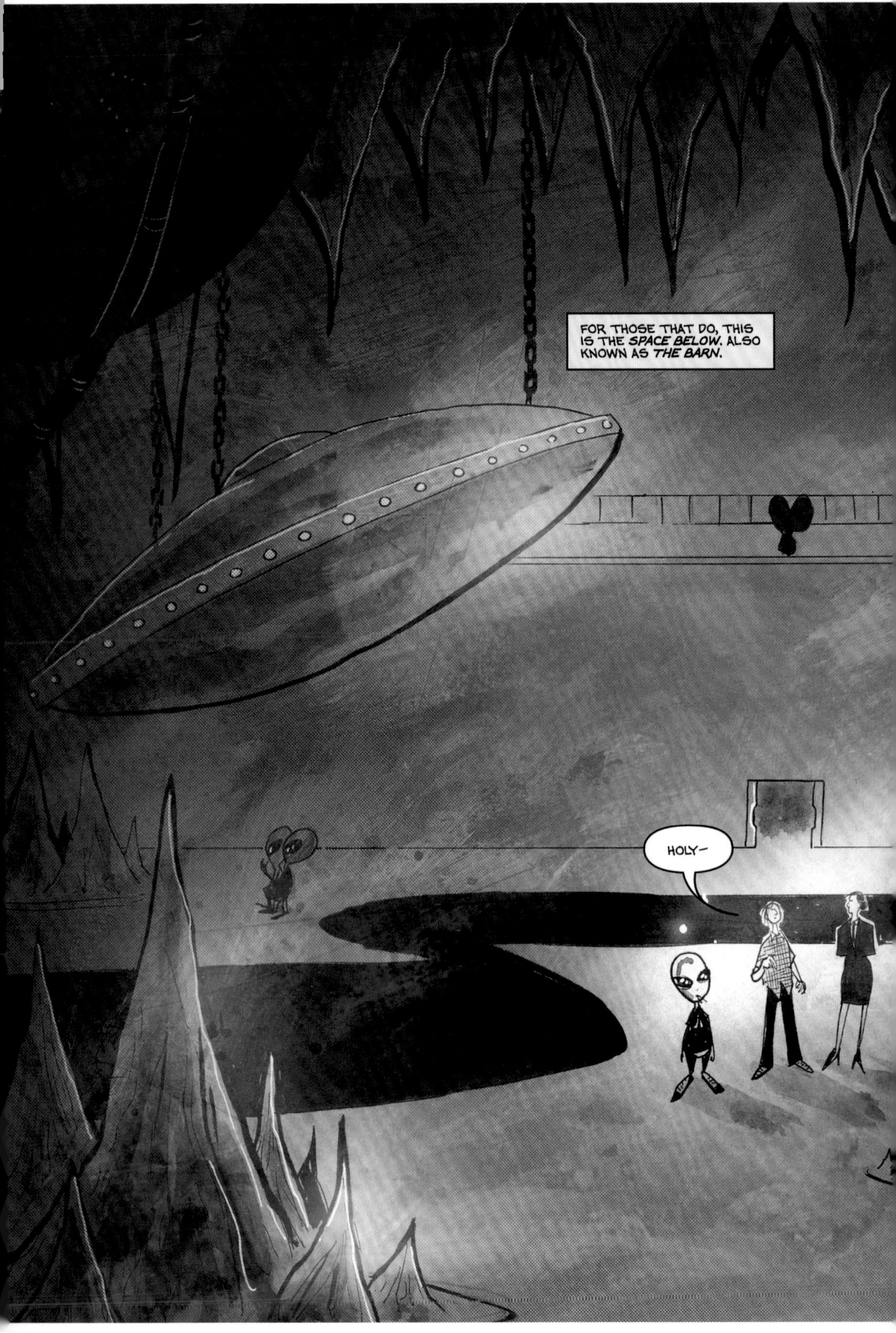
FOR THOSE THAT DO, THIS IS THE *SPACE BELOW*. ALSO KNOWN AS *THE BARN*.
HOLY–

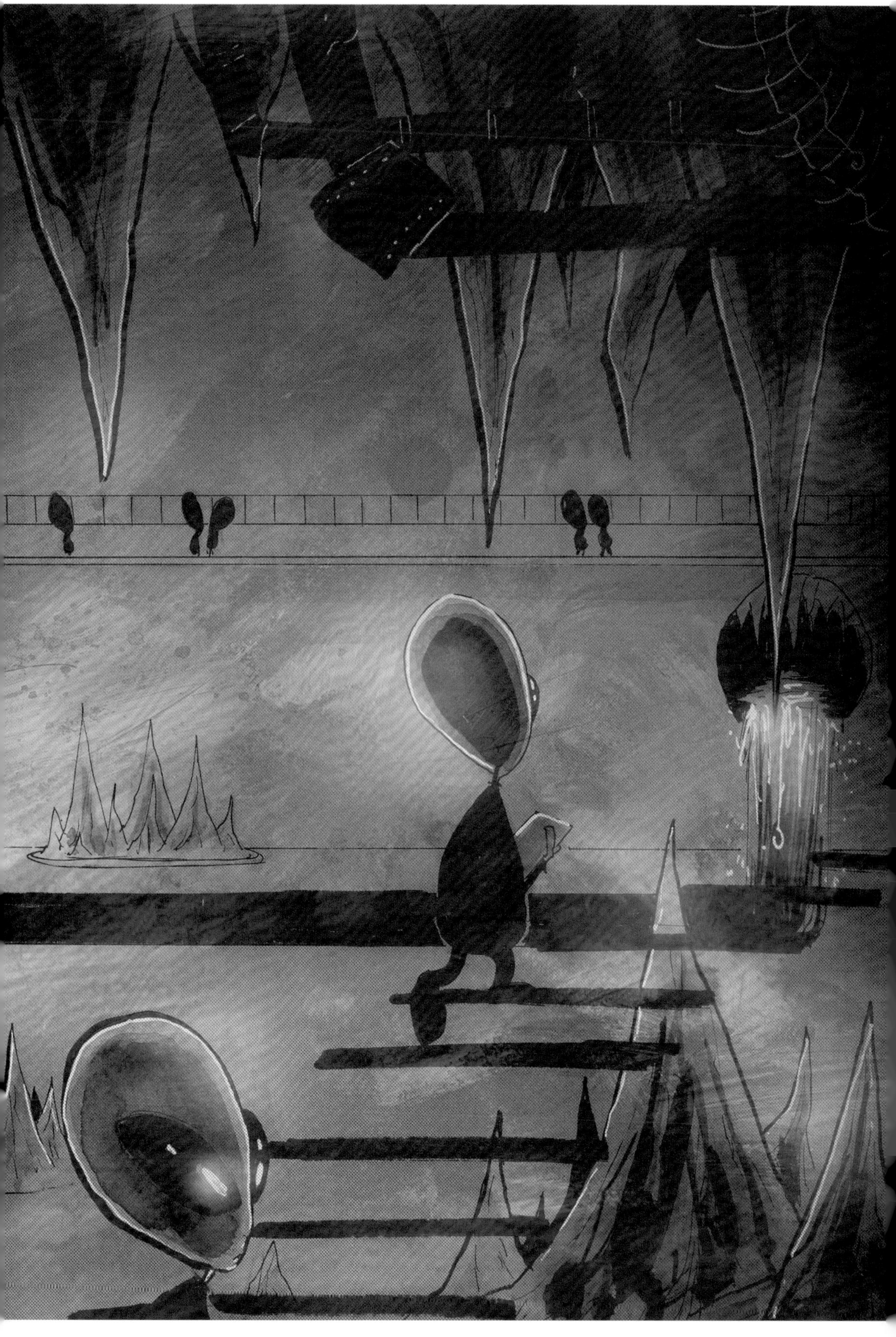

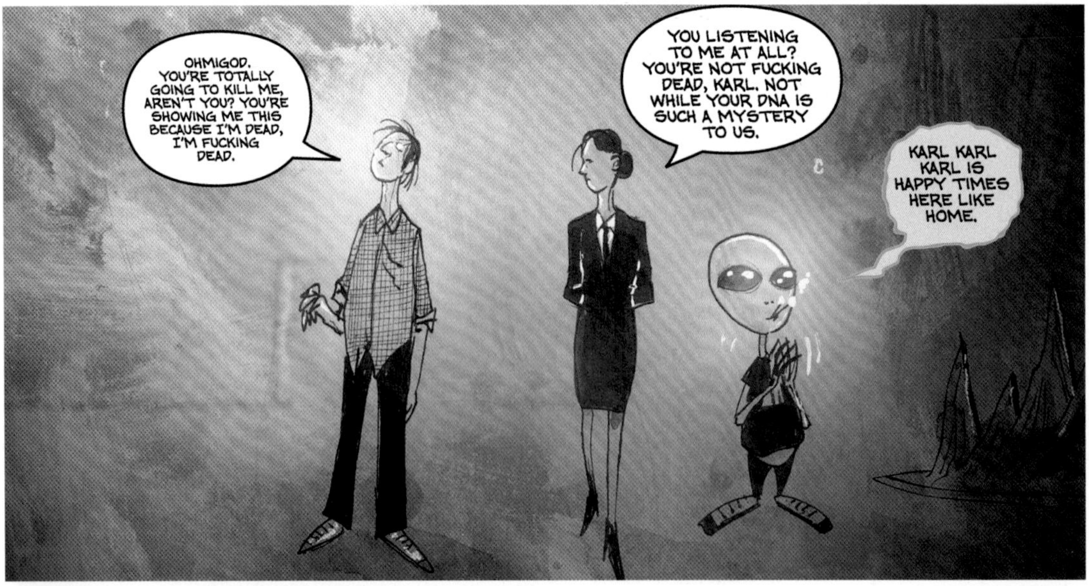
OHMIGOD. YOU'RE TOTALLY GOING TO KILL ME, AREN'T YOU? YOU'RE SHOWING ME THIS BECAUSE I'M DEAD, I'M FUCKING DEAD.
YOU LISTENING TO ME AT ALL? YOU'RE NOT FUCKING DEAD, KARL. NOT WHILE YOUR DNA IS SUCH A MYSTERY TO US.
KARL KARL KARL IS HAPPY TIMES HERE LIKE HOME.

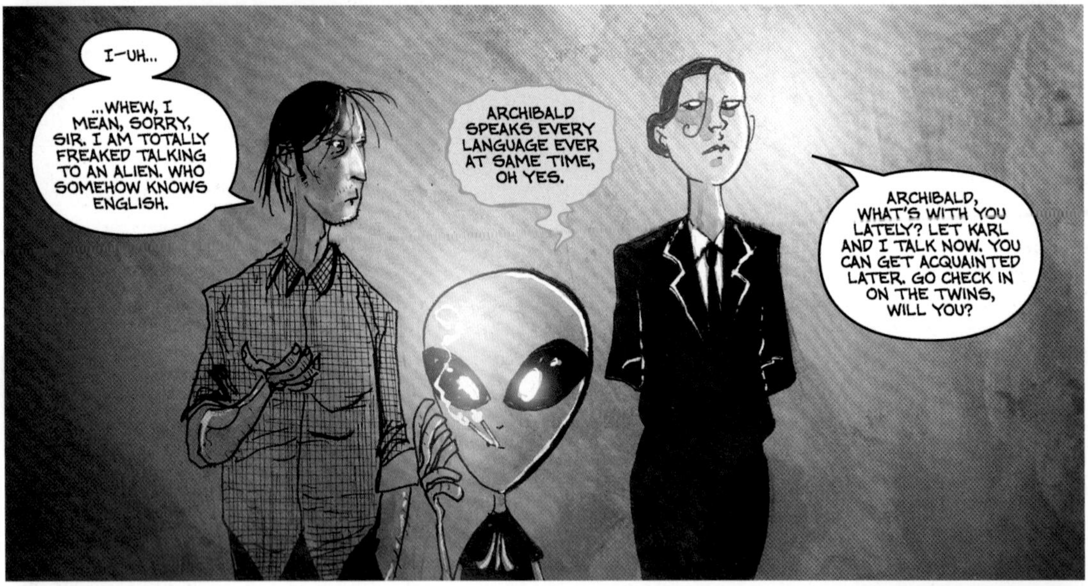
I—UH...
...WHEW, I MEAN, SORRY, SIR. I AM TOTALLY FREAKED TALKING TO AN ALIEN. WHO SOMEHOW KNOWS ENGLISH.
ARCHIBALD SPEAKS EVERY LANGUAGE EVER AT SAME TIME, OH YES.
ARCHIBALD, WHAT'S WITH YOU LATELY? LET KARL AND I TALK NOW. YOU CAN GET ACQUAINTED LATER. GO CHECK IN ON THE TWINS, WILL YOU?

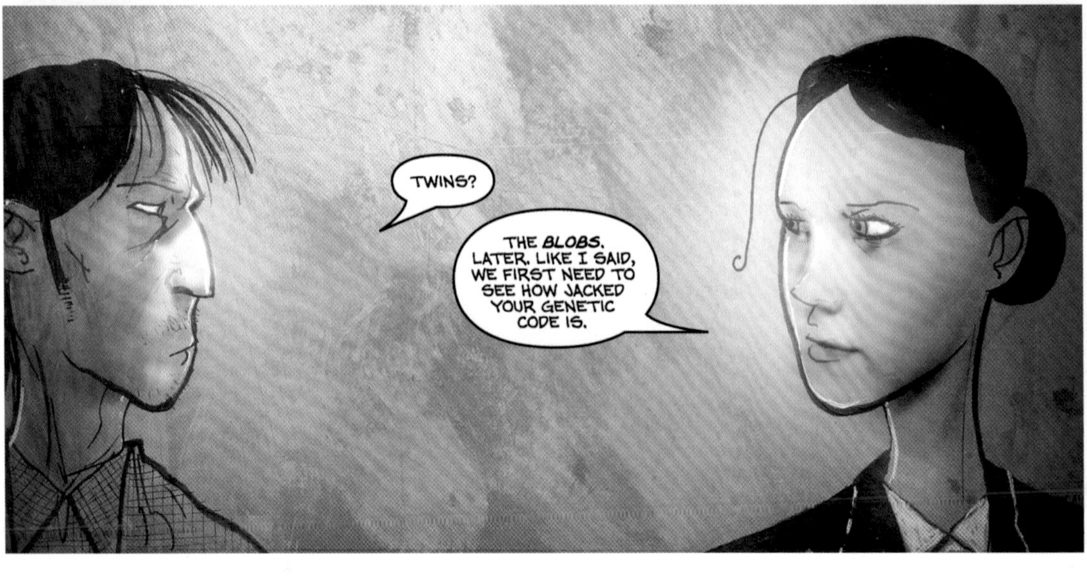
TWINS?
THE *BLOBS*. LATER. LIKE I SAID, WE FIRST NEED TO SEE HOW JACKED YOUR GENETIC CODE IS.

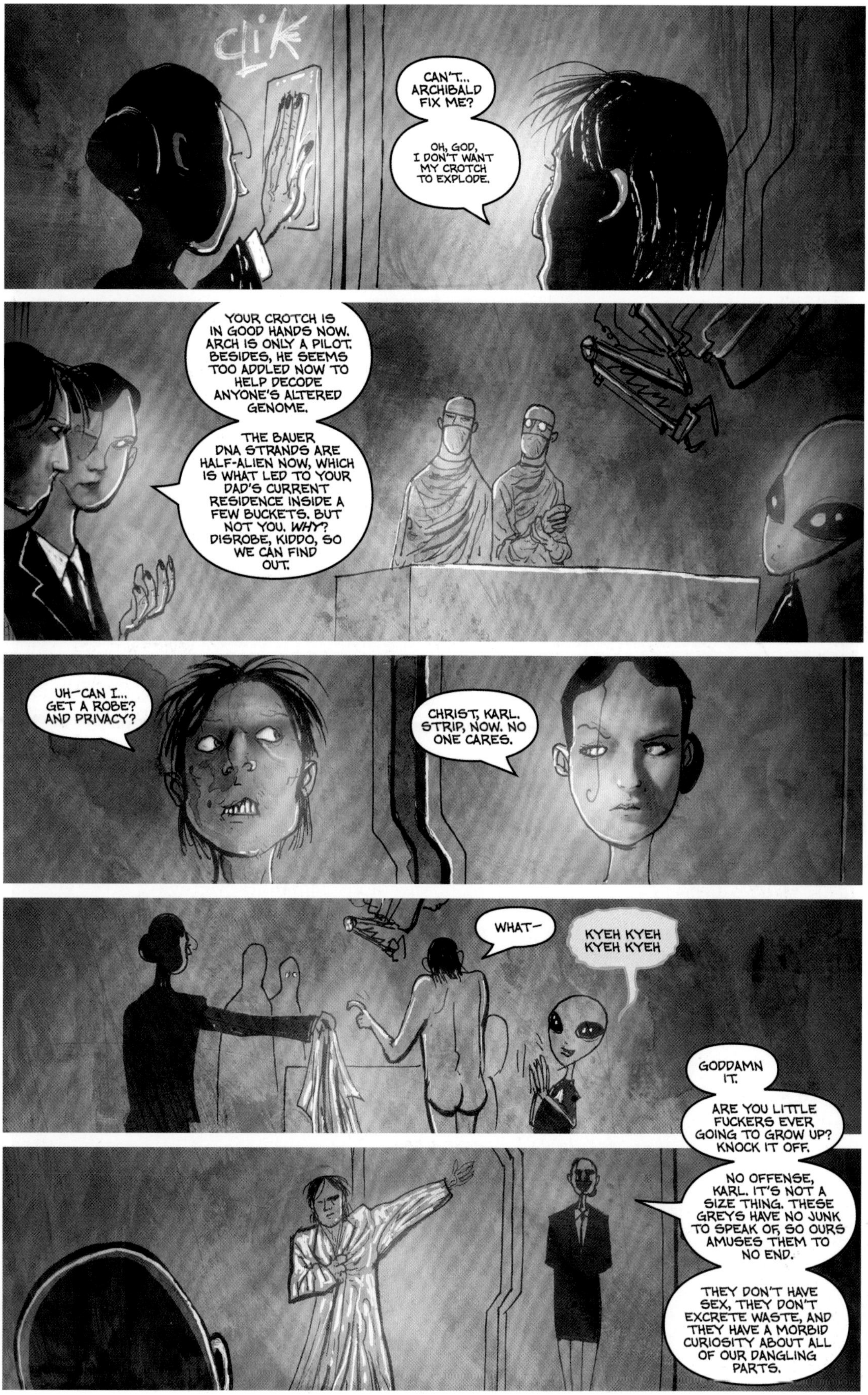
CLIK
CAN'T... ARCHIBALD FIX ME?
OH, GOD, I DON'T WANT MY CROTCH TO EXPLODE.
YOUR CROTCH IS IN GOOD HANDS NOW. ARCH IS ONLY A PILOT. BESIDES, HE SEEMS TOO ADDLED NOW TO HELP DECODE ANYONE'S ALTERED GENOME.
THE BAUER DNA STRANDS ARE HALF-ALIEN NOW, WHICH IS WHAT LED TO YOUR DAD'S CURRENT RESIDENCE INSIDE A FEW BUCKETS. BUT NOT YOU. *WHY?* DISROBE, KIDDO, SO WE CAN FIND OUT.
UH--CAN I... GET A ROBE? AND PRIVACY?
CHRIST, KARL. STRIP, NOW. NO ONE CARES.
WHAT--
KYEH KYEH KYEH KYEH
GODDAMN IT.
ARE YOU LITTLE FUCKERS EVER GOING TO GROW UP? KNOCK IT OFF.
NO OFFENSE, KARL. IT'S NOT A SIZE THING. THESE GREYS HAVE NO JUNK TO SPEAK OF, SO OURS AMUSES THEM TO NO END.
THEY DON'T HAVE SEX, THEY DON'T EXCRETE WASTE, AND THEY HAVE A MORBID CURIOSITY ABOUT ALL OF OUR DANGLING PARTS.

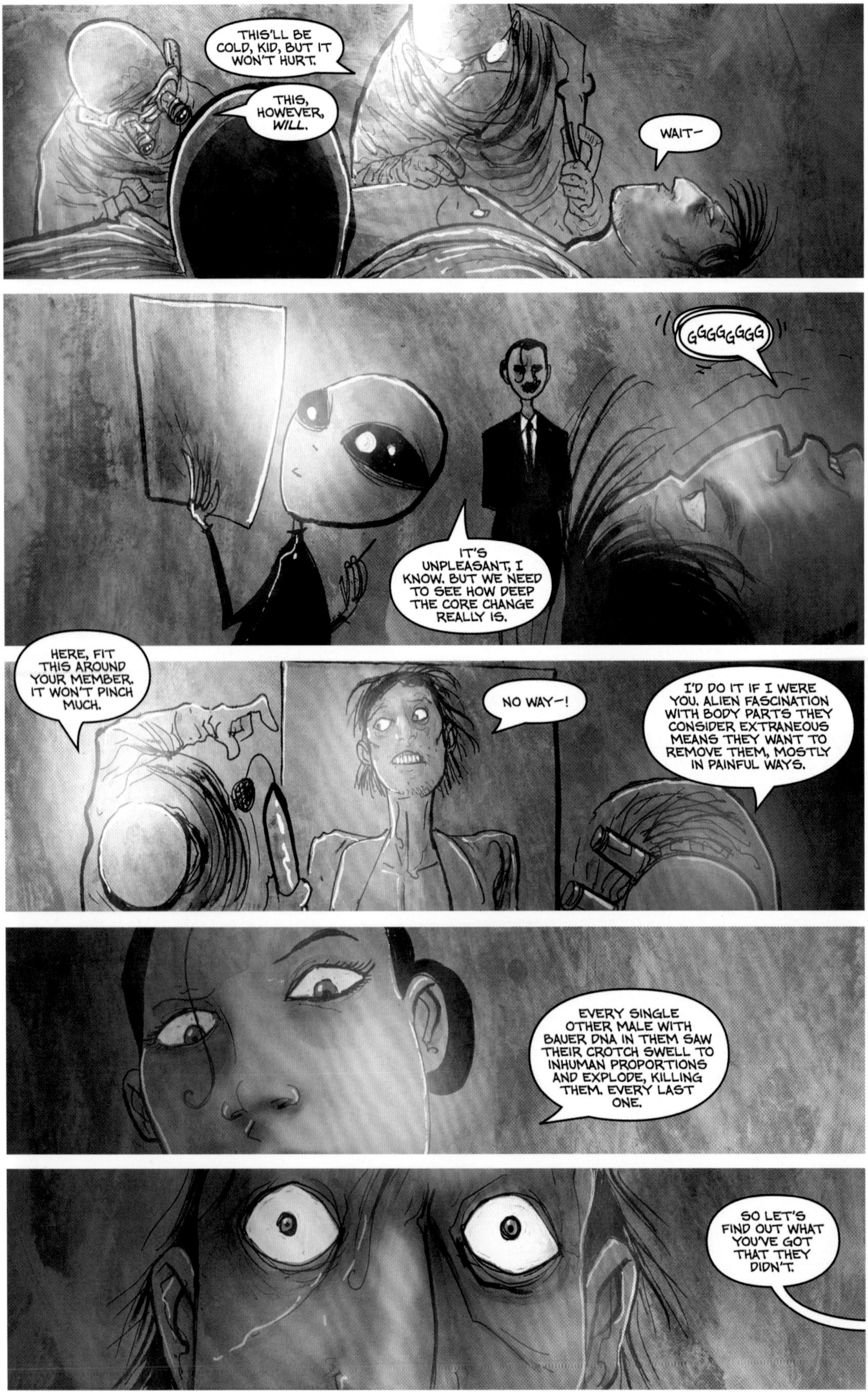
THIS'LL BE COLD, KID, BUT IT WON'T HURT.
THIS, HOWEVER, WILL.
WAIT-
GGGGGGGG
IT'S UNPLEASANT, I KNOW. BUT WE NEED TO SEE HOW DEEP THE CORE CHANGE REALLY IS.
HERE, FIT THIS AROUND YOUR MEMBER. IT WON'T PINCH MUCH.
NO WAY-!
I'D DO IT IF I WERE YOU. ALIEN FASCINATION WITH BODY PARTS THEY CONSIDER EXTRANEOUS MEANS THEY WANT TO REMOVE THEM, MOSTLY IN PAINFUL WAYS.
EVERY SINGLE OTHER MALE WITH BAUER DNA IN THEM SAW THEIR CROTCH SWELL TO INHUMAN PROPORTIONS AND EXPLODE, KILLING THEM. EVERY LAST ONE.
SO LET'S FIND OUT WHAT YOU'VE GOT THAT THEY DIDN'T.

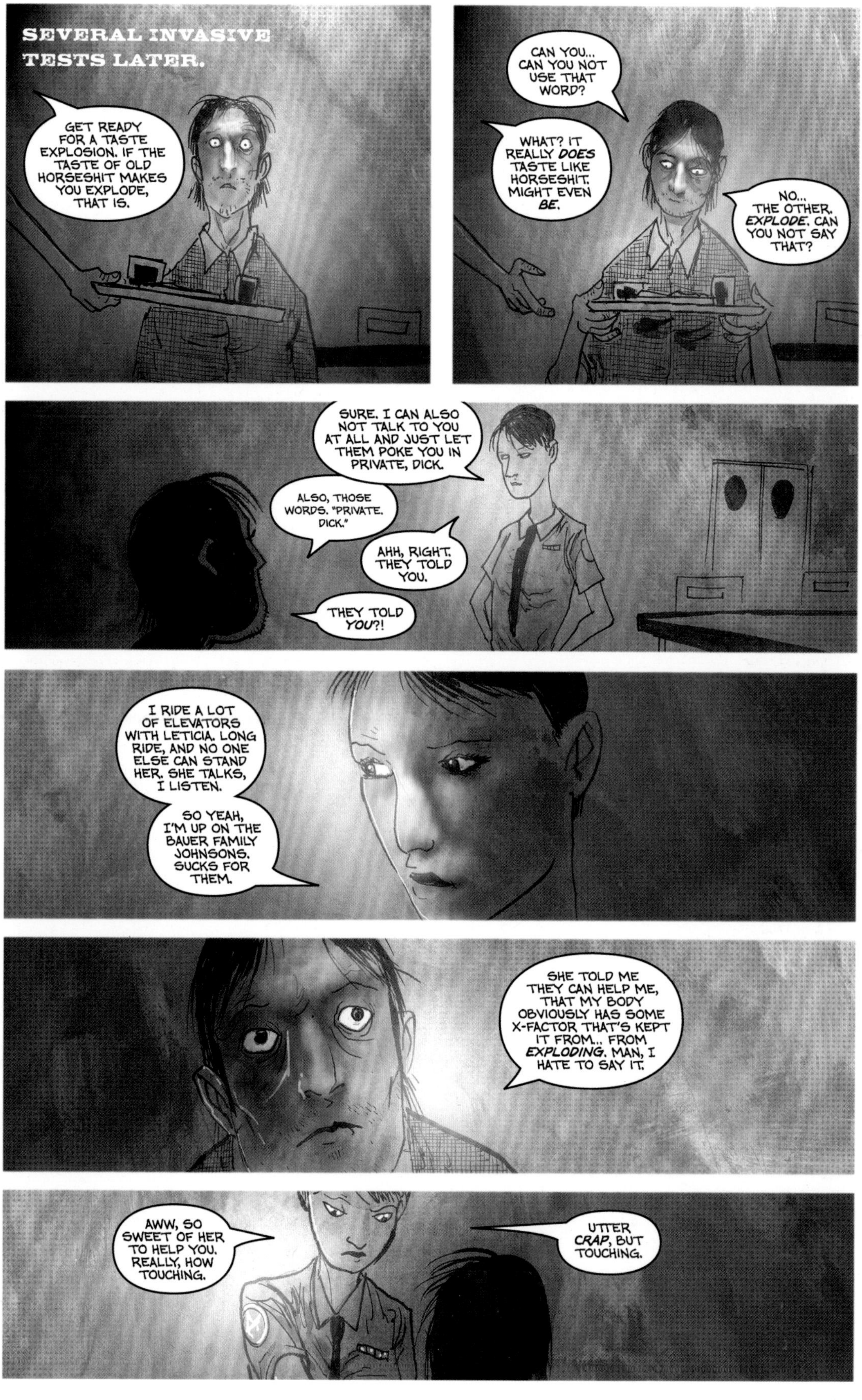
SEVERAL INVASIVE TESTS LATER.
GET READY FOR A TASTE EXPLOSION. IF THE TASTE OF OLD HORSESHIT MAKES YOU EXPLODE, THAT IS.
CAN YOU... CAN YOU NOT USE THAT WORD?
WHAT? IT REALLY *DOES* TASTE LIKE HORSESHIT. MIGHT EVEN *BE*.
NO... THE OTHER. *EXPLODE*. CAN YOU NOT SAY THAT?
SURE. I CAN ALSO NOT TALK TO YOU AT ALL AND JUST LET THEM POKE YOU IN PRIVATE, DICK.
ALSO, THOSE WORDS. "PRIVATE. DICK."
AHH, RIGHT. THEY TOLD YOU.
THEY TOLD *YOU*?!
I RIDE A LOT OF ELEVATORS WITH LETICIA. LONG RIDE, AND NO ONE ELSE CAN STAND HER. SHE TALKS, I LISTEN.
SO YEAH, I'M UP ON THE BAUER FAMILY JOHNSONS. SUCKS FOR THEM.
SHE TOLD ME THEY CAN HELP ME, THAT MY BODY OBVIOUSLY HAS SOME X-FACTOR THAT'S KEPT IT FROM... FROM *EXPLODING*. MAN, I HATE TO SAY IT.
AWW, SO SWEET OF HER TO HELP YOU. REALLY, HOW TOUCHING.
UTTER *CRAP*, BUT TOUCHING.

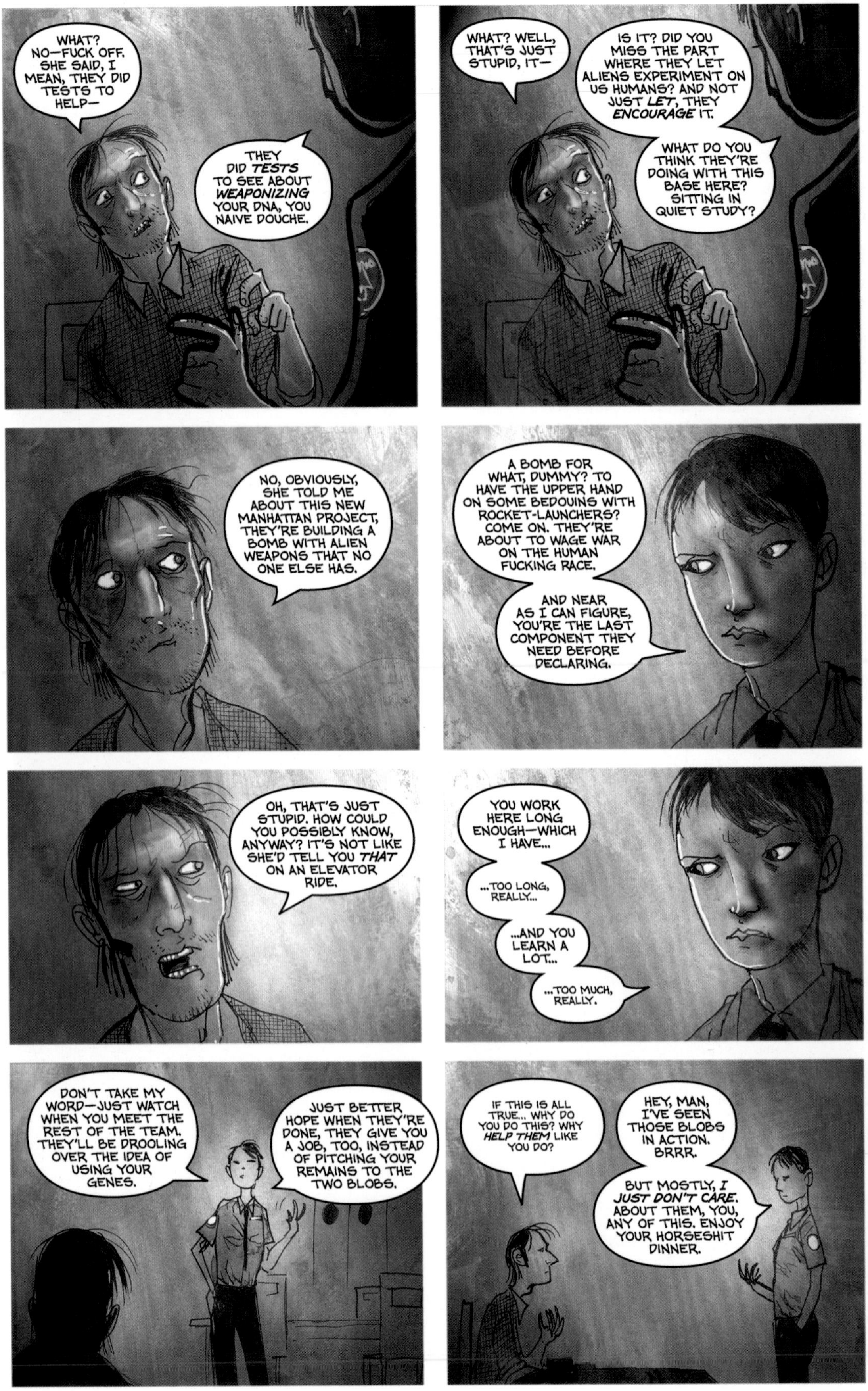
WHAT? NO—FUCK OFF. SHE SAID, I MEAN, THEY DID TESTS TO HELP—
THEY DID *TESTS* TO SEE ABOUT *WEAPONIZING* YOUR DNA, YOU NAIVE DOUCHE.
WHAT? WELL, THAT'S JUST STUPID, IT—
IS IT? DID YOU MISS THE PART WHERE THEY LET ALIENS EXPERIMENT ON US HUMANS? AND NOT JUST *LET*, THEY *ENCOURAGE* IT.
WHAT DO YOU THINK THEY'RE DOING WITH THIS BASE HERE? SITTING IN QUIET STUDY?
NO, OBVIOUSLY, SHE TOLD ME ABOUT THIS NEW MANHATTAN PROJECT, THEY'RE BUILDING A BOMB WITH ALIEN WEAPONS THAT NO ONE ELSE HAS.
A BOMB FOR WHAT, DUMMY? TO HAVE THE UPPER HAND ON SOME BEDOUINS WITH ROCKET-LAUNCHERS? COME ON. THEY'RE ABOUT TO WAGE WAR ON THE HUMAN FUCKING RACE.
AND NEAR AS I CAN FIGURE, YOU'RE THE LAST COMPONENT THEY NEED BEFORE DECLARING.
OH, THAT'S JUST STUPID. HOW COULD YOU POSSIBLY KNOW, ANYWAY? IT'S NOT LIKE SHE'D TELL YOU *THAT* ON AN ELEVATOR RIDE.
YOU WORK HERE LONG ENOUGH—WHICH I HAVE...
...TOO LONG, REALLY...
...AND YOU LEARN A LOT...
...TOO MUCH, REALLY.
DON'T TAKE MY WORD—JUST WATCH WHEN YOU MEET THE REST OF THE TEAM. THEY'LL BE DROOLING OVER THE IDEA OF USING YOUR GENES.
JUST BETTER HOPE WHEN THEY'RE DONE, THEY GIVE YOU A JOB, TOO, INSTEAD OF PITCHING YOUR REMAINS TO THE TWO BLOBS.
IF THIS IS ALL TRUE... WHY DO YOU DO THIS? WHY *HELP THEM* LIKE YOU DO?
HEY, MAN, I'VE SEEN THOSE BLOBS IN ACTION. BRRR.
BUT MOSTLY, *I JUST DON'T CARE.* ABOUT THEM, YOU, ANY OF THIS. ENJOY YOUR HORSESHIT DINNER.

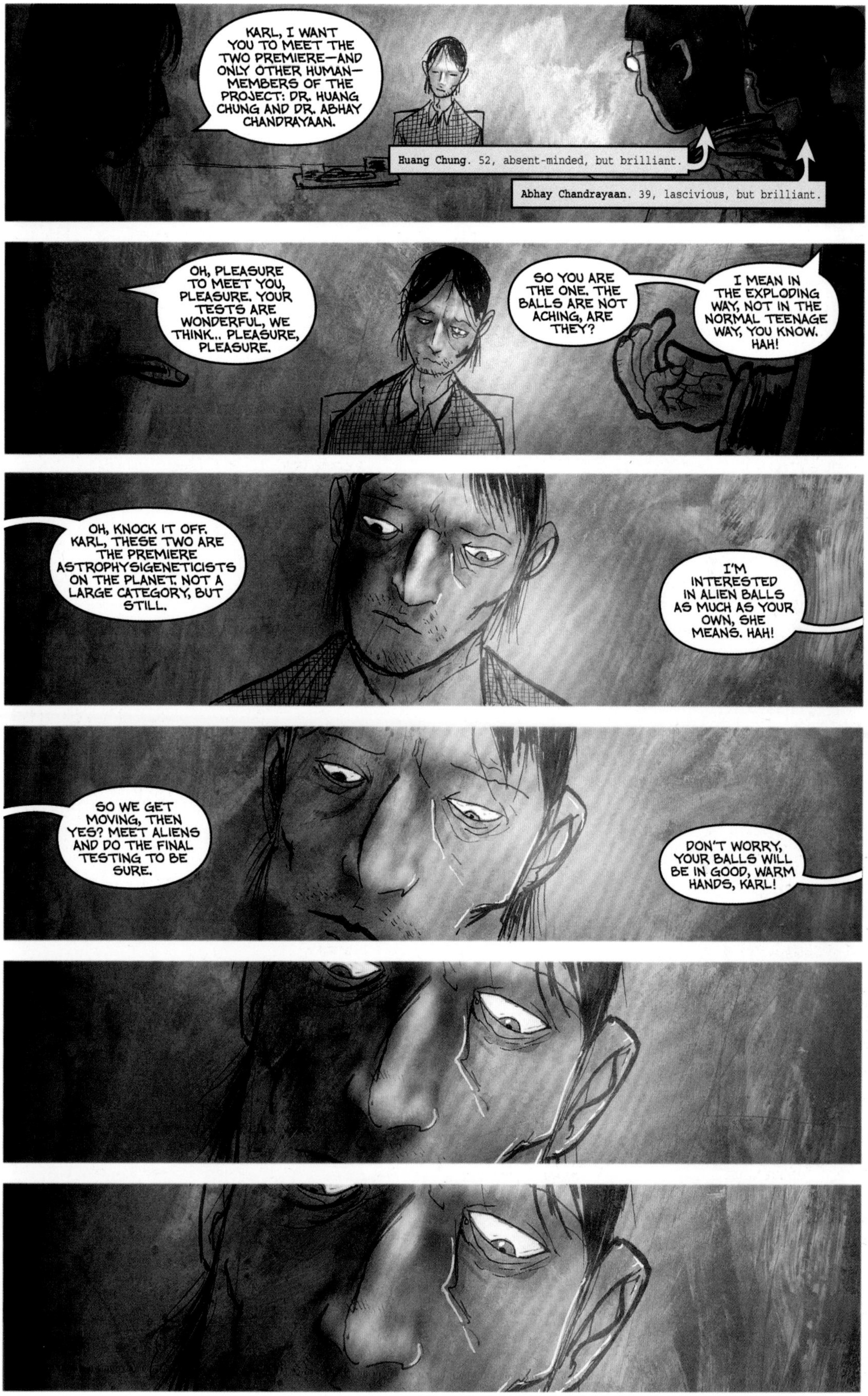
KARL, I WANT YOU TO MEET THE TWO PREMIERE—AND ONLY OTHER HUMAN—MEMBERS OF THE PROJECT: DR. HUANG CHUNG AND DR. ABHAY CHANDRAYAAN.
Huang Chung. 52, absent-minded, but brilliant.
Abhay Chandrayaan. 39, lascivious, but brilliant.
OH, PLEASURE TO MEET YOU, PLEASURE. YOUR TESTS ARE WONDERFUL, WE THINK... PLEASURE, PLEASURE.
SO YOU ARE THE ONE. THE BALLS ARE NOT ACHING, ARE THEY?
I MEAN IN THE EXPLODING WAY, NOT IN THE NORMAL TEENAGE WAY, YOU KNOW. HAH!
OH, KNOCK IT OFF. KARL, THESE TWO ARE THE PREMIERE ASTROPHYSIGENETICISTS ON THE PLANET. NOT A LARGE CATEGORY, BUT STILL.
I'M INTERESTED IN ALIEN BALLS AS MUCH AS YOUR OWN, SHE MEANS. HAH!
SO WE GET MOVING, THEN YES? MEET ALIENS AND DO THE FINAL TESTING TO BE SURE.
DON'T WORRY, YOUR BALLS WILL BE IN GOOD, WARM HANDS, KARL!

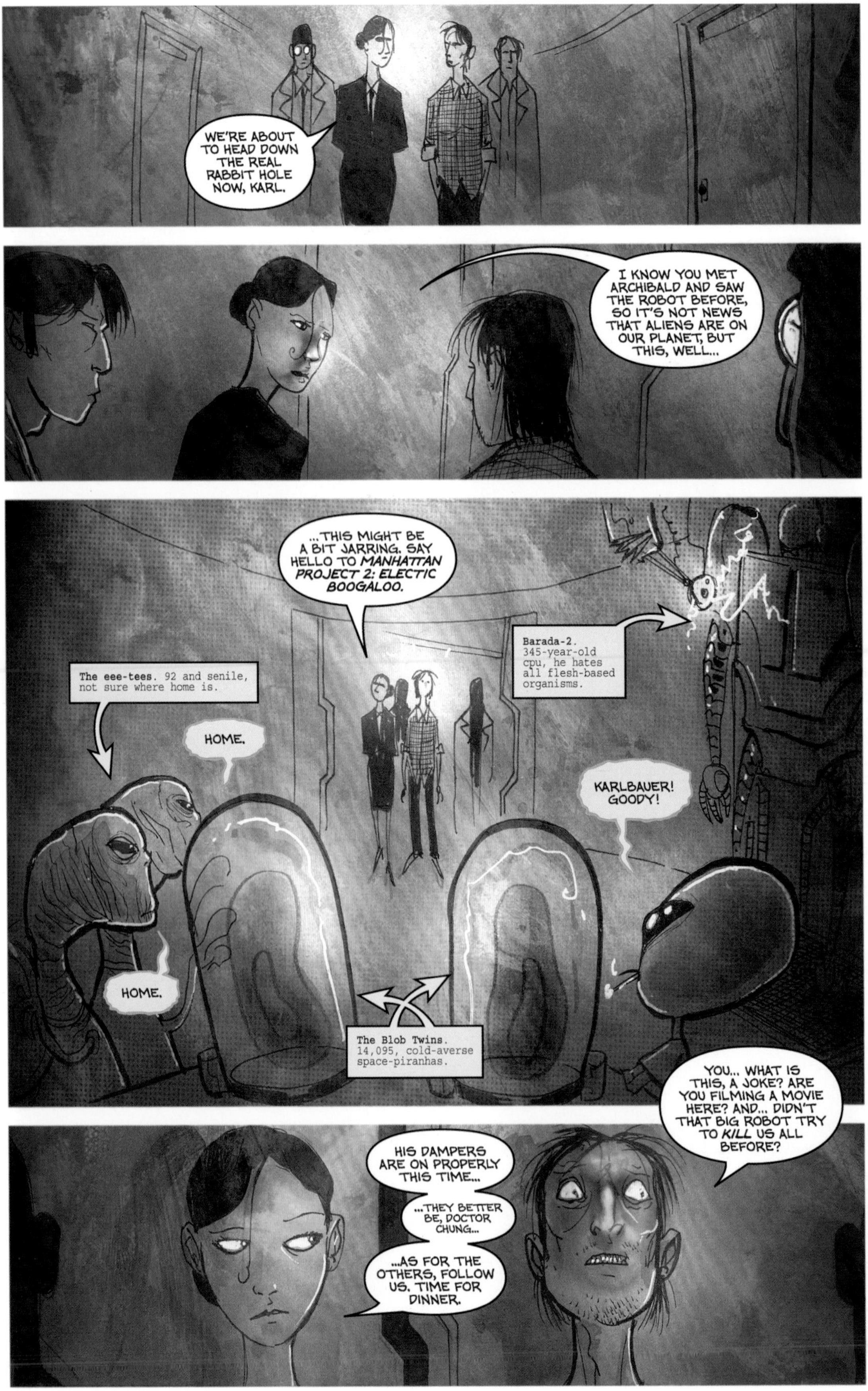
WE'RE ABOUT TO HEAD DOWN THE REAL RABBIT HOLE NOW, KARL.
I KNOW YOU MET ARCHIBALD AND SAW THE ROBOT BEFORE, SO IT'S NOT NEWS THAT ALIENS ARE ON OUR PLANET, BUT THIS, WELL...
...THIS MIGHT BE A BIT JARRING. SAY HELLO TO MANHATTAN PROJECT 2: ELECTIC BOOGALOO.
The eee-tees. 92 and senile, not sure where home is.
Barada-2. 345-year-old cpu, he hates all flesh-based organisms.
HOME.
KARLBAUER! GOODY!
HOME.
The Blob Twins. 14,095, cold-averse space-piranhas.
YOU... WHAT IS THIS, A JOKE? ARE YOU FILMING A MOVIE HERE? AND... DIDN'T THAT BIG ROBOT TRY TO KILL US ALL BEFORE?
HIS DAMPERS ARE ON PROPERLY THIS TIME...
...THEY BETTER BE, DOCTOR CHUNG...
...AS FOR THE OTHERS, FOLLOW US. TIME FOR DINNER.

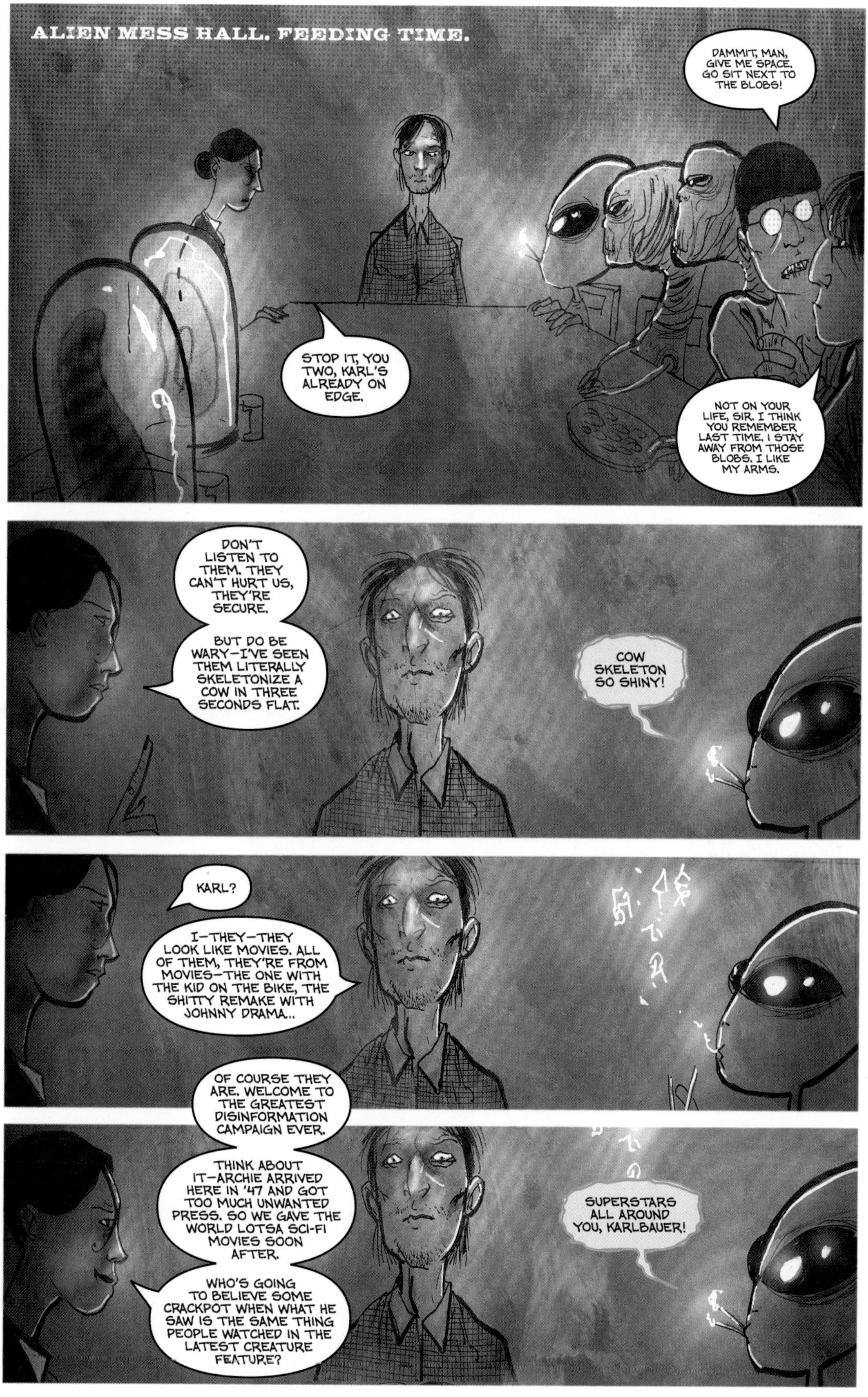

ALIEN MESS HALL. FEEDING TIME.
DAMMIT, MAN, GIVE ME SPACE. GO SIT NEXT TO THE BLOBS!
STOP IT, YOU TWO, KARL'S ALREADY ON EDGE.
NOT ON YOUR LIFE, SIR. I THINK YOU REMEMBER LAST TIME. I STAY AWAY FROM THOSE BLOBS. I LIKE MY ARMS.
DON'T LISTEN TO THEM. THEY CAN'T HURT US, THEY'RE SECURE.
BUT DO BE WARY—I'VE SEEN THEM LITERALLY SKELETONIZE A COW IN THREE SECONDS FLAT.
COW SKELETON SO SHINY!
KARL?
I—THEY—THEY LOOK LIKE MOVIES. ALL OF THEM, THEY'RE FROM MOVIES—THE ONE WITH THE KID ON THE BIKE, THE SHITTY REMAKE WITH JOHNNY DRAMA...
OF COURSE THEY ARE. WELCOME TO THE GREATEST DISINFORMATION CAMPAIGN EVER.
THINK ABOUT IT—ARCHIE ARRIVED HERE IN '47 AND GOT TOO MUCH UNWANTED PRESS. SO WE GAVE THE WORLD LOTSA SCI-FI MOVIES SOON AFTER.
WHO'S GOING TO BELIEVE SOME CRACKPOT WHEN WHAT HE SAW IS THE SAME THING PEOPLE WATCHED IN THE LATEST CREATURE FEATURE?
SUPERSTARS ALL AROUND YOU, KARLBAUER!

EVERY TIME THERE'S WORD ABOUT A NEW ARRIVAL, TIME FOR ANOTHER MOVIE. A RETIRED COLONEL BLABS ABOUT HIS ALIEN ROOMMATES? CUE THE REECE'S PIECES TIE-IN AND COLLECT THE BOX OFFICE.

THESE TWO, WE DID THAT REMAKE AFTER THEY GOT OUT ONCE. THEY KILLED SEVENTEEN... NOT COUNTING THE COW. ABSORBED 'EM IN SECONDS FLAT, GREW TO THE SIZE OF HYBRID CARS. THAT WAS SCARY.

WHAT CAN I SAY, THEY'RE SLIPPERY BUGGERS.

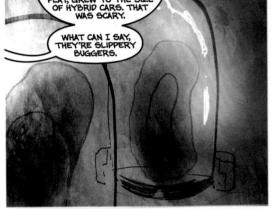

PEOPLE ARE DYING DOWN HERE? REGULARLY? AND THIS IS *OKAY*?

NOT *THAT* REGULARLY, KARL. PEOPLE DIE EVERYWHERE. BUT THESE SACRIFICES ARE BEING DONE FOR THE GOOD OF THE ENTIRE PLANET, AND MAYBE BEYOND.

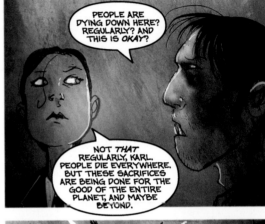

"YOU'RE POSSIBLY A BIT SLOW, OR STILL IN SHOCK, BUT AN UNDERTAKING LIKE THIS IS NECESSARY. VITAL. AND DONE UNDER THE AUSPICES OF THE GOVERNMENTS OF THE WORLD.

"WELL, THE ONES THAT MATTER, ANYWAY.

SSSSHHLLLLK

LLLLLKKKK

"WE NEED YOU ON OUR SIDE, KARL—THE HUMAN RACE'S SIDE. YOU'RE THE FINAL PIECE OF THE MOST IMPORTANT PUZZLE IN HISTORY."

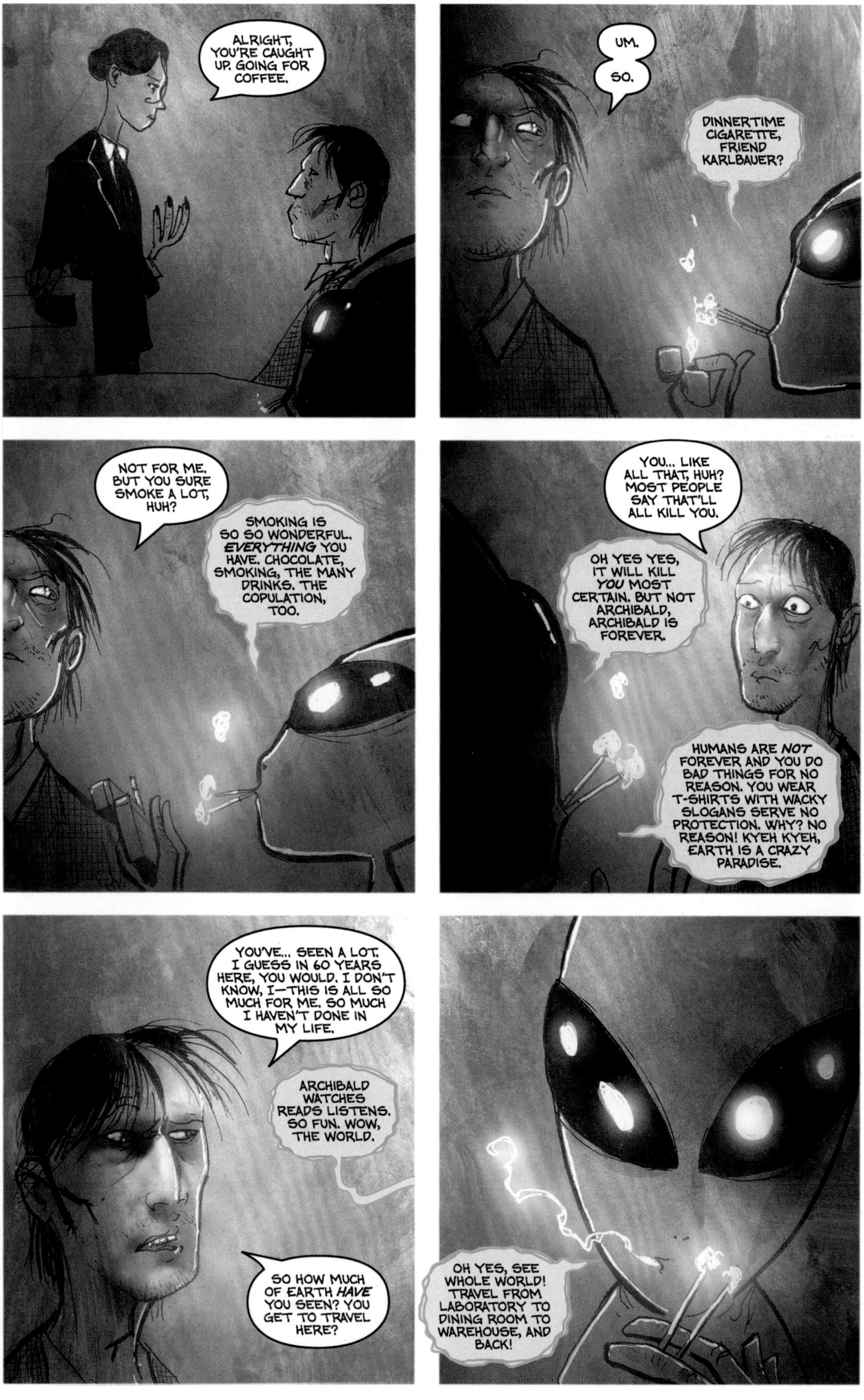
ALRIGHT, YOU'RE CAUGHT UP. GOING FOR COFFEE.
UM.
SO.
DINNERTIME CIGARETTE, FRIEND KARLBAUER?
NOT FOR ME. BUT YOU SURE SMOKE A LOT, HUH?
SMOKING IS SO SO WONDERFUL. *EVERYTHING* YOU HAVE. CHOCOLATE, SMOKING, THE MANY DRINKS. THE COPULATION, TOO.
YOU... LIKE ALL THAT, HUH? MOST PEOPLE SAY THAT'LL ALL KILL YOU.
OH YES YES, IT WILL KILL *YOU* MOST CERTAIN. BUT NOT ARCHIBALD, ARCHIBALD IS FOREVER.
HUMANS ARE *NOT* FOREVER AND YOU DO BAD THINGS FOR NO REASON. YOU WEAR T-SHIRTS WITH WACKY SLOGANS SERVE NO PROTECTION. WHY? NO REASON! KYEH KYEH, EARTH IS A CRAZY PARADISE.
YOU'VE... SEEN A LOT. I GUESS IN 60 YEARS HERE, YOU WOULD. I DON'T KNOW, I—THIS IS ALL SO MUCH FOR ME. SO MUCH I HAVEN'T DONE IN MY LIFE.
ARCHIBALD WATCHES READS LISTENS. SO FUN. WOW, THE WORLD.
SO HOW MUCH OF EARTH *HAVE* YOU SEEN? YOU GET TO TRAVEL HERE?
OH YES, SEE WHOLE WORLD! TRAVEL FROM LABORATORY TO DINING ROOM TO WAREHOUSE, AND BACK!

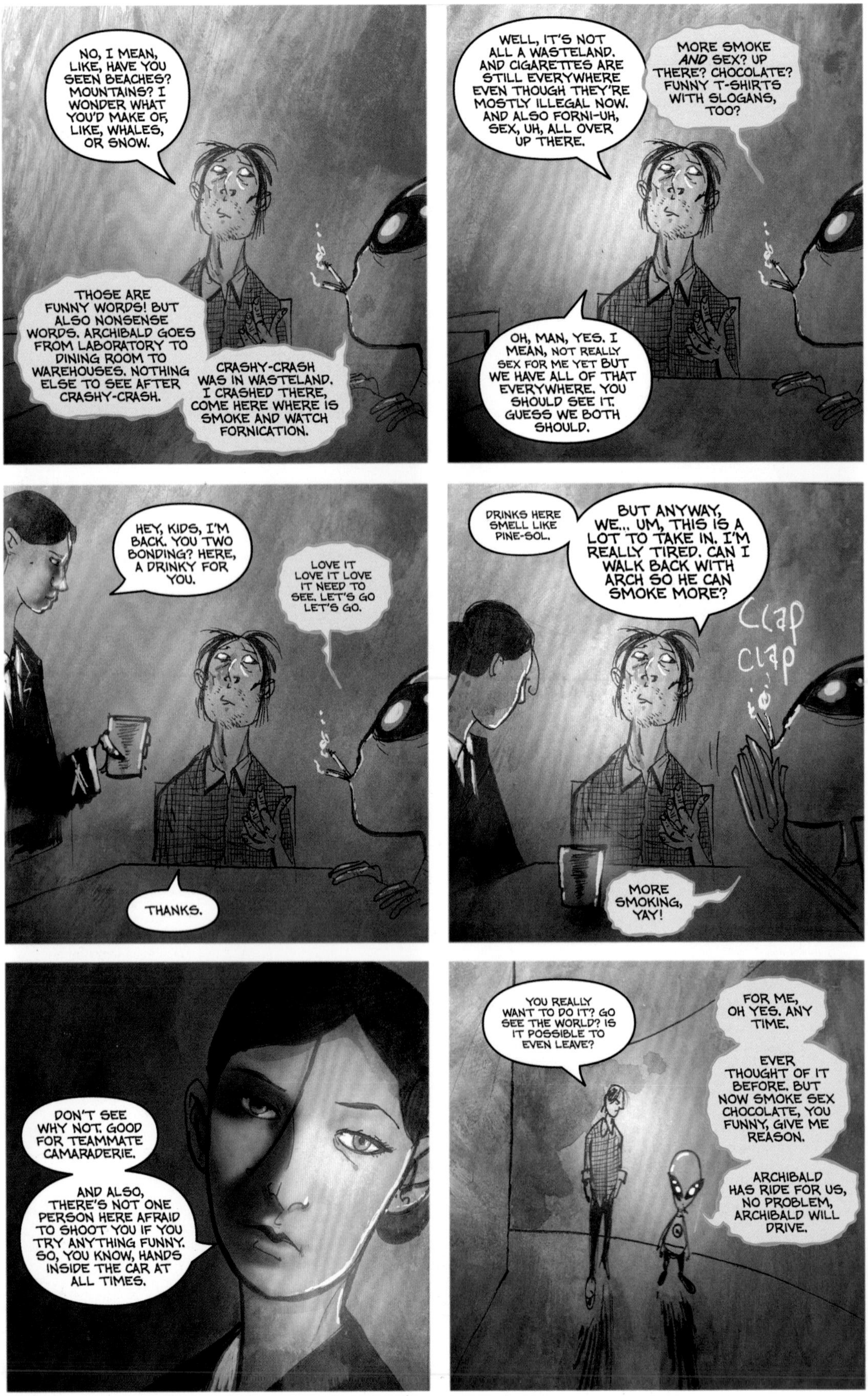
NO, I MEAN, LIKE, HAVE YOU SEEN BEACHES? MOUNTAINS? I WONDER WHAT YOU'D MAKE OF, LIKE, WHALES, OR SNOW.
THOSE ARE FUNNY WORDS! BUT ALSO NONSENSE WORDS. ARCHIBALD GOES FROM LABORATORY TO DINING ROOM TO WAREHOUSES. NOTHING ELSE TO SEE AFTER CRASHY-CRASH.
CRASHY-CRASH WAS IN WASTELAND. I CRASHED THERE, COME HERE WHERE IS SMOKE AND WATCH FORNICATION.
WELL, IT'S NOT ALL A WASTELAND. AND CIGARETTES ARE STILL EVERYWHERE EVEN THOUGH THEY'RE MOSTLY ILLEGAL NOW. AND ALSO FORNI-UH, SEX, UH, ALL OVER UP THERE.
MORE SMOKE AND SEX? UP THERE? CHOCOLATE? FUNNY T-SHIRTS WITH SLOGANS, TOO?
OH, MAN, YES. I MEAN, NOT REALLY SEX FOR ME YET BUT WE HAVE ALL OF THAT EVERYWHERE. YOU SHOULD SEE IT. GUESS WE BOTH SHOULD.
HEY, KIDS, I'M BACK. YOU TWO BONDING? HERE, A DRINKY FOR YOU.
LOVE IT LOVE IT LOVE IT NEED TO SEE. LET'S GO LET'S GO.
THANKS.
DRINKS HERE SMELL LIKE PINE-SOL.
BUT ANYWAY, WE... UM, THIS IS A LOT TO TAKE IN. I'M REALLY TIRED. CAN I WALK BACK WITH ARCH SO HE CAN SMOKE MORE?
Clap
clap
MORE SMOKING, YAY!
DON'T SEE WHY NOT. GOOD FOR TEAMMATE CAMARADERIE.
AND ALSO, THERE'S NOT ONE PERSON HERE AFRAID TO SHOOT YOU IF YOU TRY ANYTHING FUNNY. SO, YOU KNOW, HANDS INSIDE THE CAR AT ALL TIMES.
YOU REALLY WANT TO DO IT? GO SEE THE WORLD? IS IT POSSIBLE TO EVEN LEAVE?
FOR ME, OH YES. ANY TIME.
EVER THOUGHT OF IT BEFORE. BUT NOW SMOKE SEX CHOCOLATE, YOU FUNNY, GIVE ME REASON.
ARCHIBALD HAS RIDE FOR US, NO PROBLEM, ARCHIBALD WILL DRIVE.

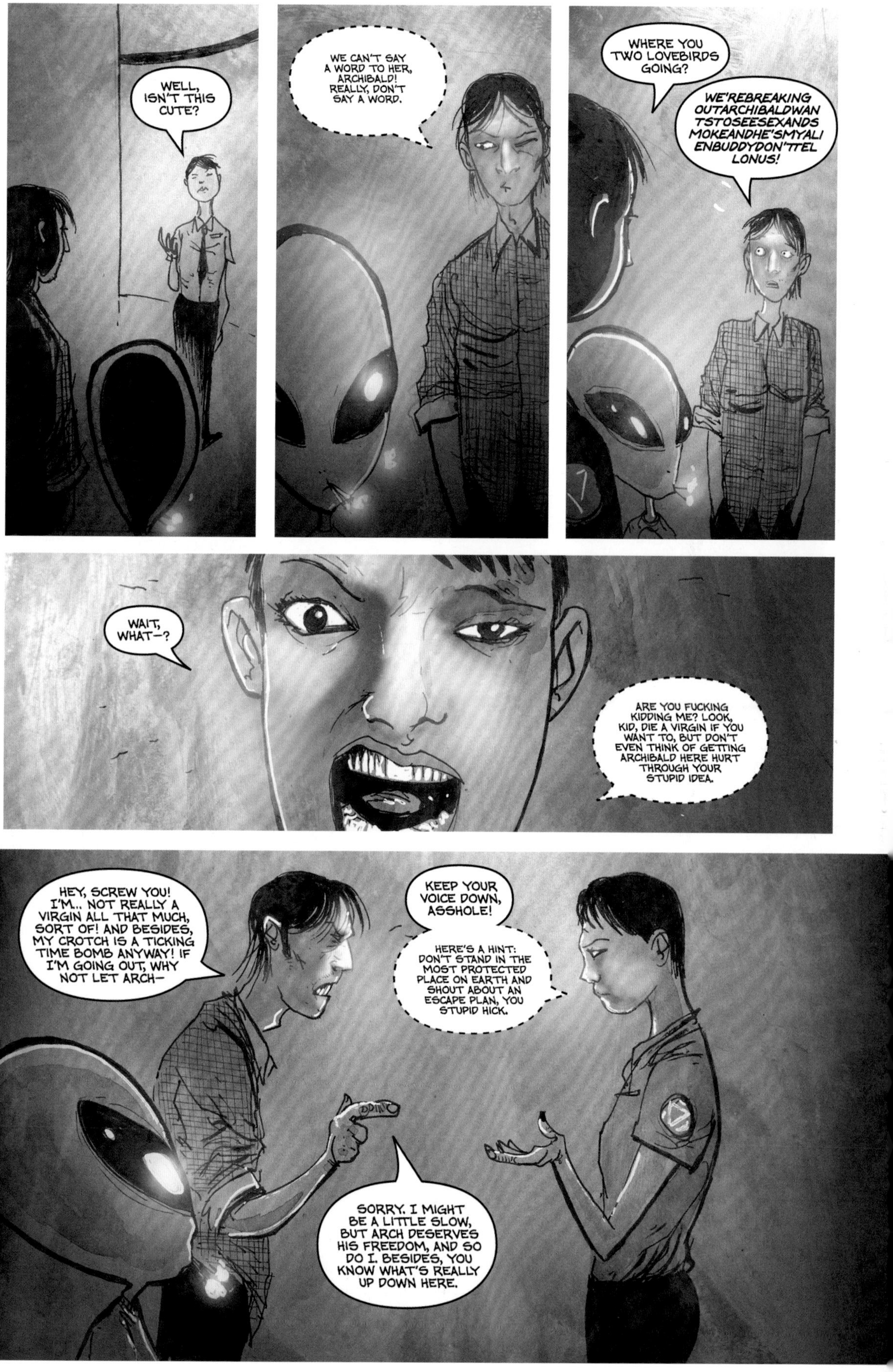
WELL, ISN'T THIS CUTE?
WE CAN'T SAY A WORD TO HER, ARCHIBALD! REALLY, DON'T SAY A WORD.
WHERE YOU TWO LOVEBIRDS GOING?
WE'REBREAKING OUTARCHIBALDWAN TSTOSEESEXANDS MOKEANDHE'SMYALI ENBUDDYDON'TTEL LONUS!
WAIT, WHAT—?
ARE YOU FUCKING KIDDING ME? LOOK, KID, DIE A VIRGIN IF YOU WANT TO, BUT DON'T EVEN THINK OF GETTING ARCHIBALD HERE HURT THROUGH YOUR STUPID IDEA.
HEY, SCREW YOU! I'M.. NOT REALLY A VIRGIN ALL THAT MUCH, SORT OF! AND BESIDES, MY CROTCH IS A TICKING TIME BOMB ANYWAY! IF I'M GOING OUT, WHY NOT LET ARCH—
KEEP YOUR VOICE DOWN, ASSHOLE!
HERE'S A HINT: DON'T STAND IN THE MOST PROTECTED PLACE ON EARTH AND SHOUT ABOUT AN ESCAPE PLAN, YOU STUPID HICK.
SORRY. I MIGHT BE A LITTLE SLOW, BUT ARCH DESERVES HIS FREEDOM, AND SO DO I. BESIDES, YOU KNOW WHAT'S REALLY UP DOWN HERE.

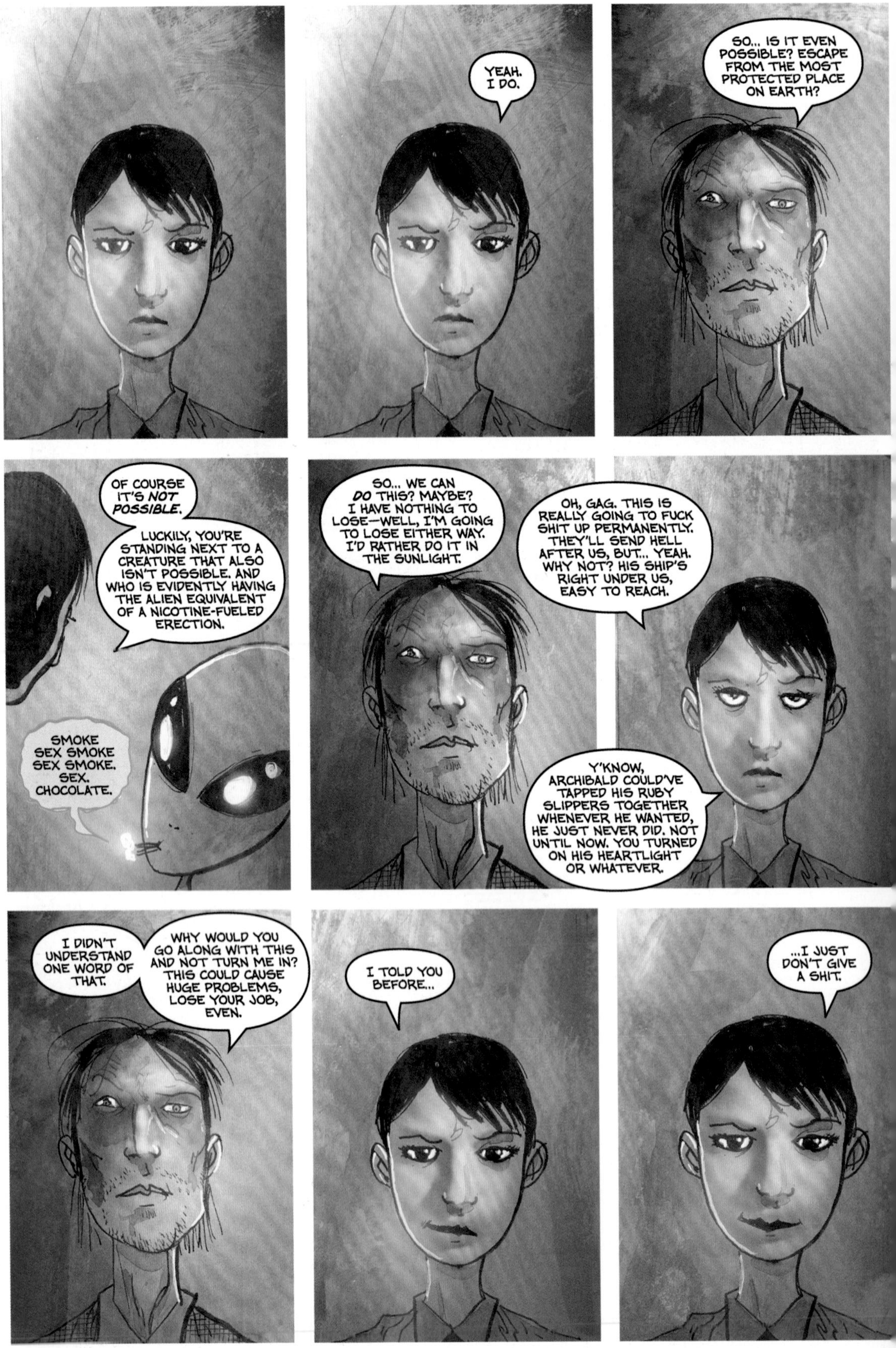
YEAH. I DO.
SO... IS IT EVEN POSSIBLE? ESCAPE FROM THE MOST PROTECTED PLACE ON EARTH?
OF COURSE IT'S *NOT POSSIBLE*.
LUCKILY, YOU'RE STANDING NEXT TO A CREATURE THAT ALSO ISN'T POSSIBLE. AND WHO IS EVIDENTLY HAVING THE ALIEN EQUIVALENT OF A NICOTINE-FUELED ERECTION.
SMOKE SEX SMOKE SEX SMOKE. SEX. CHOCOLATE.
SO... WE CAN *DO* THIS? MAYBE? I HAVE NOTHING TO LOSE—WELL, I'M GOING TO LOSE EITHER WAY. I'D RATHER DO IT IN THE SUNLIGHT.
OH, GAG. THIS IS REALLY GOING TO FUCK SHIT UP PERMANENTLY. THEY'LL SEND HELL AFTER US, BUT... YEAH. WHY NOT? HIS SHIP'S RIGHT UNDER US, EASY TO REACH.
Y'KNOW, ARCHIBALD COULD'VE TAPPED HIS RUBY SLIPPERS TOGETHER WHENEVER HE WANTED, HE JUST NEVER DID. NOT UNTIL NOW. YOU TURNED ON HIS HEARTLIGHT OR WHATEVER.
I DIDN'T UNDERSTAND ONE WORD OF THAT.
WHY WOULD YOU GO ALONG WITH THIS AND NOT TURN ME IN? THIS COULD CAUSE HUGE PROBLEMS, LOSE YOUR JOB, EVEN.
I TOLD YOU BEFORE...
...I JUST DON'T GIVE A SHIT.

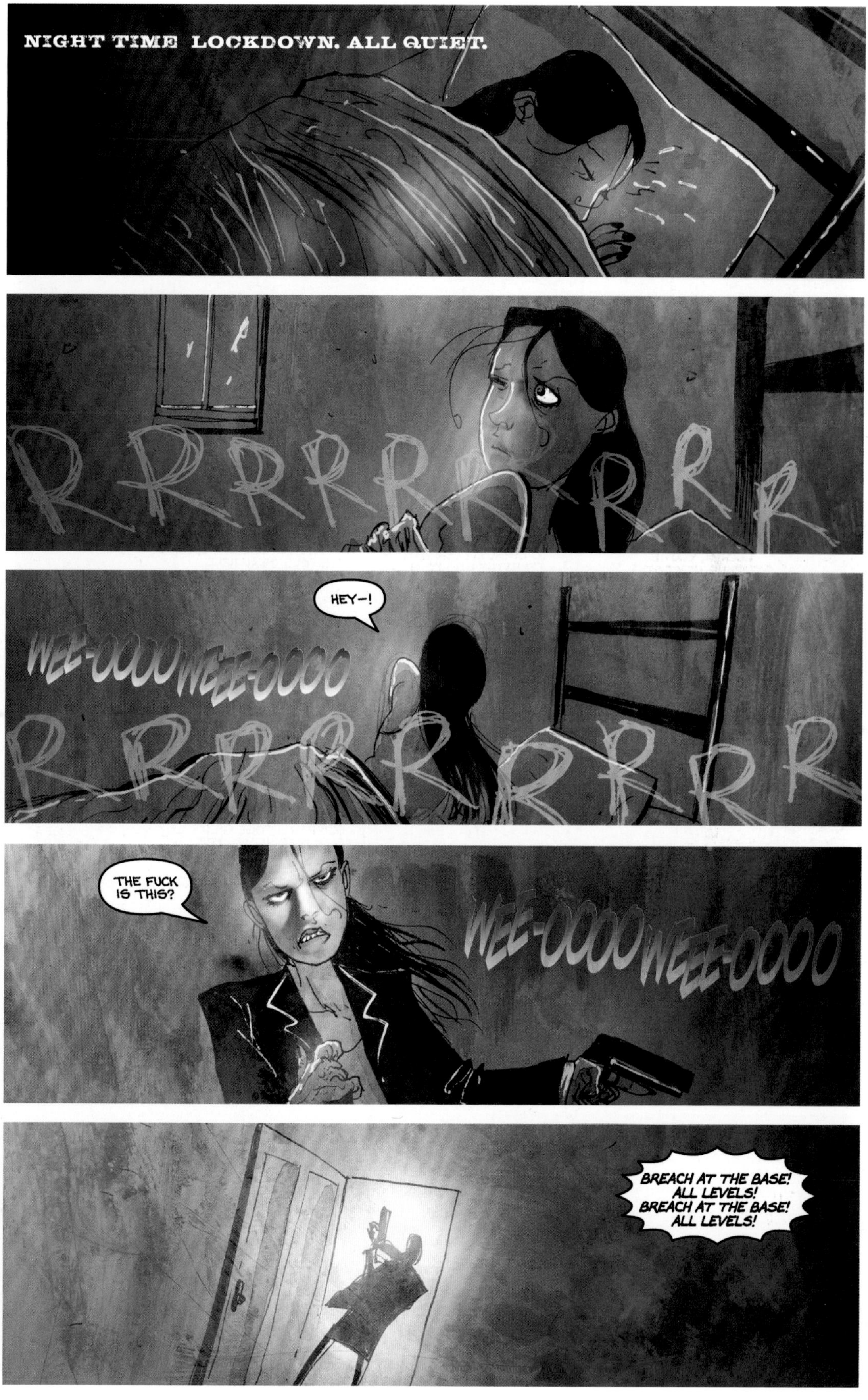
NIGHT TIME LOCKDOWN. ALL QUIET.
RRRRRRRRRR
WEE-OOOO WEEE-OOOO
HEY—!
RRRRRRRRRRR
THE FUCK IS THIS?
WEE-OOOO WEEE-OOOO
BREACH AT THE BASE! ALL LEVELS! BREACH AT THE BASE! ALL LEVELS!

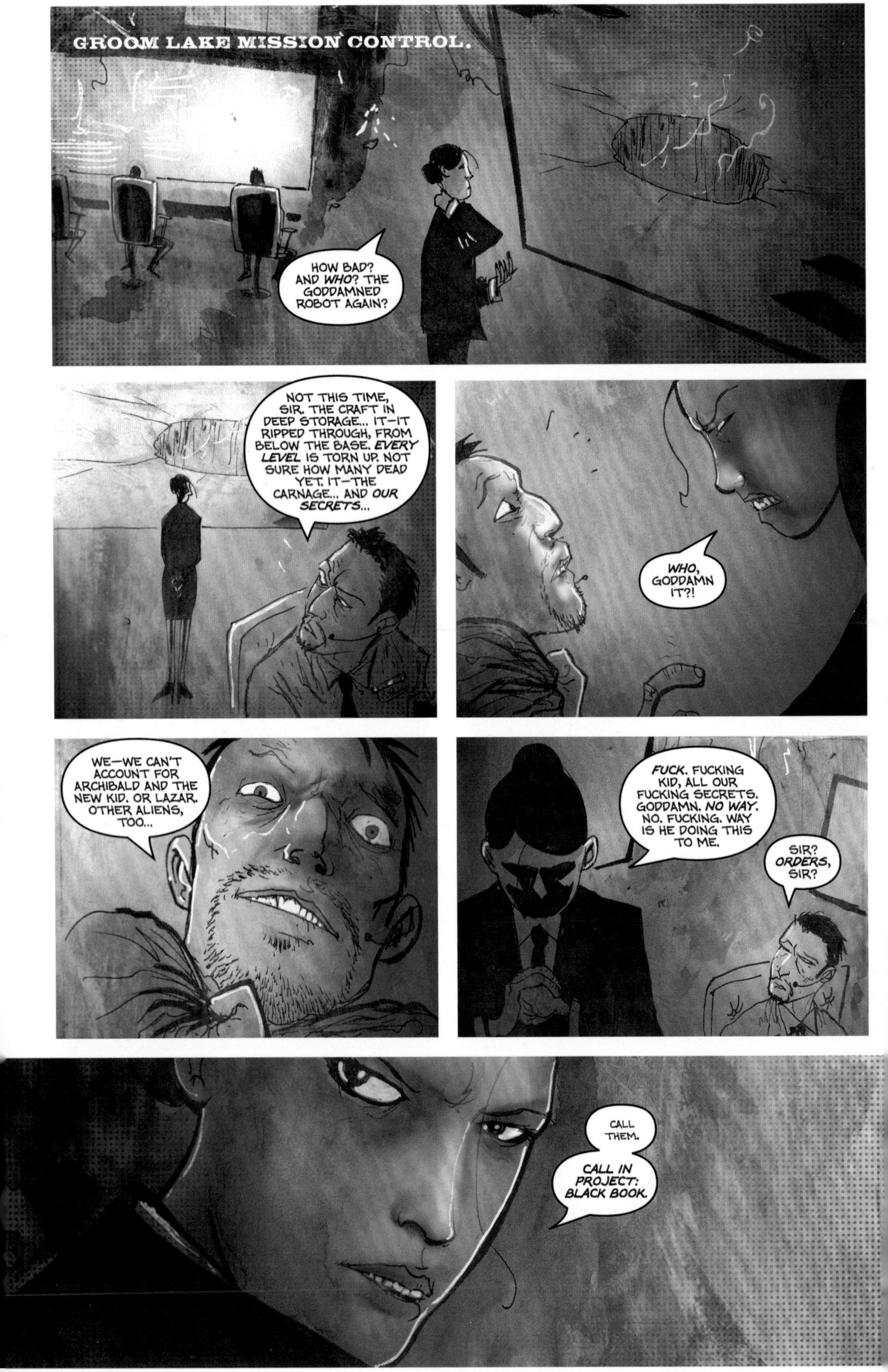
GROOM LAKE MISSION CONTROL.
HOW BAD? AND WHO? THE GODDAMNED ROBOT AGAIN?
NOT THIS TIME, SIR. THE CRAFT IN DEEP STORAGE... IT—IT RIPPED THROUGH, FROM BELOW THE BASE. EVERY LEVEL IS TORN UP. NOT SURE HOW MANY DEAD YET. IT—THE CARNAGE... AND OUR SECRETS...
WHO, GODDAMN IT?!
WE—WE CAN'T ACCOUNT FOR ARCHIBALD AND THE NEW KID. OR LAZAR. OTHER ALIENS, TOO...
FUCK. FUCKING KID, ALL OUR FUCKING SECRETS. GODDAMN. NO WAY. NO. FUCKING. WAY IS HE DOING THIS TO ME.
SIR? ORDERS, SIR?
CALL THEM.
CALL IN PROJECT: BLACK BOOK.

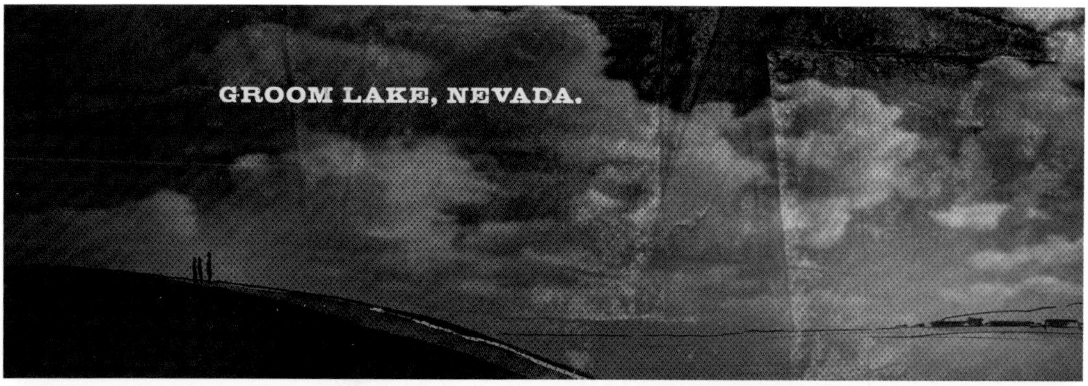
GROOM LAKE, NEVADA.

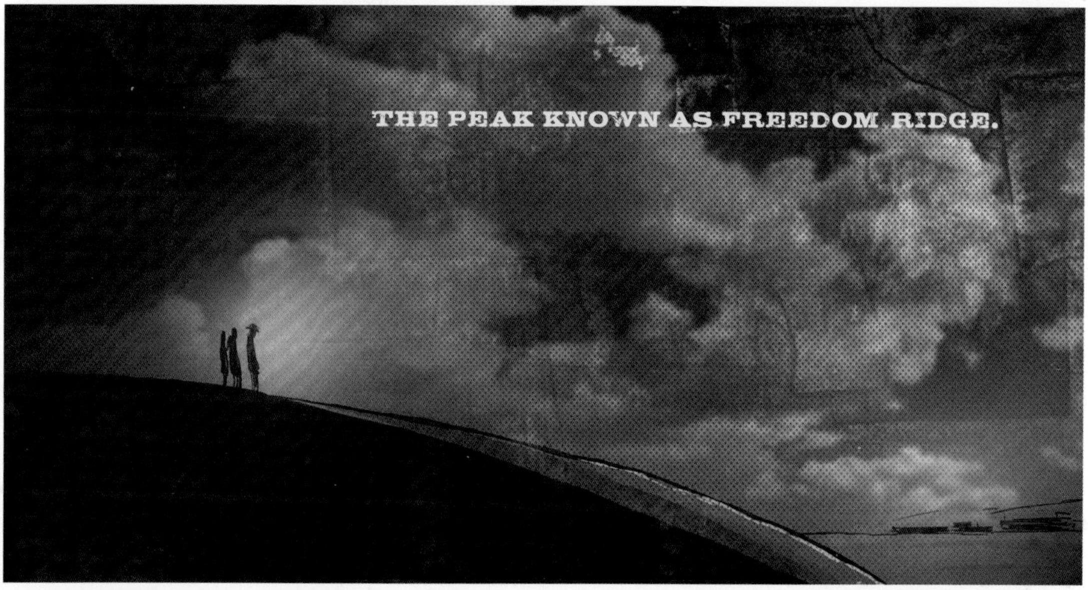
THE PEAK KNOWN AS FREEDOM RIDGE.

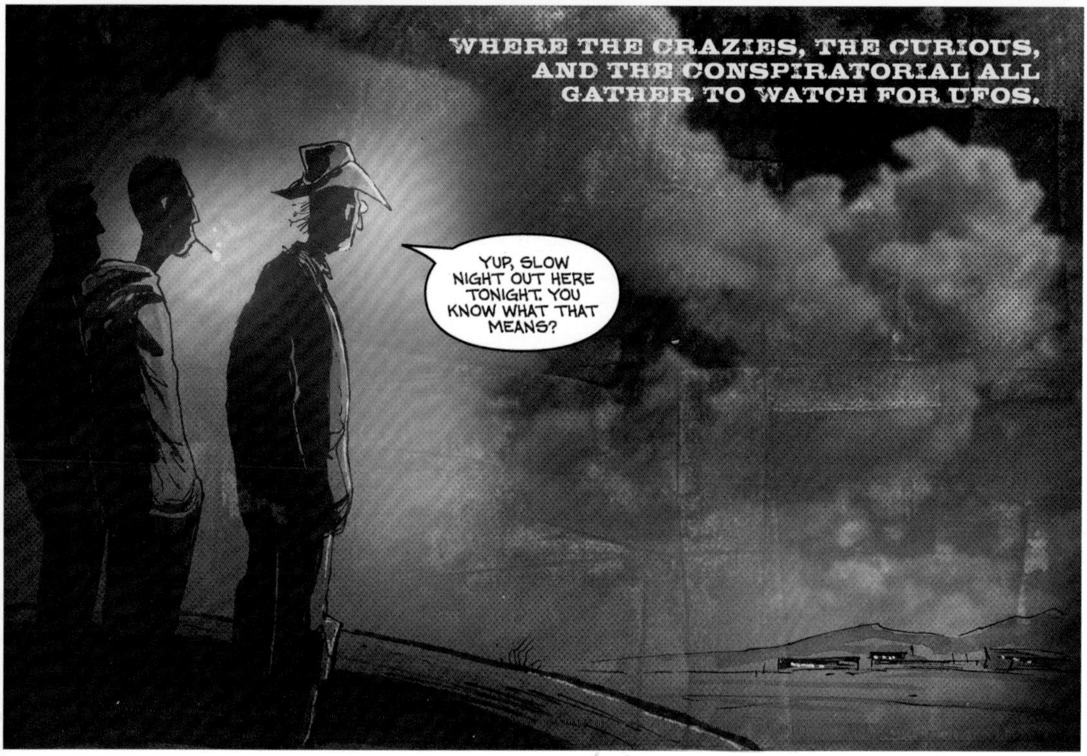
WHERE THE CRAZIES, THE CURIOUS, AND THE CONSPIRATORIAL ALL GATHER TO WATCH FOR UFOS.
YUP, SLOW NIGHT OUT HERE TONIGHT. YOU KNOW WHAT THAT MEANS?

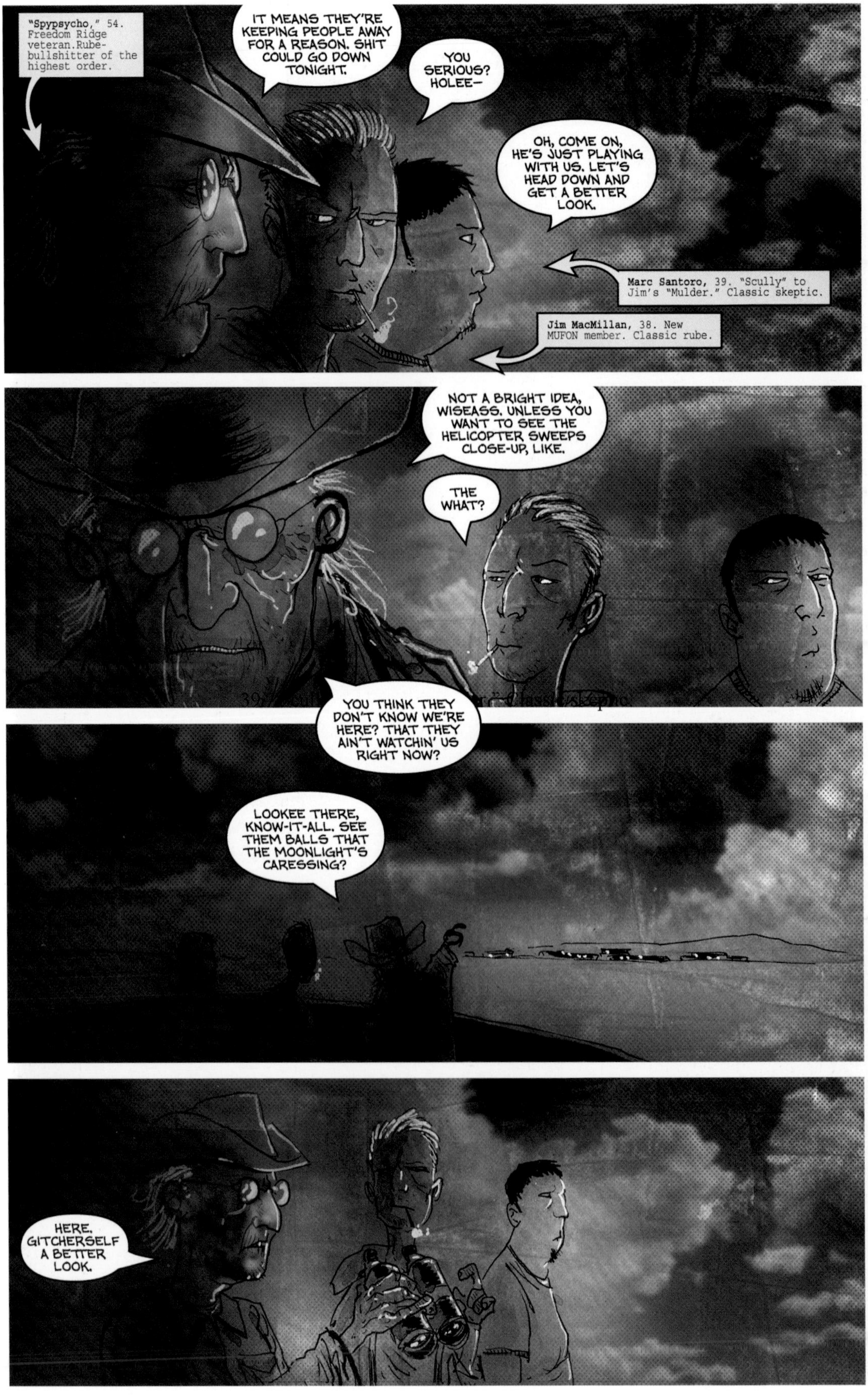
"Spypsycho," 54. Freedom Ridge veteran. Rube-bullshitter of the highest order.
IT MEANS THEY'RE KEEPING PEOPLE AWAY FOR A REASON. SHIT COULD GO DOWN TONIGHT.
YOU SERIOUS? HOLEE—
OH, COME ON, HE'S JUST PLAYING WITH US. LET'S HEAD DOWN AND GET A BETTER LOOK.
Marc Santoro, 39. "Scully" to Jim's "Mulder." Classic skeptic.
Jim MacMillan, 38. New MUFON member. Classic rube.
NOT A BRIGHT IDEA, WISEASS. UNLESS YOU WANT TO SEE THE HELICOPTER SWEEPS CLOSE-UP, LIKE.
THE WHAT?
YOU THINK THEY DON'T KNOW WE'RE HERE? THAT THEY AIN'T WATCHIN' US RIGHT NOW?
LOOKEE THERE, KNOW-IT-ALL. SEE THEM BALLS THAT THE MOONLIGHT'S CARESSING?
HERE. GITCHERSELF A BETTER LOOK.

"YEAH, THE SILVER BALLS? SENSORS. THEY CAN TELL A HUMAN FROM A COW OR OTHERWISE JUST BY THE GASSES YOU'RE SQUEEZING OUT OF YOUR BUNGS, FELLAS. SO YOU WATCH YOURSELVES.

"WE'RE ALL JUST LUCKY THAT THE DAMNED THINGS DON'T SEEM TO BE ACTIVE ANYMORE. EVEN NOVICES LIKE YOU DON'T SEEM TO GIVE OFF ANY—

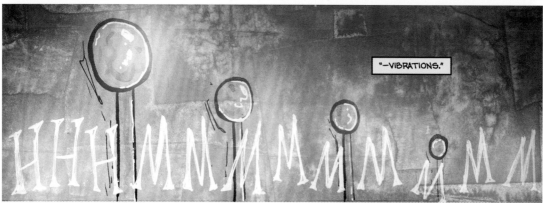

"—VIBRATIONS."

HHHHMMMMMMMMM

UH-OH.

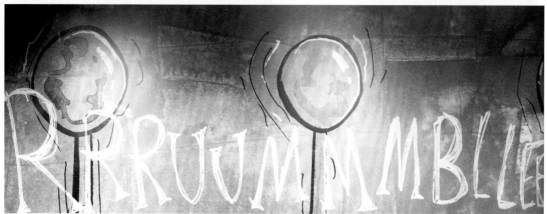

RRRUUMMMBLLE

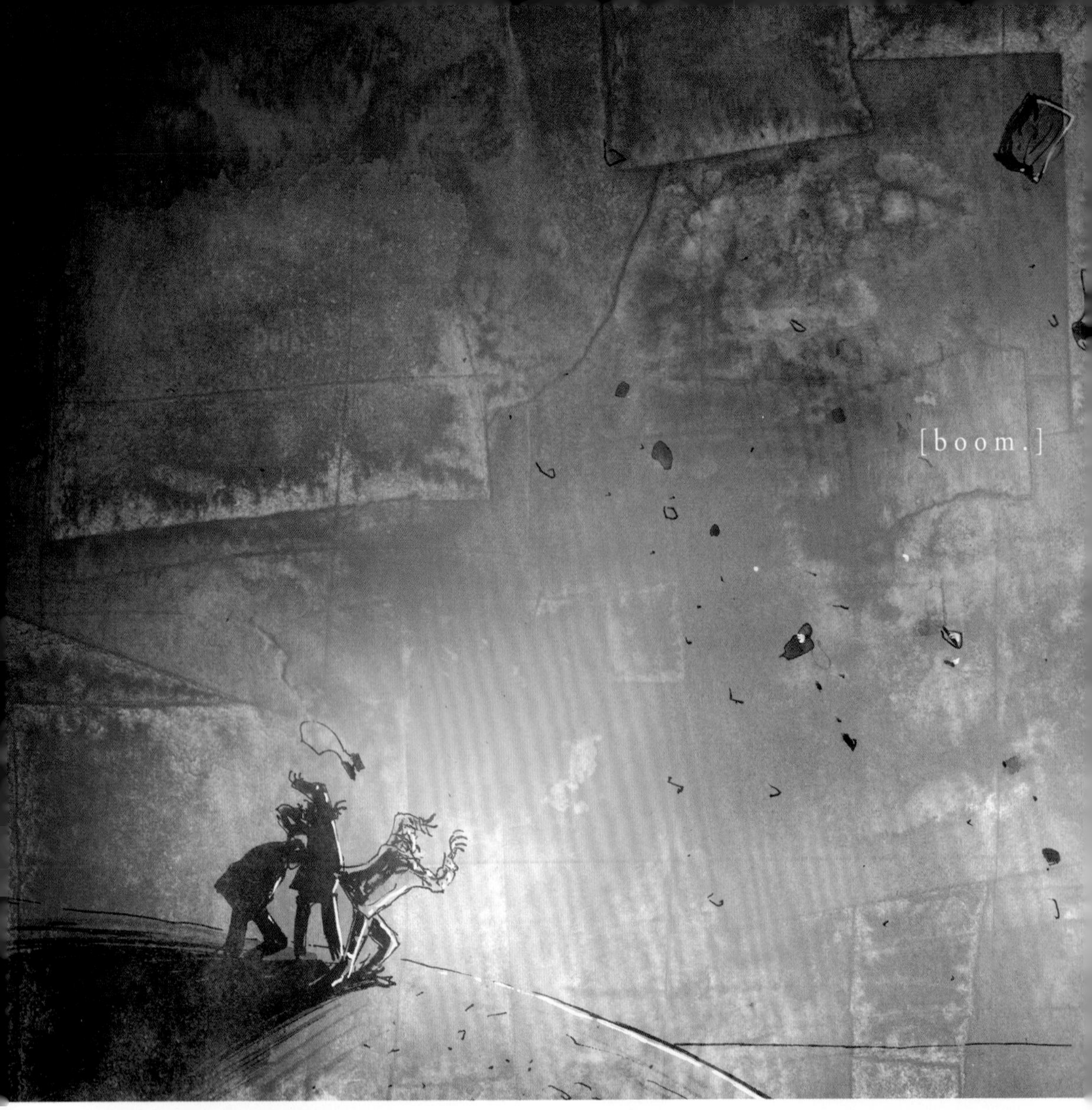
[boom.]

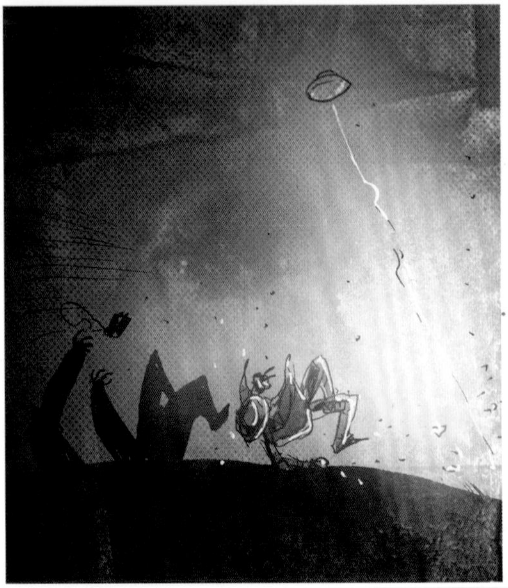

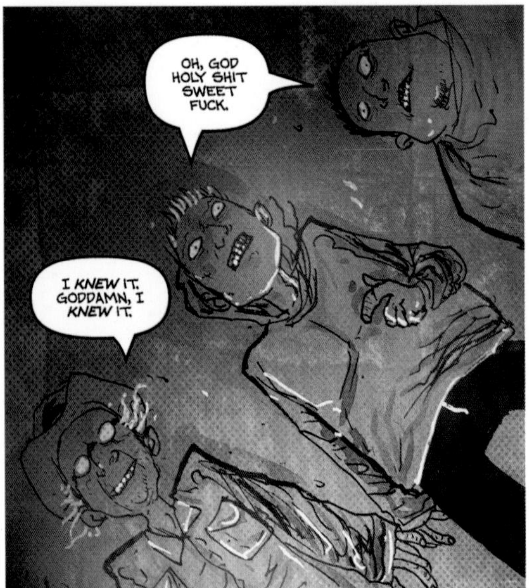
OH, GOD HOLY SHIT SWEET FUCK.
I KNEW IT. GODDAMN, I KNEW IT.

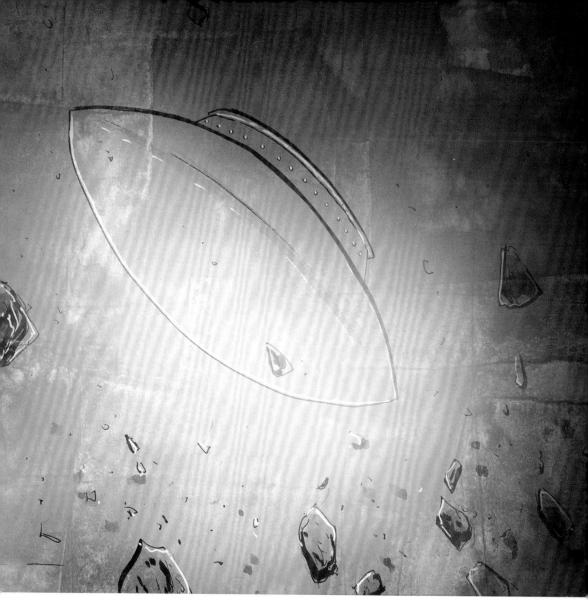

I *KNEW* IT! HAHA, GUESS YOUR NEXT *MUFON* MEETING WILL BE PRETTY EXCITING, WON'T—

—HEY, WHERE YOU TWO PUSSIES GOIN'? THIS IS IT, BABY, THE GAME'S AFOOT!

LATER, OLD MAN! THERE MIGHT BE MORE!

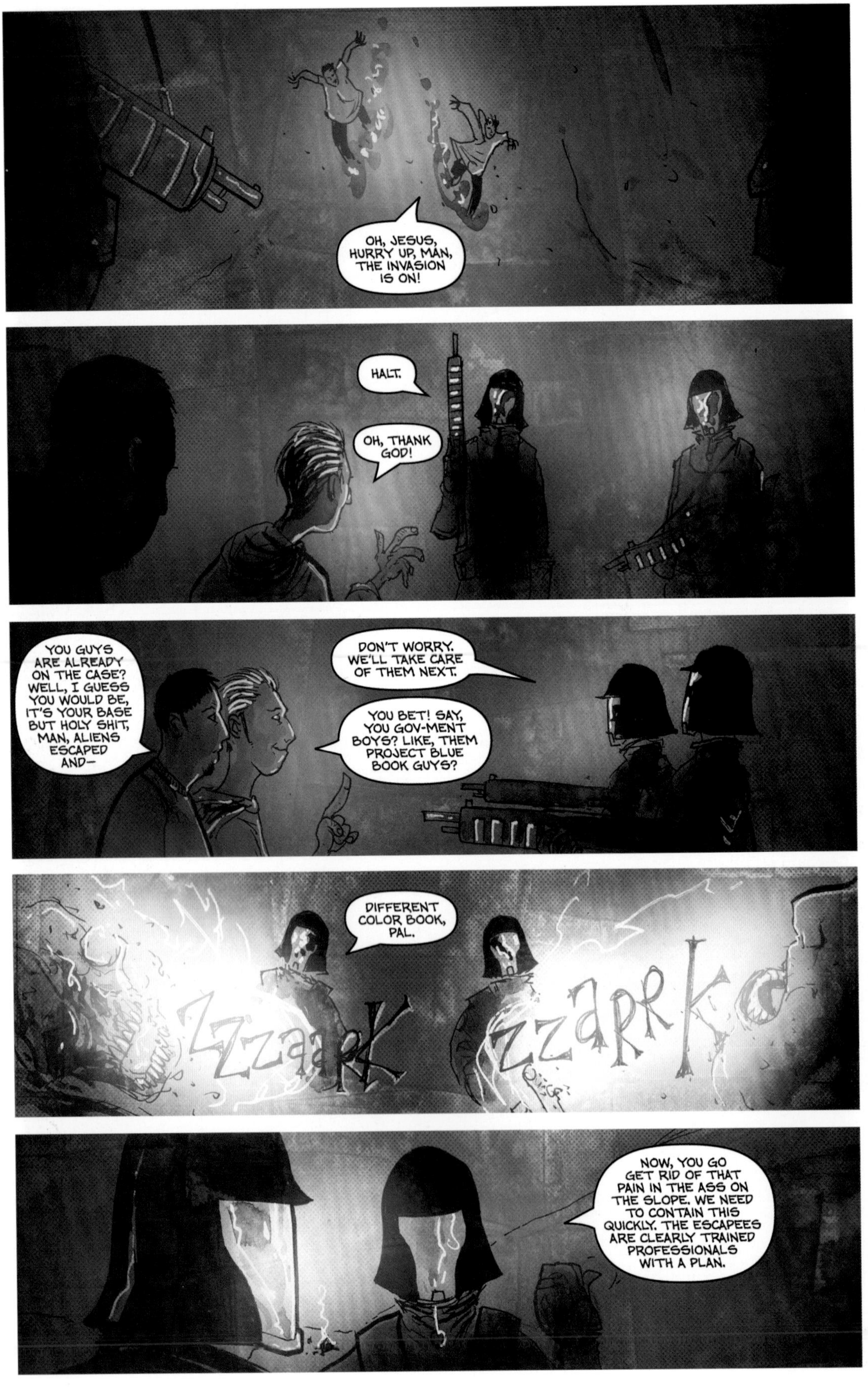
OH, JESUS, HURRY UP, MAN, THE INVASION IS ON!
HALT.
OH, THANK GOD!
YOU GUYS ARE ALREADY ON THE CASE? WELL, I GUESS YOU WOULD BE, IT'S YOUR BASE BUT HOLY SHIT, MAN, ALIENS ESCAPED AND—
DON'T WORRY. WE'LL TAKE CARE OF THEM NEXT.
YOU BET! SAY, YOU GOV-MENT BOYS? LIKE, THEM PROJECT BLUE BOOK GUYS?
DIFFERENT COLOR BOOK, PAL.
ZZZARK
ZZARRK
NOW, YOU GO GET RID OF THAT PAIN IN THE ASS ON THE SLOPE. WE NEED TO CONTAIN THIS QUICKLY. THE ESCAPEES ARE CLEARLY TRAINED PROFESSIONALS WITH A PLAN.

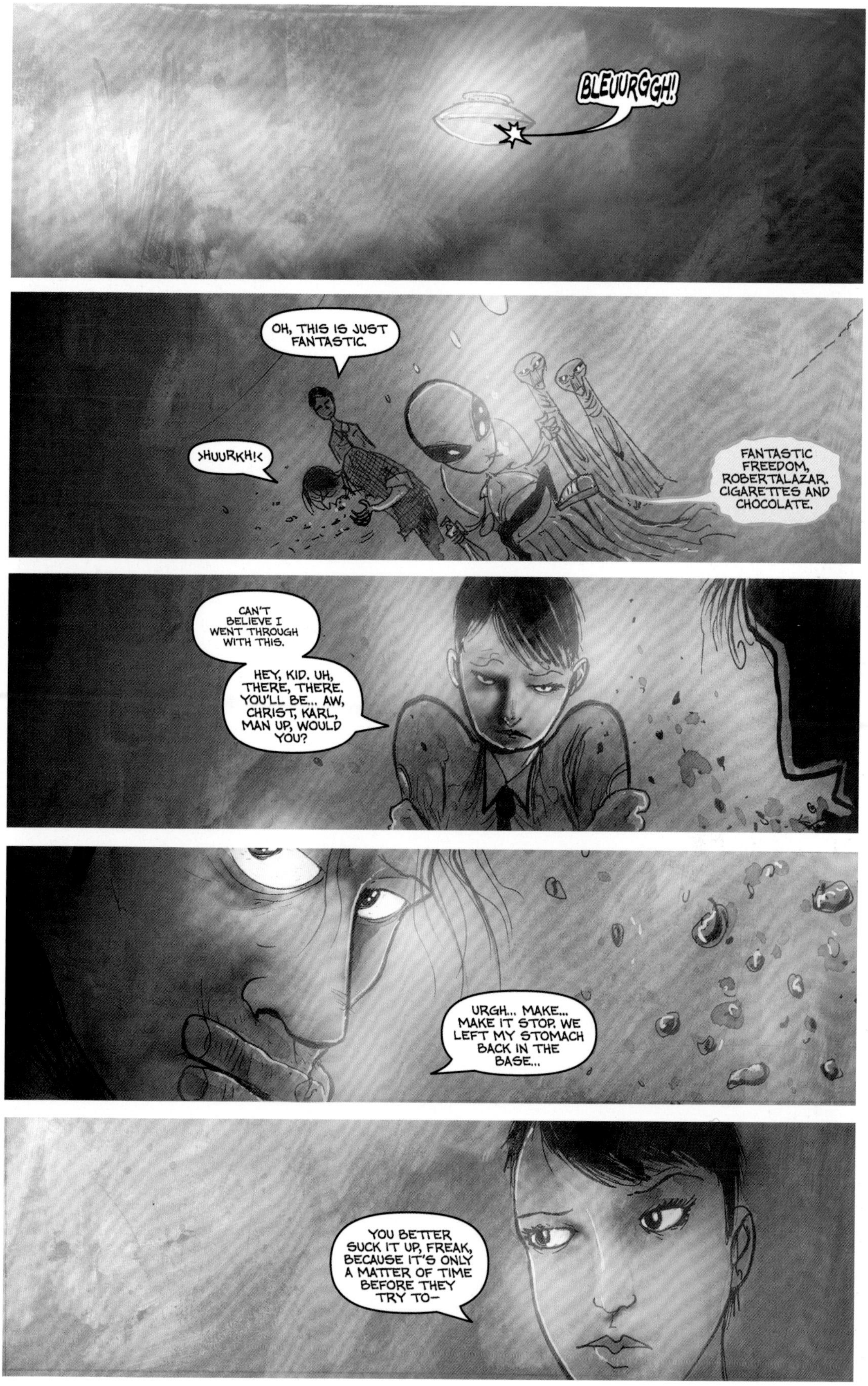
BLEUURGGH!
OH, THIS IS JUST FANTASTIC.
>HUURKH!<
FANTASTIC FREEDOM, ROBERTALAZAR. CIGARETTES AND CHOCOLATE.
CAN'T BELIEVE I WENT THROUGH WITH THIS.
HEY, KID. UH, THERE, THERE. YOU'LL BE... AW, CHRIST, KARL, MAN UP, WOULD YOU?
URGH... MAKE... MAKE IT STOP. WE LEFT MY STOMACH BACK IN THE BASE...
YOU BETTER SUCK IT UP, FREAK, BECAUSE IT'S ONLY A MATTER OF TIME BEFORE THEY TRY TO—

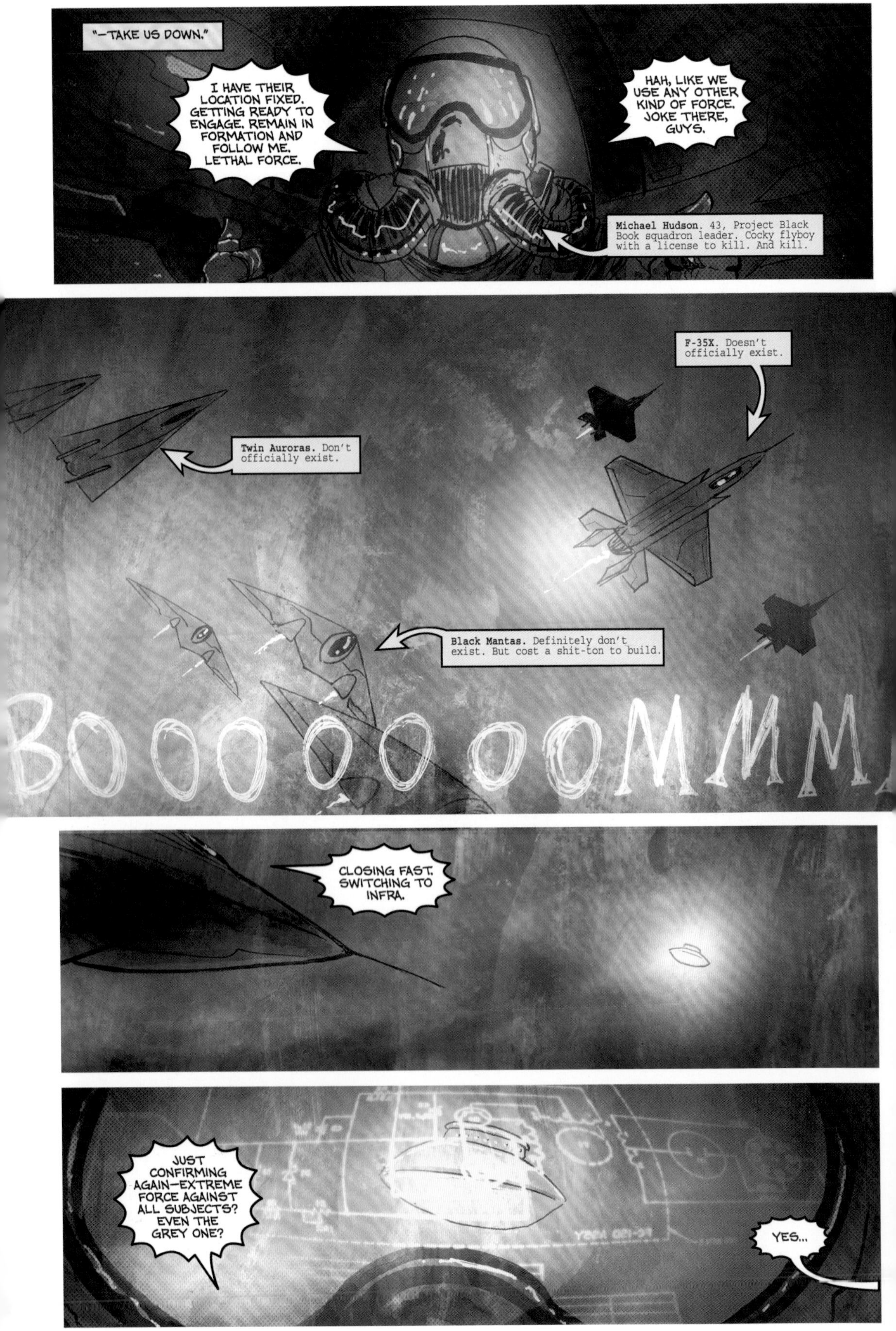
"—TAKE US DOWN."
I HAVE THEIR LOCATION FIXED. GETTING READY TO ENGAGE. REMAIN IN FORMATION AND FOLLOW ME. LETHAL FORCE.
HAH, LIKE WE USE ANY OTHER KIND OF FORCE. JOKE THERE, GUYS.
Michael Hudson. 43, Project Black Book squadron leader. Cocky flyboy with a license to kill. And kill.
F-35X. Doesn't officially exist.
Twin Auroras. Don't officially exist.
Black Mantas. Definitely don't exist. But cost a shit-ton to build.
BOOOOOOOMMM
CLOSING FAST. SWITCHING TO INFRA.
JUST CONFIRMING AGAIN—EXTREME FORCE AGAINST ALL SUBJECTS? EVEN THE GREY ONE?
YES...

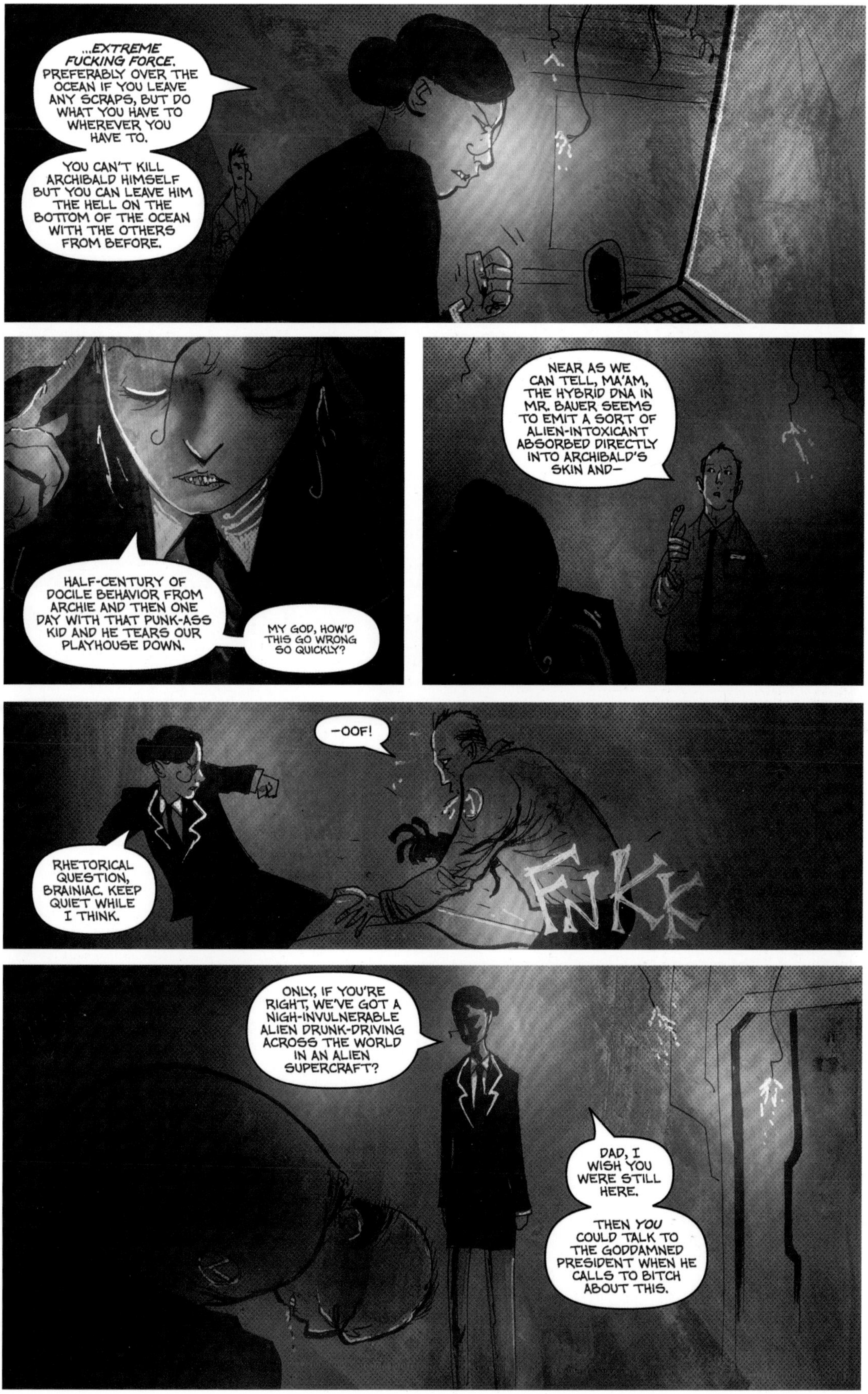
...EXTREME FUCKING FORCE. PREFERABLY OVER THE OCEAN IF YOU LEAVE ANY SCRAPS, BUT DO WHAT YOU HAVE TO WHEREVER YOU HAVE TO.
YOU CAN'T KILL ARCHIBALD HIMSELF BUT YOU CAN LEAVE HIM THE HELL ON THE BOTTOM OF THE OCEAN WITH THE OTHERS FROM BEFORE.
HALF-CENTURY OF DOCILE BEHAVIOR FROM ARCHIE AND THEN ONE DAY WITH THAT PUNK-ASS KID AND HE TEARS OUR PLAYHOUSE DOWN.
MY GOD, HOW'D THIS GO WRONG SO QUICKLY?
NEAR AS WE CAN TELL, MA'AM, THE HYBRID DNA IN MR. BAUER SEEMS TO EMIT A SORT OF ALIEN-INTOXICANT ABSORBED DIRECTLY INTO ARCHIBALD'S SKIN AND—
RHETORICAL QUESTION, BRAINIAC. KEEP QUIET WHILE I THINK.
—OOF!
FNKK
ONLY, IF YOU'RE RIGHT, WE'VE GOT A NIGH-INVULNERABLE ALIEN DRUNK-DRIVING ACROSS THE WORLD IN AN ALIEN SUPERCRAFT?
DAD, I WISH YOU WERE STILL HERE.
THEN YOU COULD TALK TO THE GODDAMNED PRESIDENT WHEN HE CALLS TO BITCH ABOUT THIS.

IT'S DONE, MA'AM, THE SPECTATORS'RE NOTHING BUT ASH.

OH, *THANK HEAVEN*. YOU KNOCKED OFF TWO OR THREE LONERS UP ON A HILL? WELL, NOW NO ONE WILL KNOW THAT A *GIANT FUCKING SPACESHIP* TORE OUT OF THE NEVADA DESERT, WILL THEY?

AND YES, THAT WAS SARCASM. GET OUT MY SIGHT NOW. GO KILL A FEW MORE LOSERS AND *THEN* MAYBE I'LL SUCK YOUR DICKS.

DON'T WORRY ABOUT IT, MAN. *HER CAREER'S DONE* AND SHE'S TAKING IT OUT ON US.

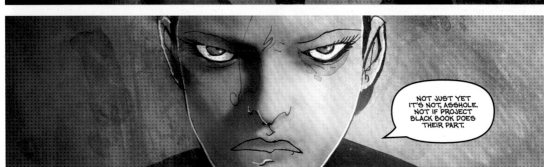

NOT JUST YET IT'S NOT, ASSHOLE. NOT IF PROJECT BLACK BOOK DOES THEIR PART.

PROJECT BLACK BOOK, DOING THEIR PART.

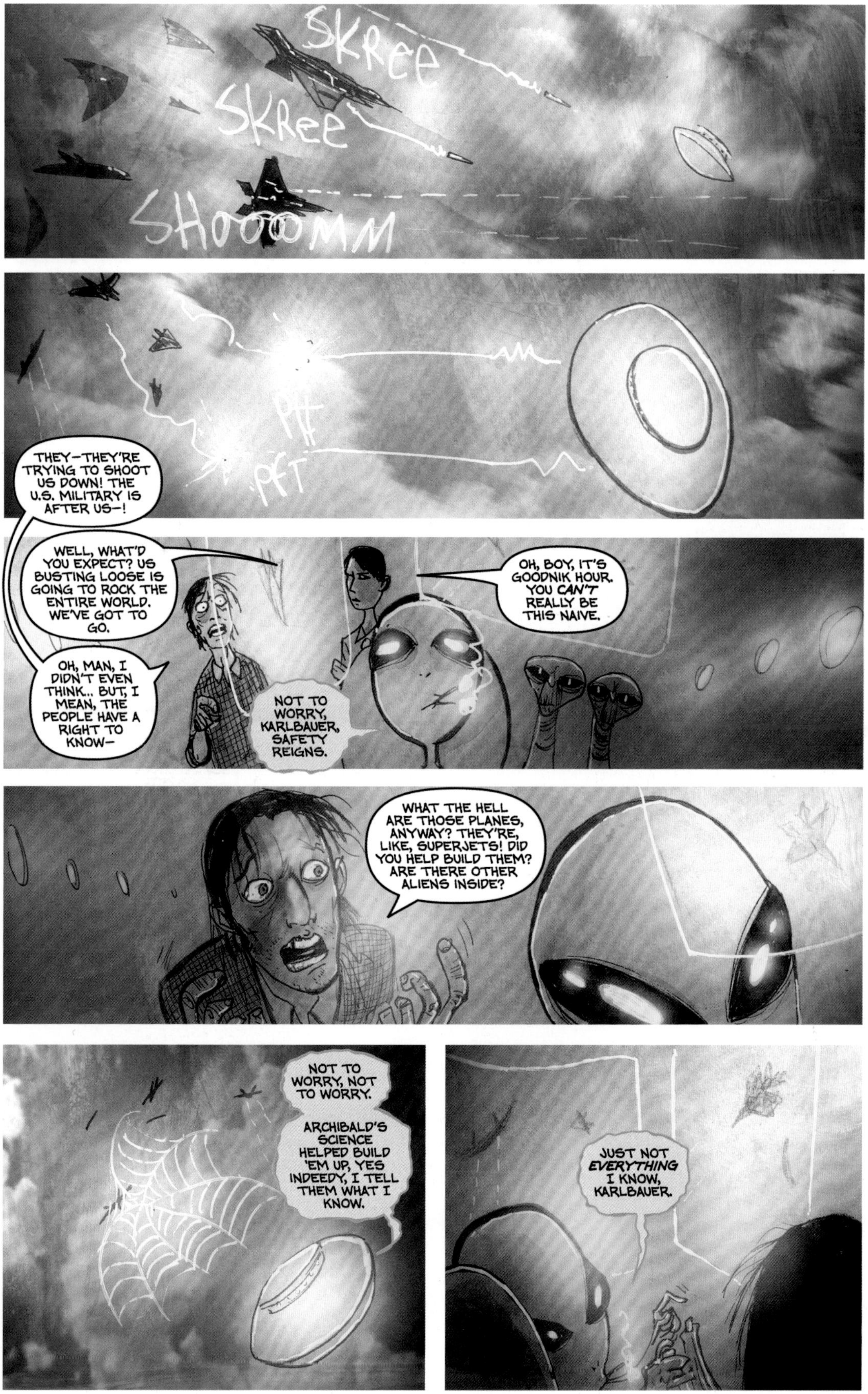
SKREE
SKREE
SHOOOOMM
PFT
PFT
THEY—THEY'RE TRYING TO SHOOT US DOWN! THE U.S. MILITARY IS AFTER US—!
WELL, WHAT'D YOU EXPECT? US BUSTING LOOSE IS GOING TO ROCK THE ENTIRE WORLD. WE'VE GOT TO GO.
OH, BOY, IT'S GOODNIK HOUR. YOU CAN'T REALLY BE THIS NAIVE.
OH, MAN, I DIDN'T EVEN THINK.. BUT, I MEAN, THE PEOPLE HAVE A RIGHT TO KNOW—
NOT TO WORRY, KARLBAUER, SAFETY REIGNS.
WHAT THE HELL ARE THOSE PLANES, ANYWAY? THEY'RE, LIKE, SUPERJETS! DID YOU HELP BUILD THEM? ARE THERE OTHER ALIENS INSIDE?
NOT TO WORRY, NOT TO WORRY.
ARCHIBALD'S SCIENCE HELPED BUILD 'EM UP, YES INDEEDY, I TELL THEM WHAT I KNOW.
JUST NOT EVERYTHING I KNOW, KARLBAUER.

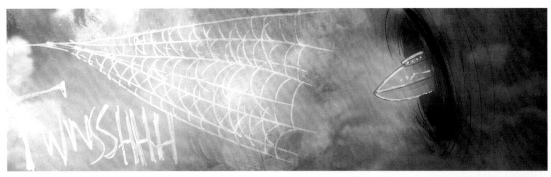

WOW, NICE!

WORMHOLEY FUN! TAKE THAT, BLACK MANTAS.

UH, HEY, WHAT'S WITH THE ETS BACK THERE? NOT MUCH HELP SO FAR, ARE THEY?

EMPATHS. THEIR SHIT GLOWS WHEN THEY SENSE STRONG EMOTIONS. NO USE IN A FIGHT. LONG AS THEY DON'T TURN OFF THE DAMPERS KEEPING THE ROBOT DOWN BECAUSE THEY FEEL BAD FOR HIM, THEY'RE HARMLESS. AND WORTHLESS.

HEY, ARCHIBALD, I'M ALL FOR A FIGHT, BUT... GOT ANY SEATBELTS ON THIS THING? THIS COULD GET ROUGH.

OHH, NO. NOT NEEDED, GOOD TIMES. GYRO-SCOPO-STABILIZING FOR ALL PASSENGERS...

...SAFETY FIRST, SAFETY FIRST.

'KAY, WE FIGHT BACK NOW, YOU BETCHA.
TOO MANY PLANES. AURORAS, WHEW, TROUBLE, TOO. BUT AN EASY FIX FOR US. BLOBS!
Putt Putt Putt Putt
TIME FOR FOOD, LITTLE BLOB-FRIENDS. EAT 'EM UP!
TICKLISH BLOBS. READY FOR CRAZY RIDE?

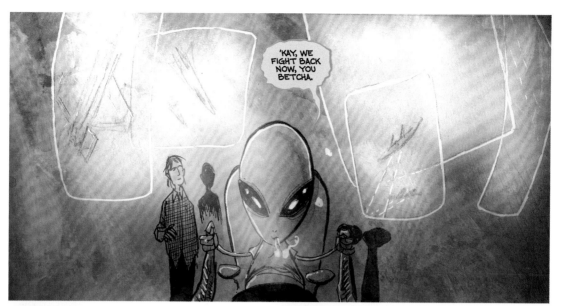

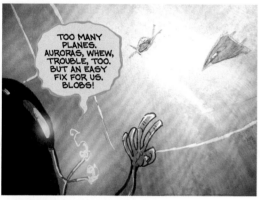

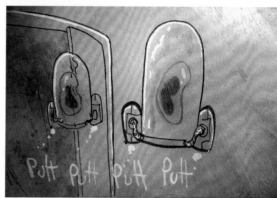

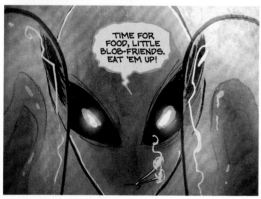

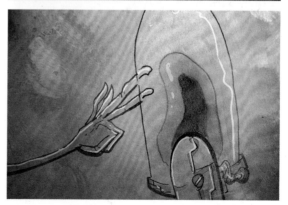

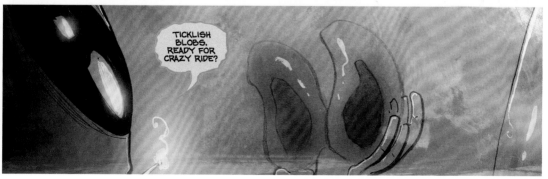

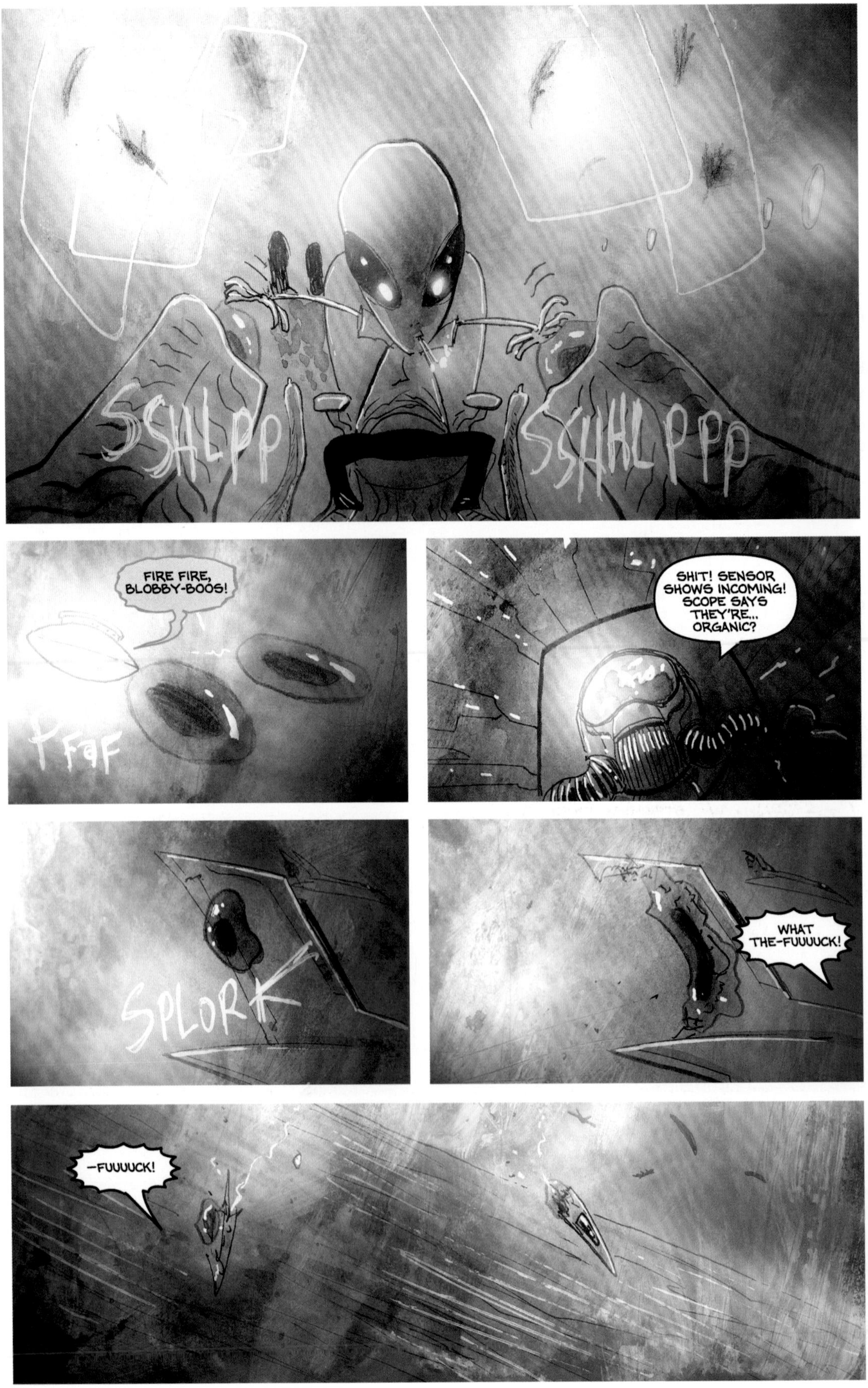

SSHLPP
SSHHLPPP
FIRE FIRE, BLOBBY-BOOS!
PFAF
SHIT! SENSOR SHOWS INCOMING! SCOPE SAYS THEY'RE... ORGANIC?
SPLORK
WHAT THE-FUUUUCK!
-FUUUUCK!

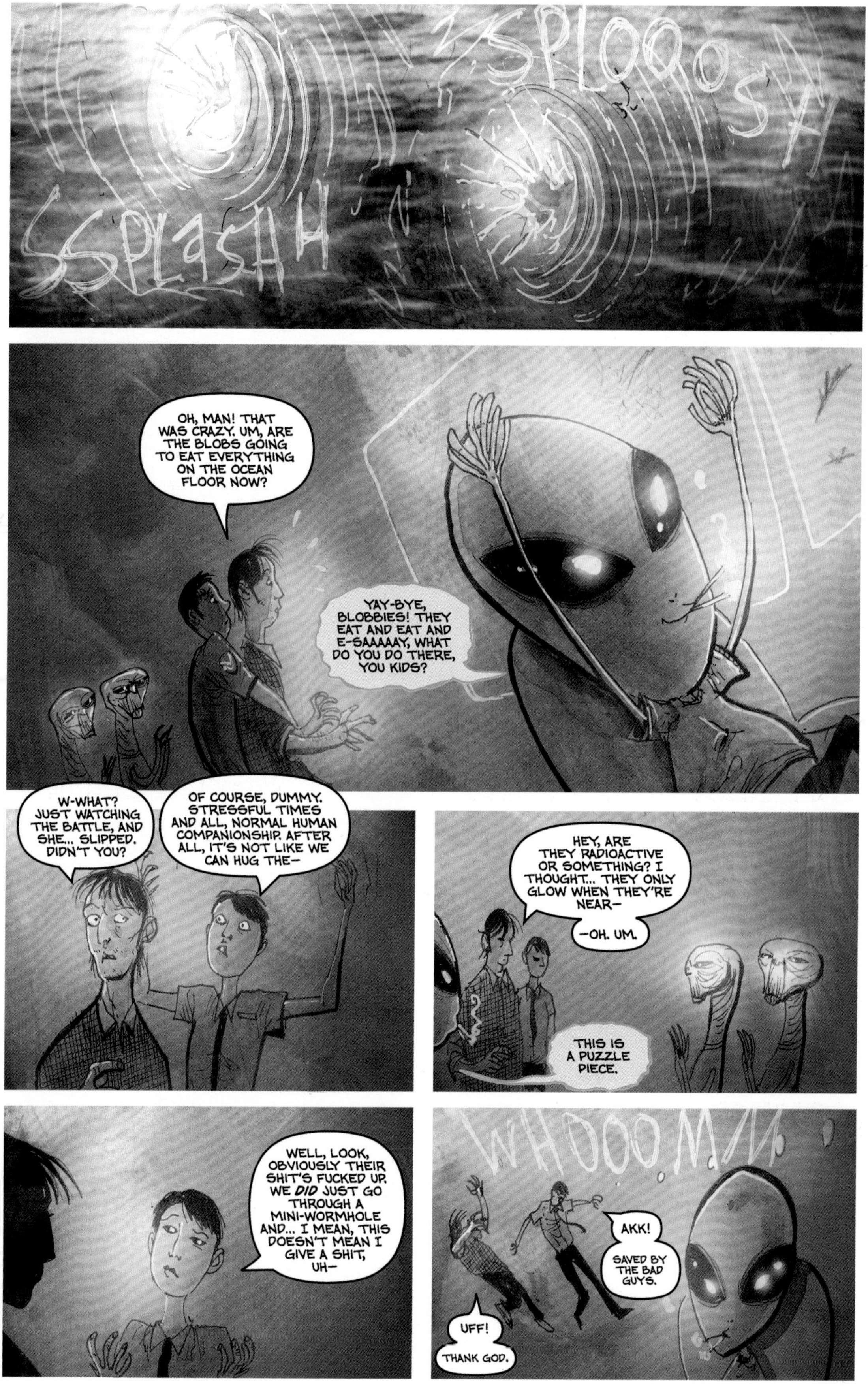
SPLASHH
SPLOOOSH
OH, MAN! THAT WAS CRAZY. UM, ARE THE BLOBS GOING TO EAT EVERYTHING ON THE OCEAN FLOOR NOW?
YAY-BYE, BLOBBIES! THEY EAT AND EAT AND E-SAAAAAY, WHAT DO YOU DO THERE, YOU KIDS?
W-WHAT? JUST WATCHING THE BATTLE, AND SHE... SLIPPED. DIDN'T YOU?
OF COURSE, DUMMY. STRESSFUL TIMES AND ALL, NORMAL HUMAN COMPANIONSHIP. AFTER ALL, IT'S NOT LIKE WE CAN HUG THE–
HEY, ARE THEY RADIOACTIVE OR SOMETHING? I THOUGHT... THEY ONLY GLOW WHEN THEY'RE NEAR–
–OH. UM.
THIS IS A PUZZLE PIECE.
WELL, LOOK, OBVIOUSLY THEIR SHIT'S FUCKED UP. WE *DID* JUST GO THROUGH A MINI-WORMHOLE AND... I MEAN, THIS DOESN'T MEAN I GIVE A SHIT, UH–
WHOOOMM
AKK!
SAVED BY THE BAD GUYS.
UFF!
THANK GOD.

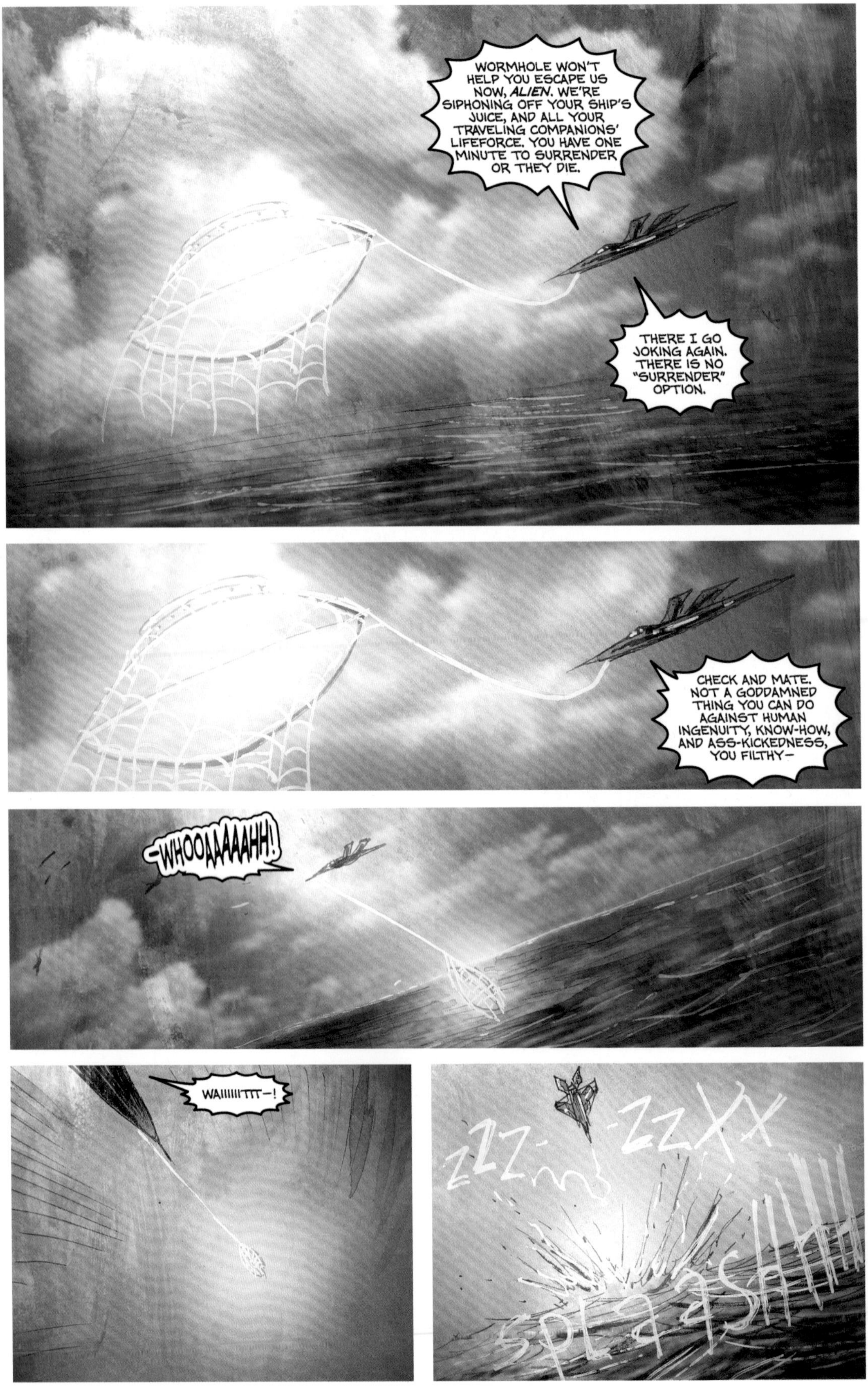
WORMHOLE WON'T HELP YOU ESCAPE US NOW, *ALIEN*. WE'RE SIPHONING OFF YOUR SHIP'S JUICE, AND ALL YOUR TRAVELING COMPANIONS' LIFEFORCE. YOU HAVE ONE MINUTE TO SURRENDER OR THEY DIE.
THERE I GO JOKING AGAIN. THERE IS NO "SURRENDER" OPTION.
CHECK AND MATE. NOT A GODDAMNED THING YOU CAN DO AGAINST HUMAN INGENUITY, KNOW-HOW, AND ASS-KICKEDNESS, YOU FILTHY—
-WHOOAAAAAHH!
WAIIIIIITTT—!
ZZZ--ZZXX
SPLAASH!!

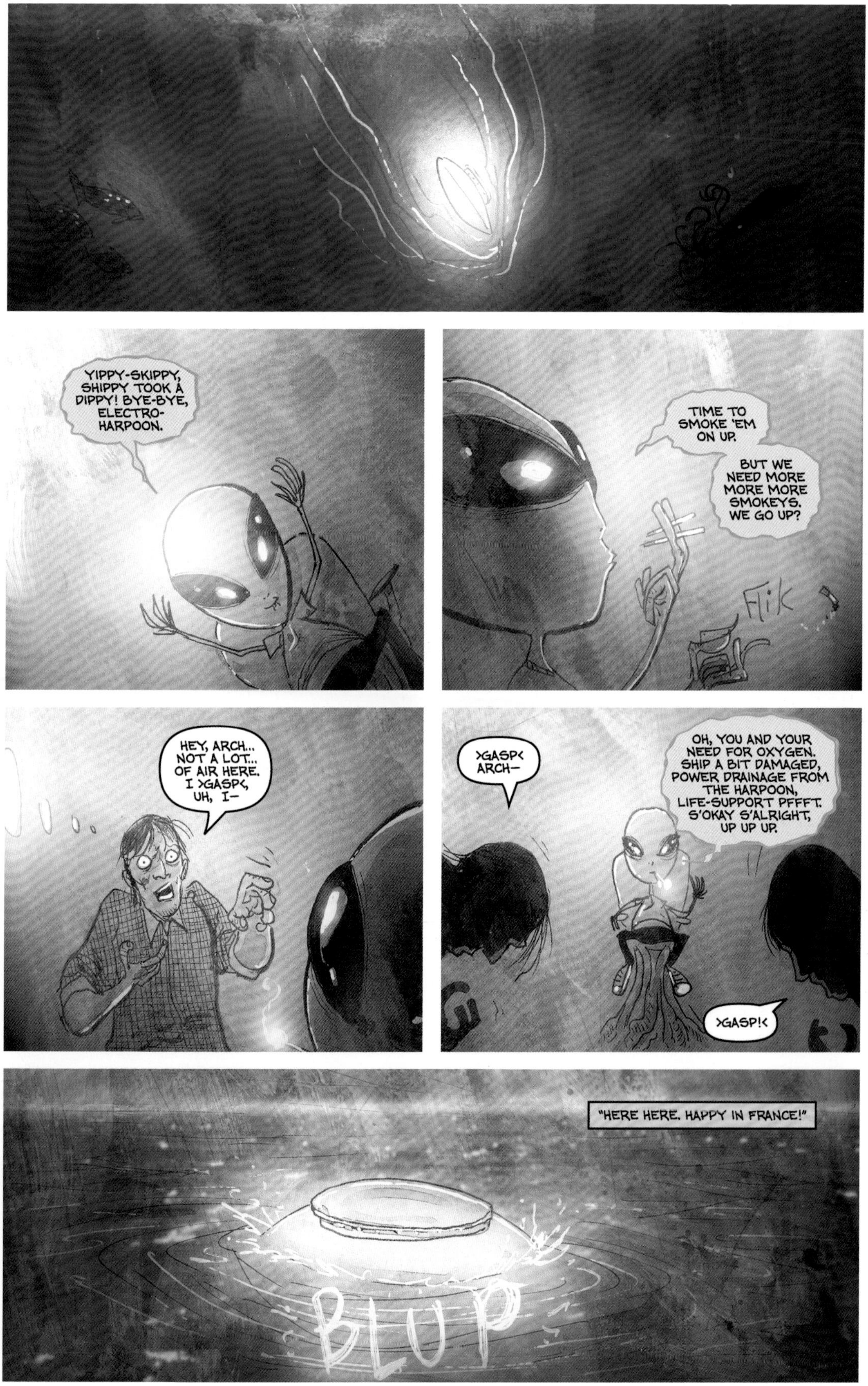
YIPPY-SKIPPY, SHIPPY TOOK A DIPPY! BYE-BYE, ELECTRO-HARPOON.
TIME TO SMOKE 'EM ON UP.
BUT WE NEED MORE MORE MORE SMOKEYS. WE GO UP?
HEY, ARCH... NOT A LOT... OF AIR HERE. I >GASP<, UH, I—
>GASP< ARCH—
OH, YOU AND YOUR NEED FOR OXYGEN. SHIP A BIT DAMAGED, POWER DRAINAGE FROM THE HARPOON, LIFE-SUPPORT PFFFT. S'OKAY S'ALRIGHT, UP UP UP.
>GASP!<
"HERE HERE. HAPPY IN FRANCE!"
BLUP

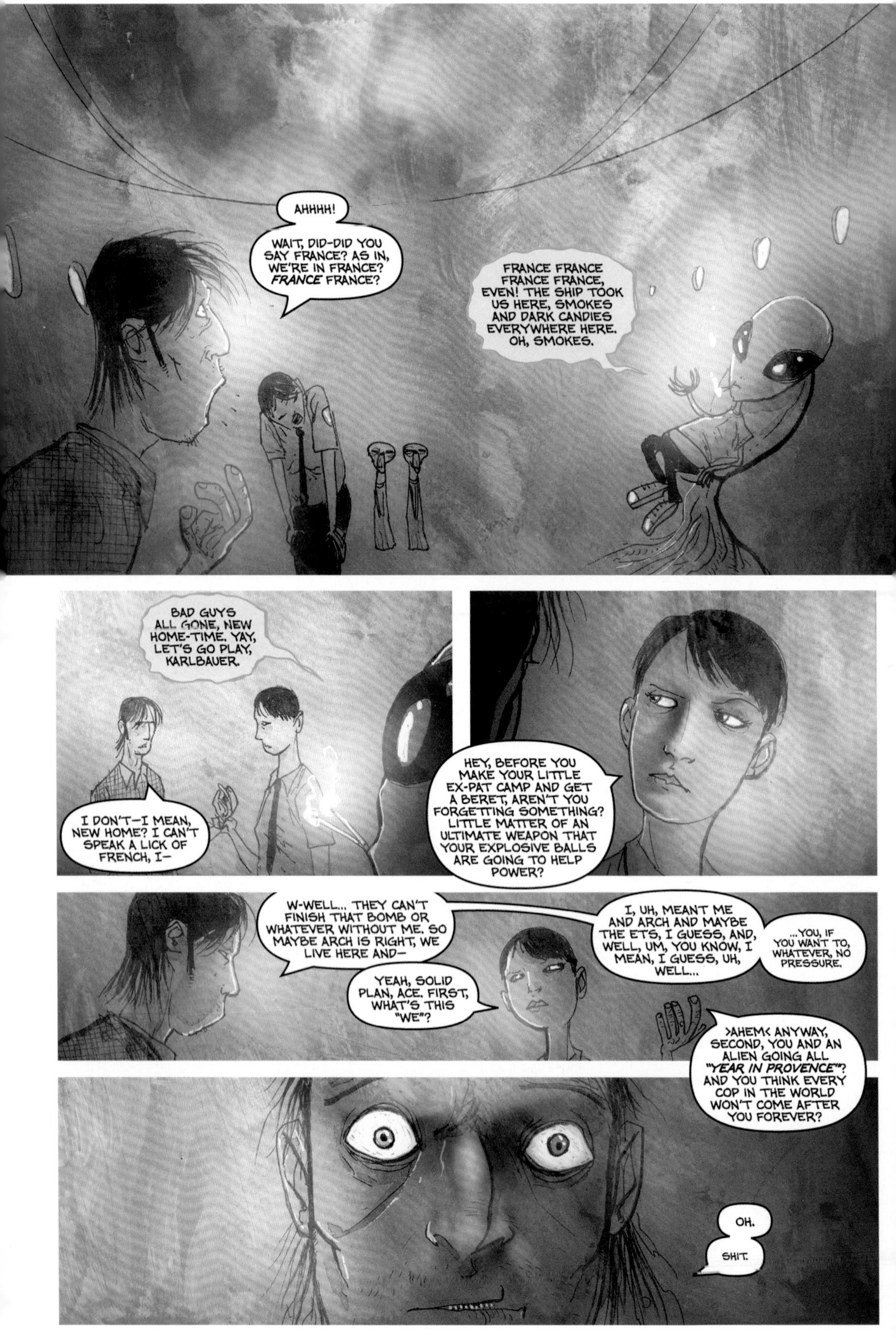
AHHHH!
WAIT, DID-DID YOU SAY FRANCE? AS IN, WE'RE IN FRANCE? *FRANCE* FRANCE?
FRANCE FRANCE FRANCE FRANCE, EVEN! THE SHIP TOOK US HERE, SMOKES AND DARK CANDIES EVERYWHERE HERE. OH, SMOKES.
BAD GUYS ALL GONE, NEW HOME-TIME. YAY, LET'S GO PLAY, KARLBAUER.
I DON'T—I MEAN, NEW HOME? I CAN'T SPEAK A LICK OF FRENCH, I—
HEY, BEFORE YOU MAKE YOUR LITTLE EX-PAT CAMP AND GET A BERET, AREN'T YOU FORGETTING SOMETHING? LITTLE MATTER OF AN ULTIMATE WEAPON THAT YOUR EXPLOSIVE BALLS ARE GOING TO HELP POWER?
W-WELL... THEY CAN'T FINISH THAT BOMB OR WHATEVER WITHOUT ME. SO MAYBE ARCH IS RIGHT, WE LIVE HERE AND—
YEAH, SOLID PLAN, ACE. FIRST, WHAT'S THIS "WE"?
I, UH, MEANT ME AND ARCH AND MAYBE THE ETS, I GUESS, AND, WELL, UM, YOU KNOW, I MEAN, I GUESS, UH, WELL...
...YOU, IF YOU WANT TO, WHATEVER, NO PRESSURE.
>AHEM< ANYWAY, SECOND, YOU AND AN ALIEN GOING ALL *"YEAR IN PROVENCE"*? AND YOU THINK EVERY COP IN THE WORLD WON'T COME AFTER YOU FOREVER?
OH.
SHIT.

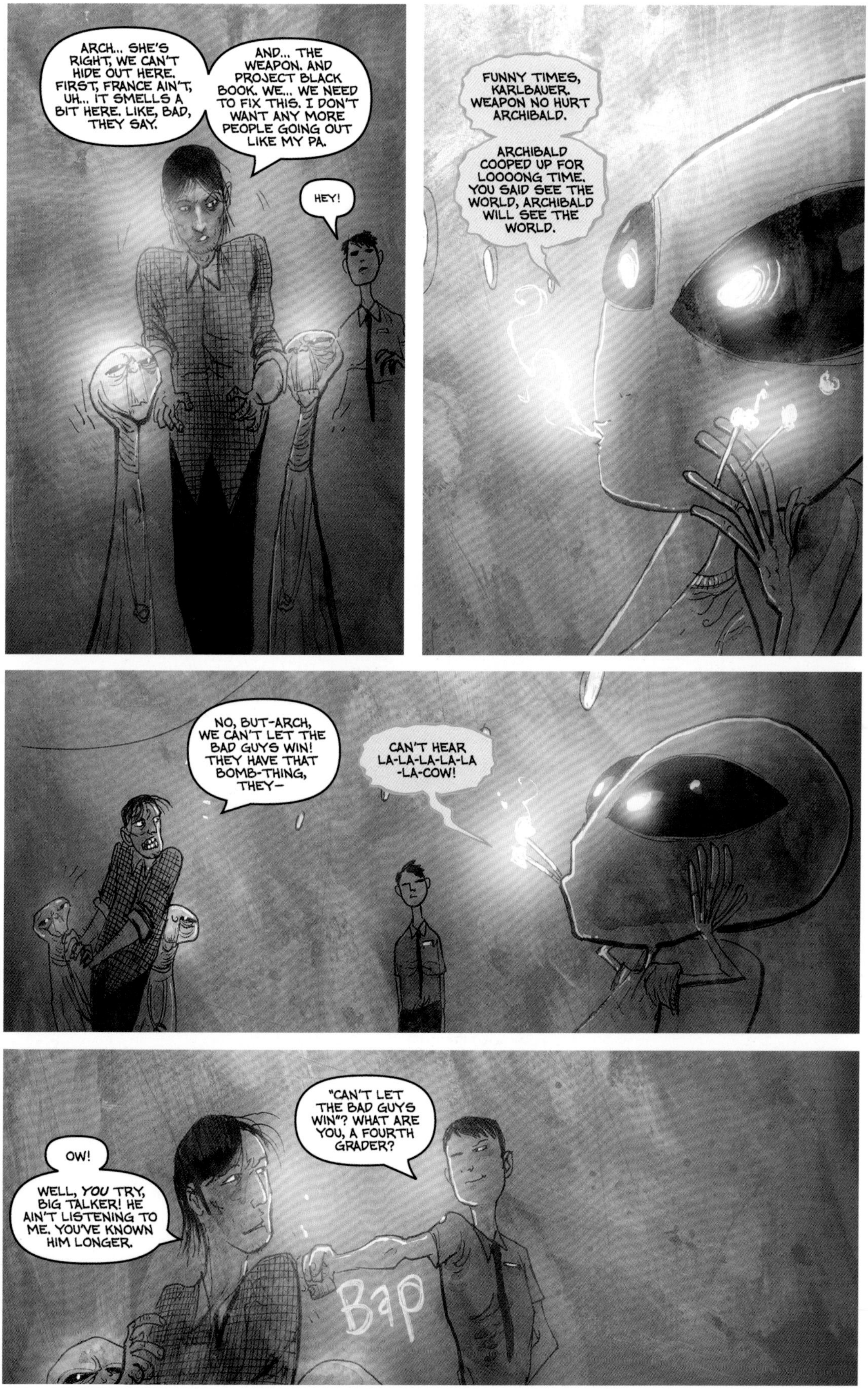

ARCH... SHE'S RIGHT, WE CAN'T HIDE OUT HERE. FIRST, FRANCE AIN'T, UH... IT SMELLS A BIT HERE. LIKE, BAD, THEY SAY.
AND... THE WEAPON. AND PROJECT BLACK BOOK. WE... WE NEED TO FIX THIS. I DON'T WANT ANY MORE PEOPLE GOING OUT LIKE MY PA.
HEY!
FUNNY TIMES, KARLBAUER. WEAPON NO HURT ARCHIBALD.
ARCHIBALD COOPED UP FOR LOOOONG TIME. YOU SAID SEE THE WORLD, ARCHIBALD WILL SEE THE WORLD.
NO, BUT-ARCH, WE CAN'T LET THE BAD GUYS WIN! THEY HAVE THAT BOMB-THING, THEY–
CAN'T HEAR LA-LA-LA-LA-LA -LA-COW!
OW!
WELL, *YOU* TRY, BIG TALKER! HE AIN'T LISTENING TO ME. YOU'VE KNOWN HIM LONGER.
"CAN'T LET THE BAD GUYS WIN"? WHAT ARE YOU, A FOURTH GRADER?
Bap

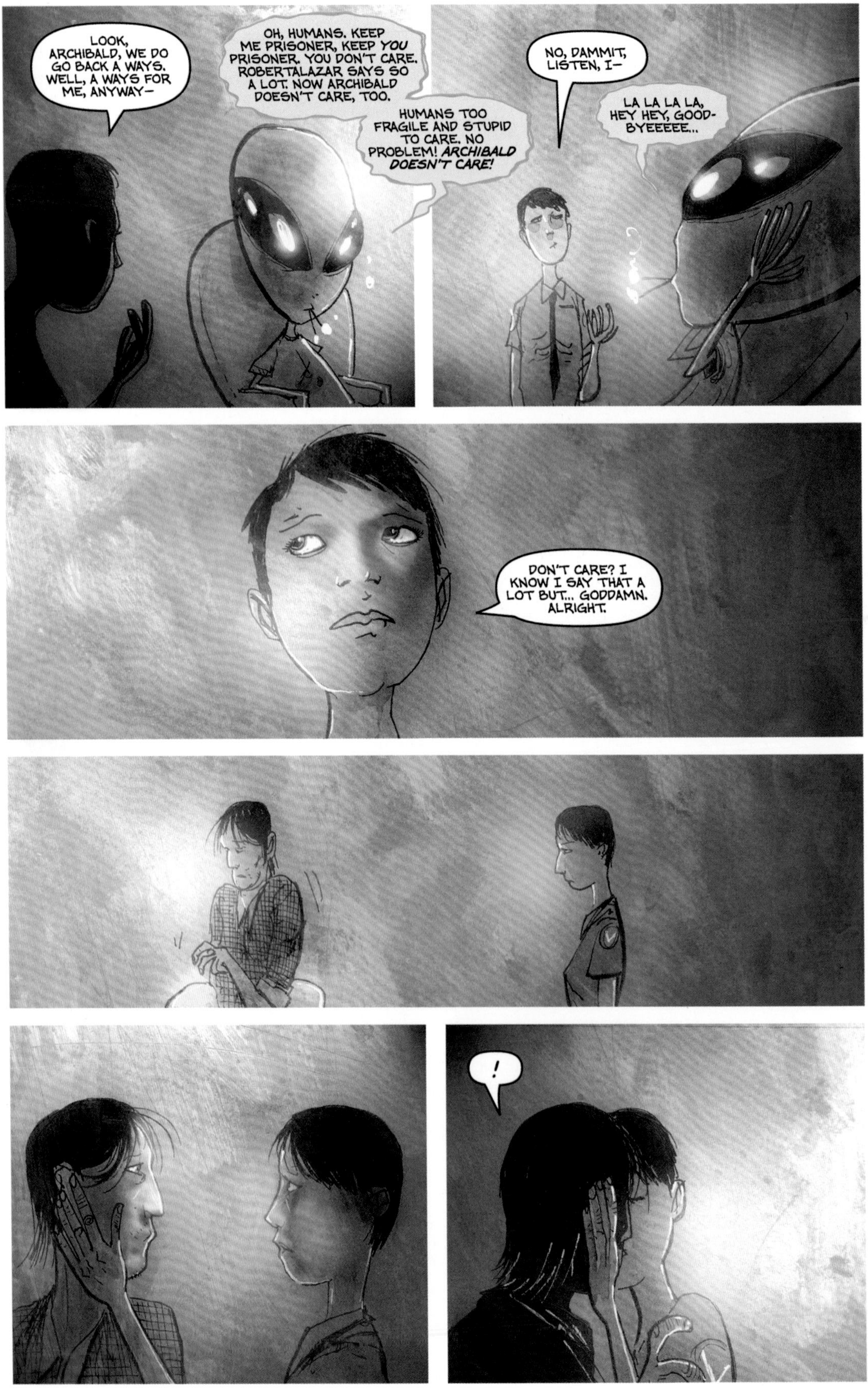
LOOK, ARCHIBALD, WE DO GO BACK A WAYS. WELL, A WAYS FOR ME, ANYWAY—
OH, HUMANS. KEEP ME PRISONER, KEEP YOU PRISONER. YOU DON'T CARE. ROBERTALAZAR SAYS SO A LOT. NOW ARCHIBALD DOESN'T CARE, TOO.
HUMANS TOO FRAGILE AND STUPID TO CARE. NO PROBLEM! ARCHIBALD DOESN'T CARE!
NO, DAMMIT, LISTEN, I—
LA LA LA LA, HEY HEY, GOOD-BYEEEEE...
DON'T CARE? I KNOW I SAY THAT A LOT BUT... GODDAMN. ALRIGHT.
!

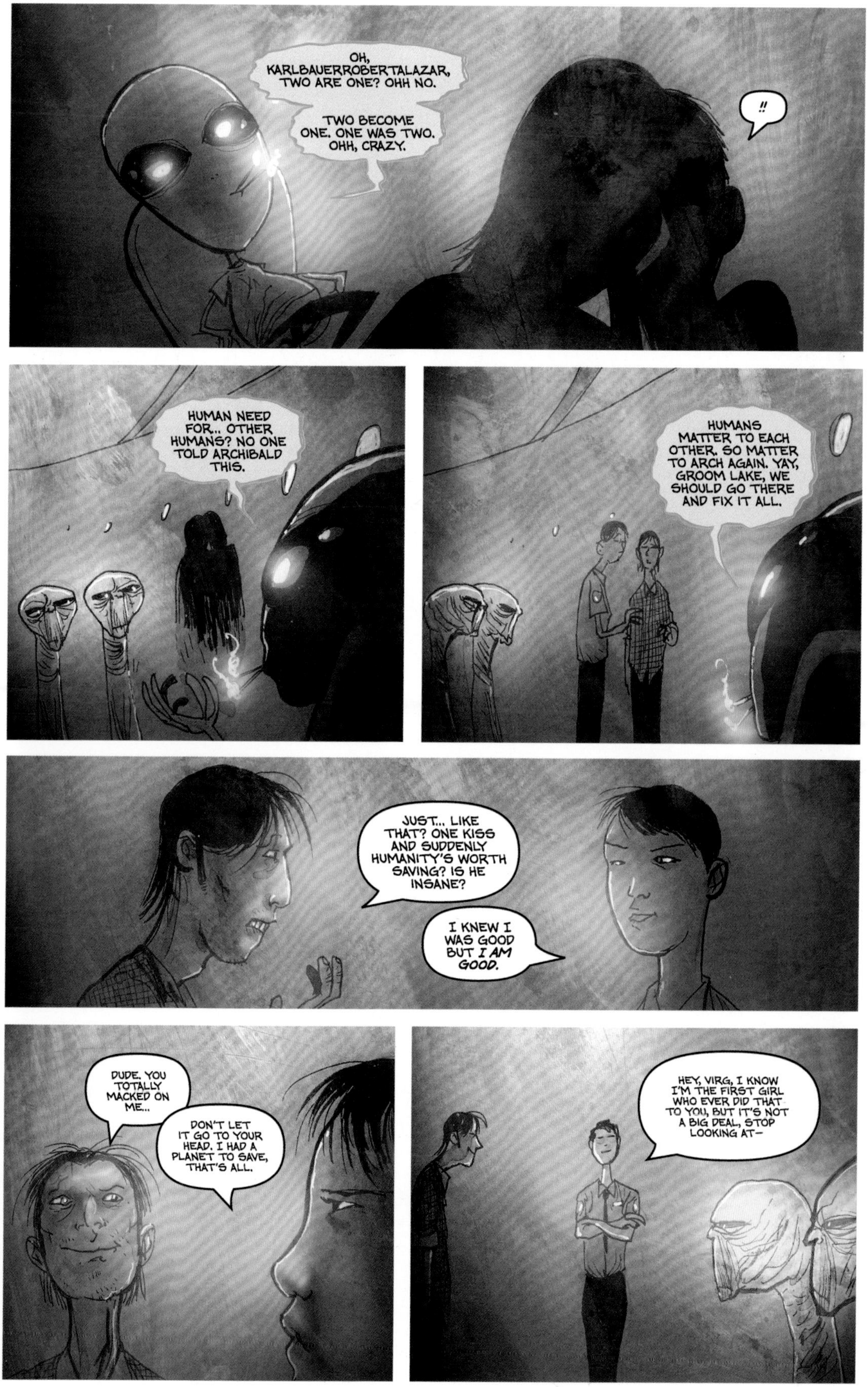
OH, KARLBAUERROBERTALAZAR, TWO ARE ONE? OHH NO.
TWO BECOME ONE. ONE WAS TWO. OHH, CRAZY.
!!
HUMAN NEED FOR.. OTHER HUMANS? NO ONE TOLD ARCHIBALD THIS.
HUMANS MATTER TO EACH OTHER. SO MATTER TO ARCH AGAIN. YAY, GROOM LAKE, WE SHOULD GO THERE AND FIX IT ALL.
JUST... LIKE THAT? ONE KISS AND SUDDENLY HUMANITY'S WORTH SAVING? IS HE INSANE?
I KNEW I WAS GOOD BUT I AM GOOD.
DUDE. YOU TOTALLY MACKED ON ME...
DON'T LET IT GO TO YOUR HEAD. I HAD A PLANET TO SAVE, THAT'S ALL.
HEY, VIRG, I KNOW I'M THE FIRST GIRL WHO EVER DID THAT TO YOU, BUT IT'S NOT A BIG DEAL, STOP LOOKING AT—

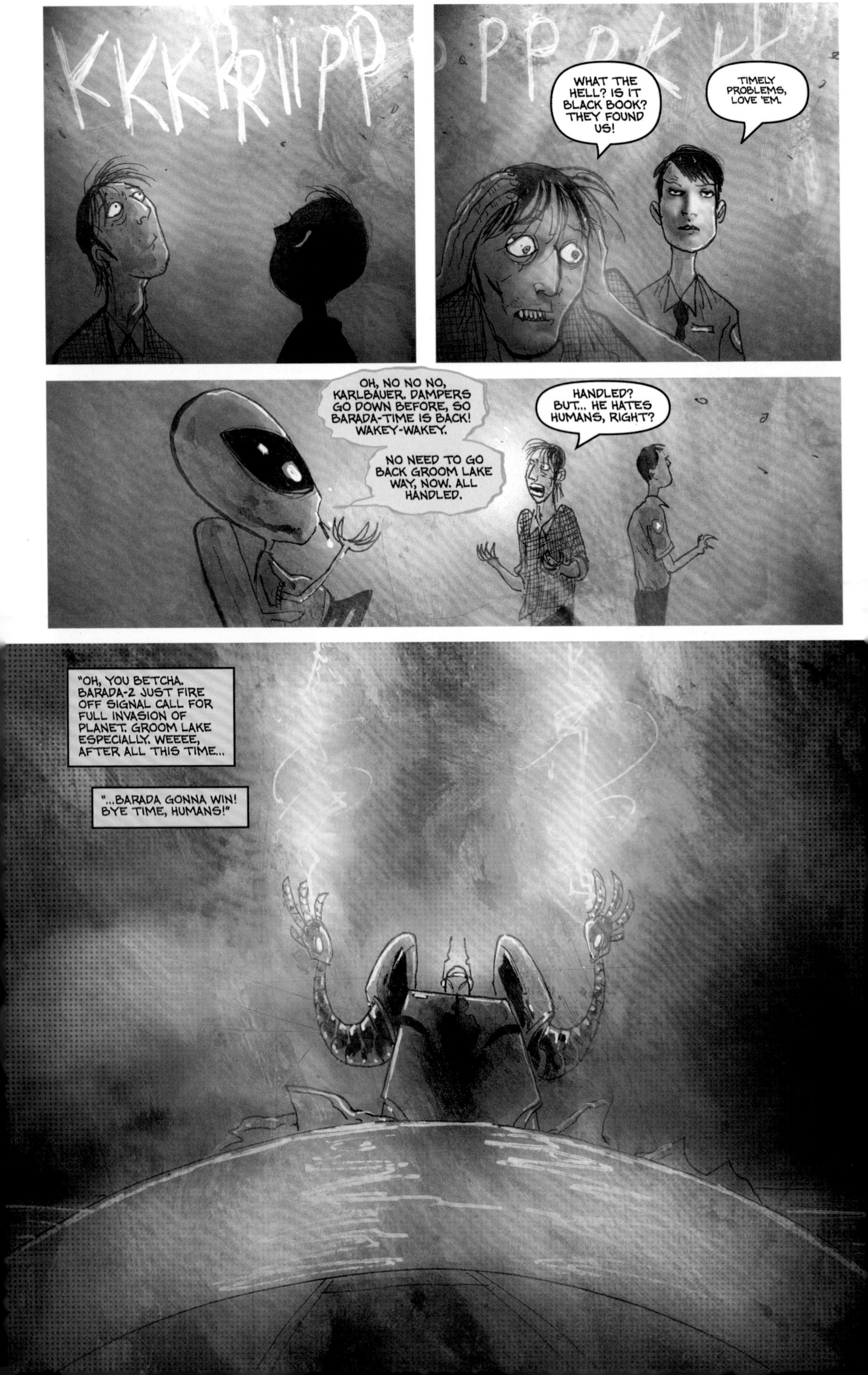
KKKRRIIPPP
PPPPKLL
WHAT THE HELL? IS IT BLACK BOOK? THEY FOUND US!
TIMELY PROBLEMS, LOVE 'EM.
OH, NO NO NO, KARLBAUER. DAMPERS GO DOWN BEFORE, SO BARADA-TIME IS BACK! WAKEY-WAKEY.
NO NEED TO GO BACK GROOM LAKE WAY, NOW. ALL HANDLED.
HANDLED? BUT... HE HATES HUMANS, RIGHT?
"OH, YOU BETCHA. BARADA-2 JUST FIRE OFF SIGNAL CALL FOR FULL INVASION OF PLANET. GROOM LAKE ESPECIALLY. WEEEE, AFTER ALL THIS TIME...
"...BARADA GONNA WIN! BYE TIME, HUMANS!"

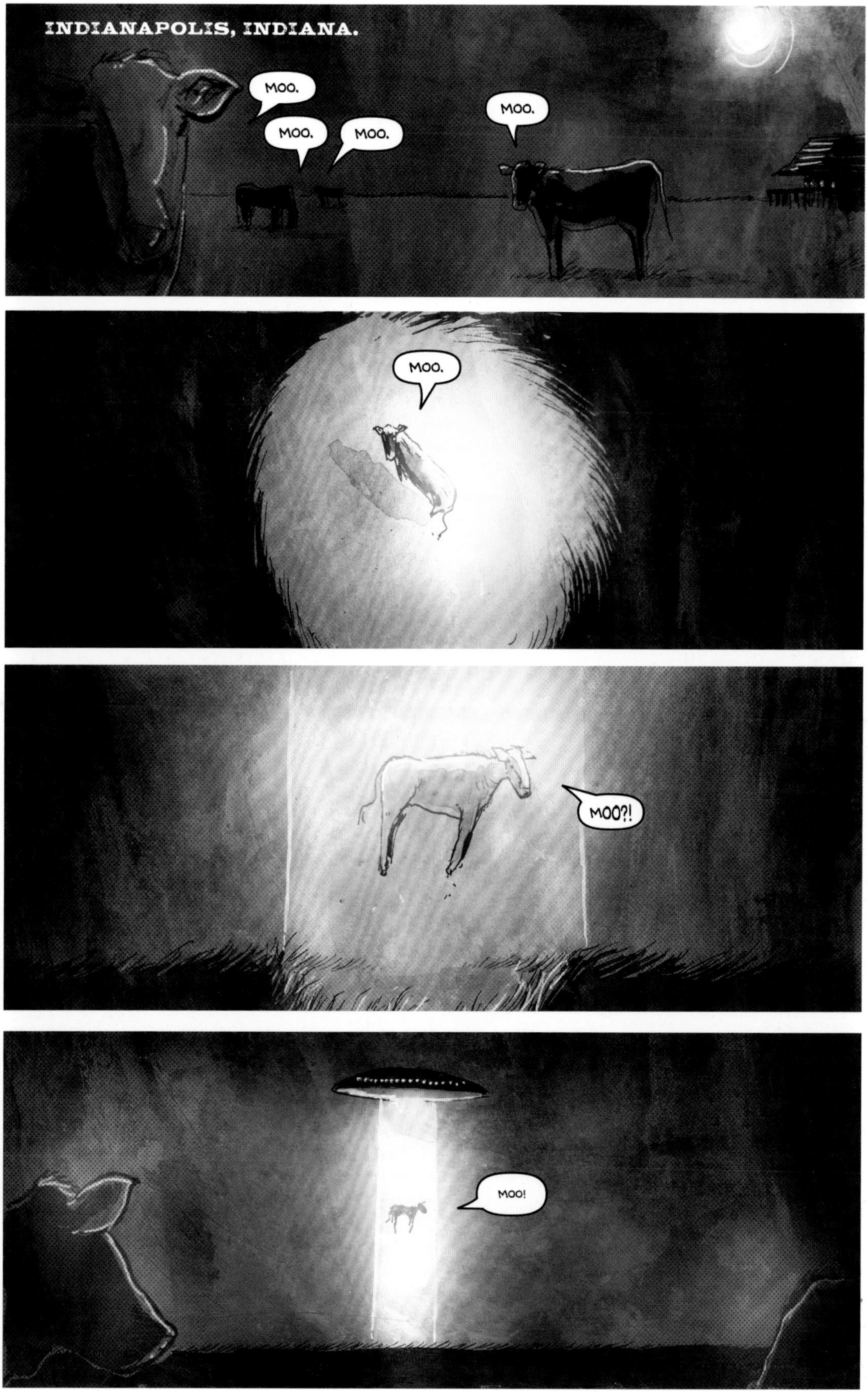
INDIANAPOLIS, INDIANA.
MOO.
MOO.
MOO.
MOO.
MOO.
MOO?!
MOO!

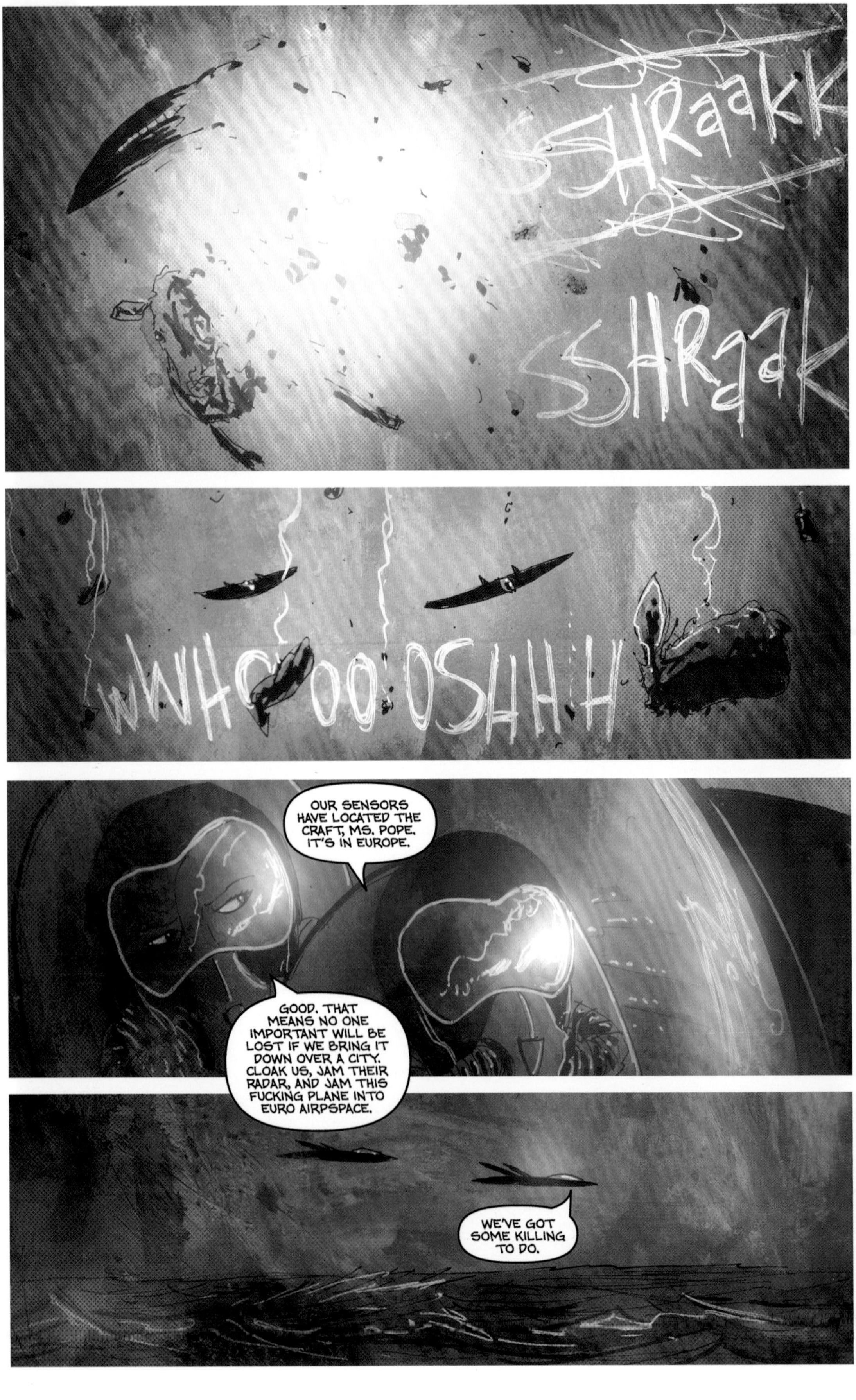
SSHRAAKK
SSHRAAK
WWHOOOOSHHH
OUR SENSORS HAVE LOCATED THE CRAFT, MS. POPE. IT'S IN EUROPE.
GOOD. THAT MEANS NO ONE IMPORTANT WILL BE LOST IF WE BRING IT DOWN OVER A CITY. CLOAK US, JAM THEIR RADAR, AND JAM THIS FUCKING PLANE INTO EURO AIRSPACE.
WE'VE GOT SOME KILLING TO DO.

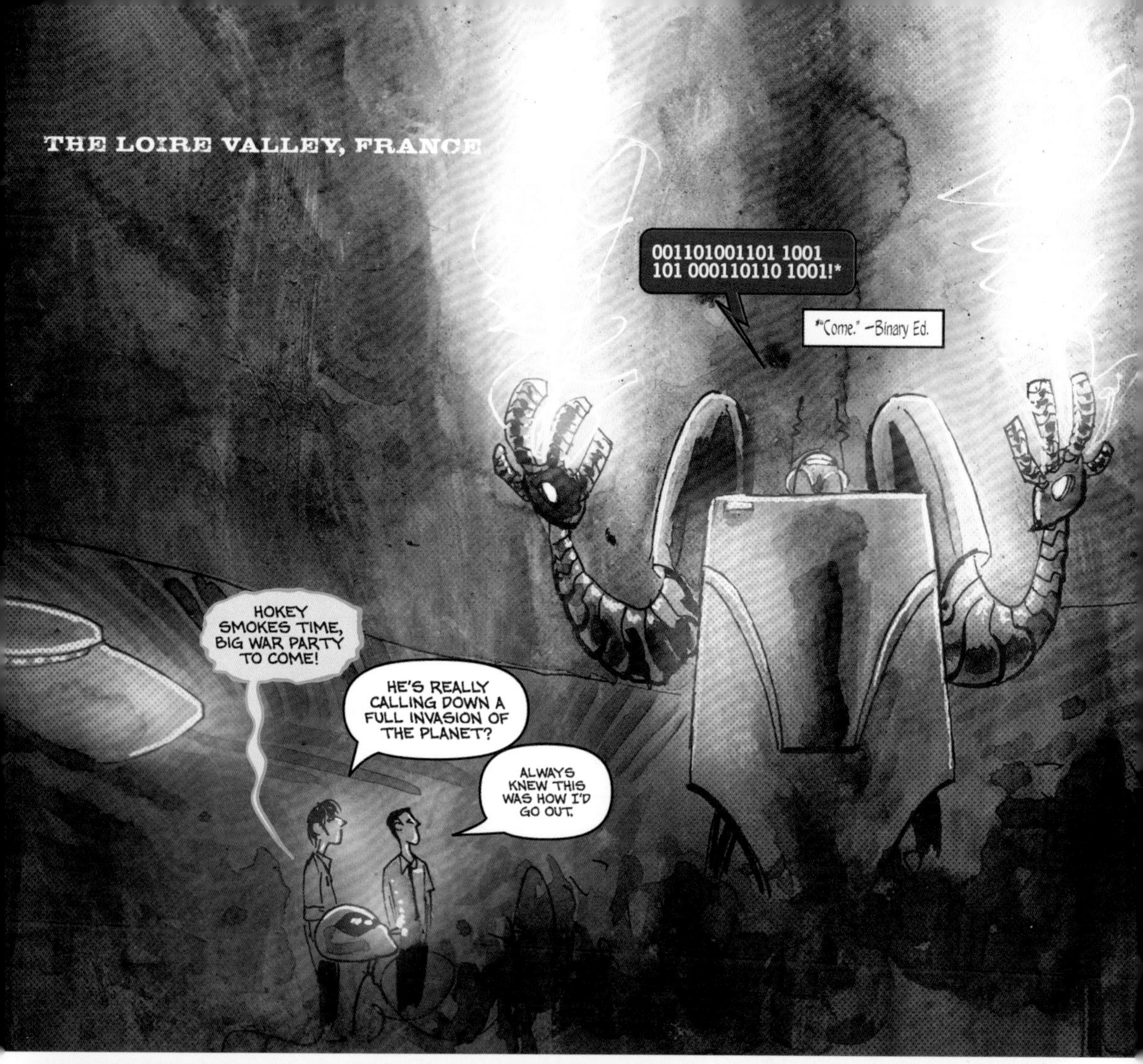
THE LOIRE VALLEY, FRANCE
001101001101 1001
101 000110110 1001!*
*"Come." —Binary Ed.
HOKEY SMOKES TIME, BIG WAR PARTY TO COME!
HE'S REALLY CALLING DOWN A FULL INVASION OF THE PLANET?
ALWAYS KNEW THIS WAS HOW I'D GO OUT.

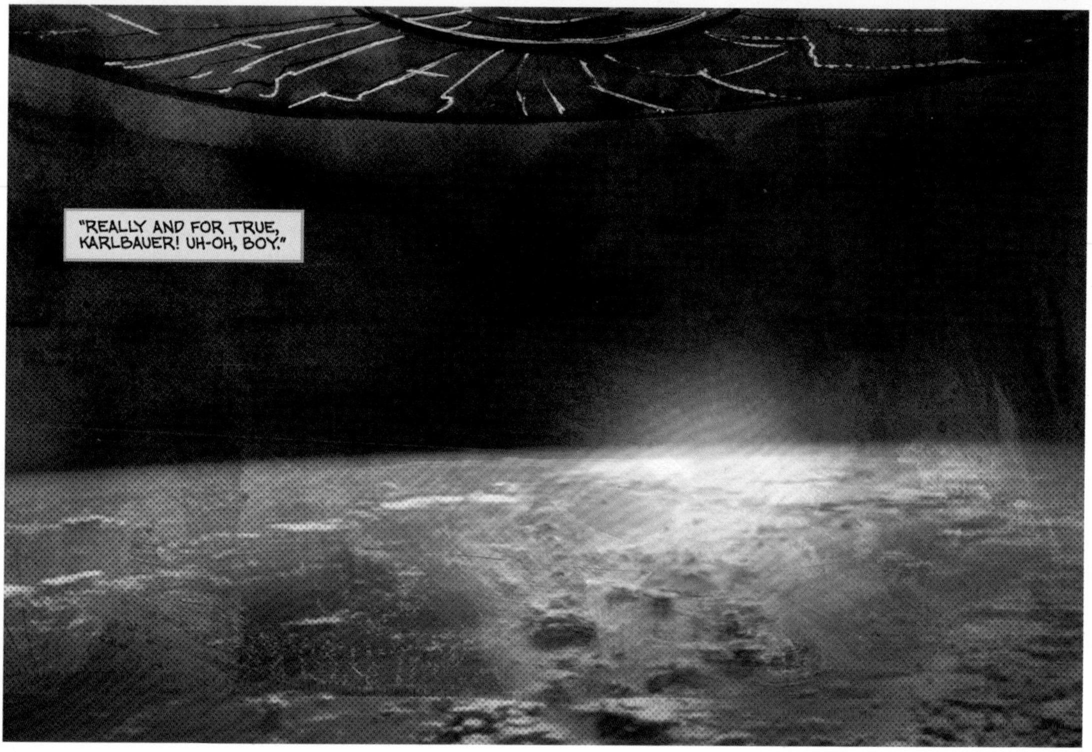
"REALLY AND FOR TRUE, KARLBAUER! UH-OH, BOY."

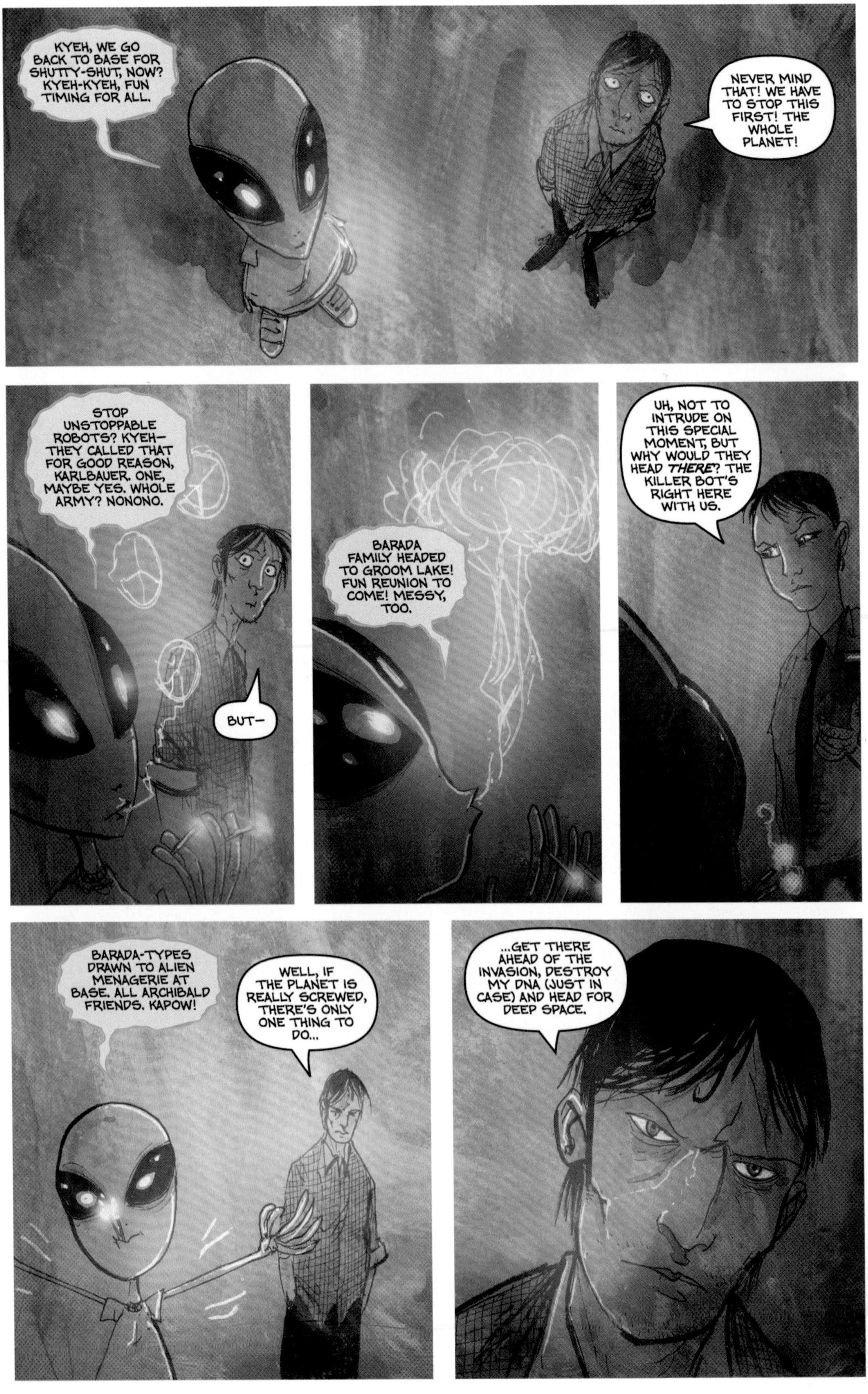
KYEH, WE GO BACK TO BASE FOR SHUTTY-SHUT, NOW? KYEH-KYEH, FUN TIMING FOR ALL.
NEVER MIND THAT! WE HAVE TO STOP THIS FIRST! THE WHOLE PLANET!
STOP UNSTOPPABLE ROBOTS? KYEH— THEY CALLED THAT FOR GOOD REASON, KARLBAUER. ONE, MAYBE YES. WHOLE ARMY? NONONO.
BUT—
BARADA FAMILY HEADED TO GROOM LAKE! FUN REUNION TO COME! MESSY, TOO.
UH, NOT TO INTRUDE ON THIS SPECIAL MOMENT, BUT WHY WOULD THEY HEAD *THERE*? THE KILLER BOT'S RIGHT HERE WITH US.
BARADA-TYPES DRAWN TO ALIEN MENAGERIE AT BASE. ALL ARCHIBALD FRIENDS. KAPOW!
WELL, IF THE PLANET IS REALLY SCREWED, THERE'S ONLY ONE THING TO DO...
...GET THERE AHEAD OF THE INVASION, DESTROY MY DNA (JUST IN CASE) AND HEAD FOR DEEP SPACE.

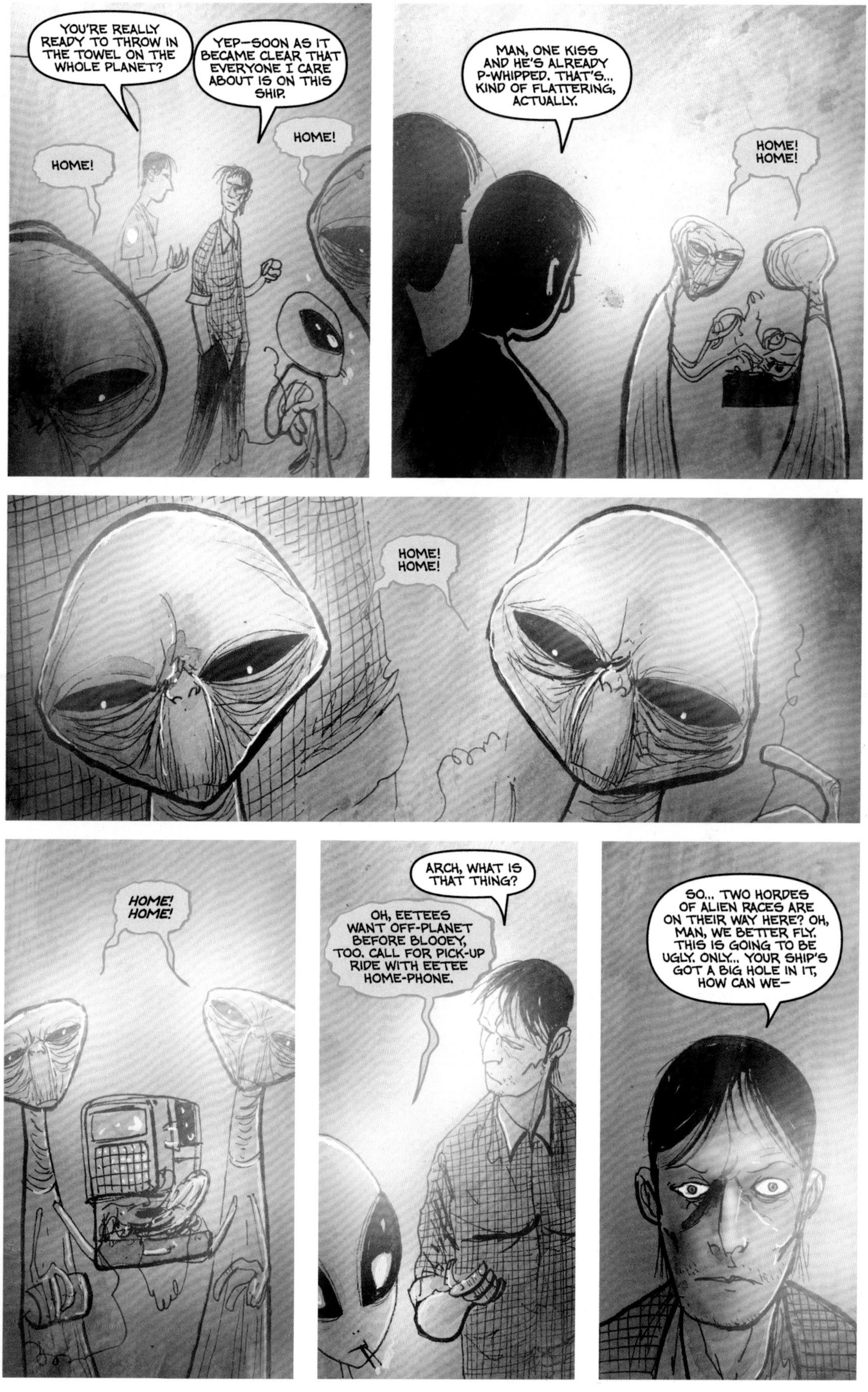

YOU'RE REALLY READY TO THROW IN THE TOWEL ON THE WHOLE PLANET?
YEP—SOON AS IT BECAME CLEAR THAT EVERYONE I CARE ABOUT IS ON THIS SHIP.
HOME!
HOME!
MAN, ONE KISS AND HE'S ALREADY P-WHIPPED. THAT'S... KIND OF FLATTERING, ACTUALLY.
HOME! HOME!
HOME! HOME!
HOME! HOME!
ARCH, WHAT IS THAT THING?
OH, EETEES WANT OFF-PLANET BEFORE BLOOEY, TOO. CALL FOR PICK-UP RIDE WITH EETEE HOME-PHONE.
SO... TWO HORDES OF ALIEN RACES ARE ON THEIR WAY HERE? OH, MAN, WE BETTER FLY. THIS IS GOING TO BE UGLY. ONLY... YOUR SHIP'S GOT A BIG HOLE IN IT, HOW CAN WE—

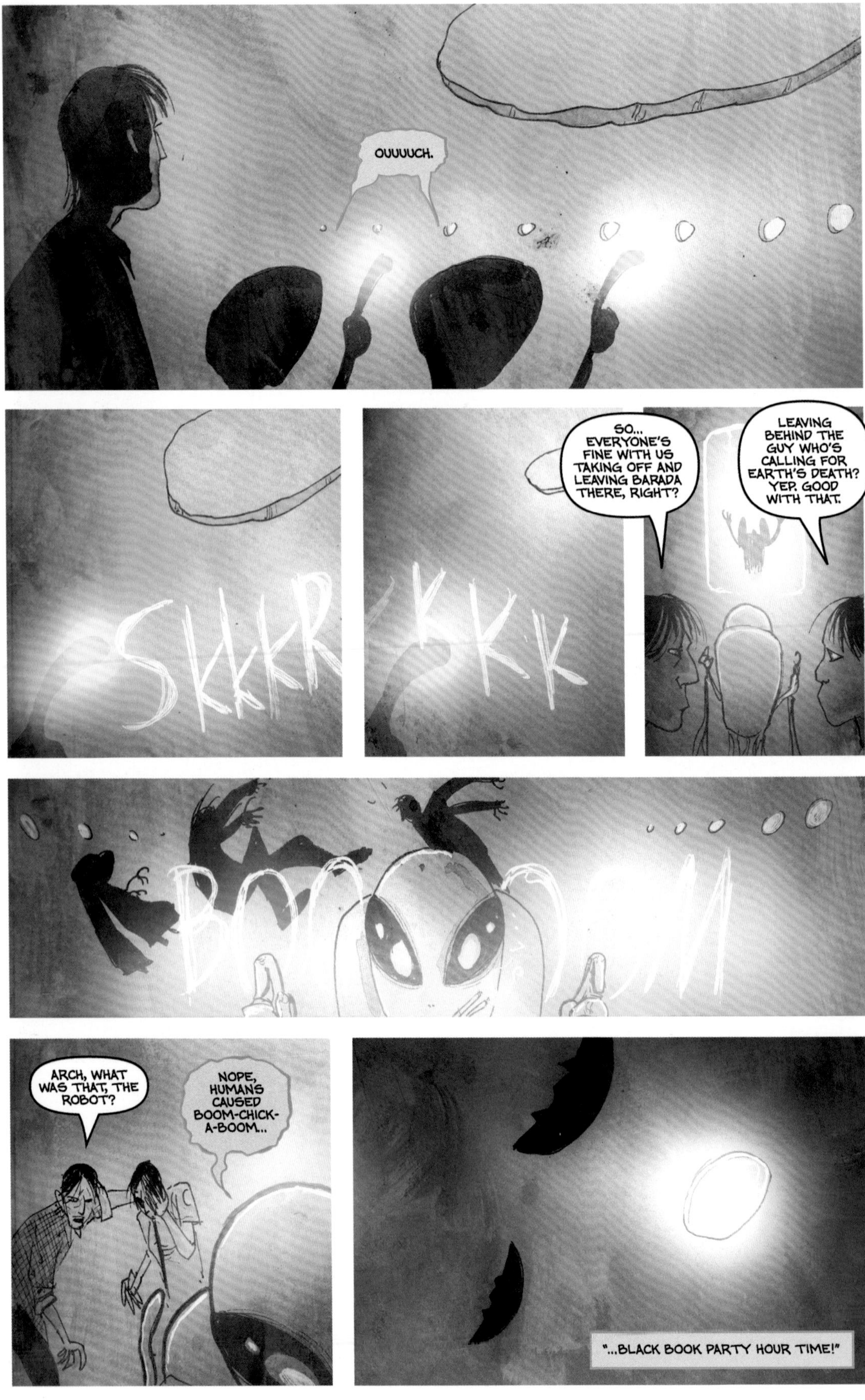
OUUUUCH.
SKKKRKKKK
SO... EVERYONE'S FINE WITH US TAKING OFF AND LEAVING BARADA THERE, RIGHT?
LEAVING BEHIND THE GUY WHO'S CALLING FOR EARTH'S DEATH? YEP. GOOD WITH THAT.
ARCH, WHAT WAS THAT, THE ROBOT?
NOPE, HUMANS CAUSED BOOM-CHICK-A-BOOM...
"...BLACK BOOK PARTY HOUR TIME!"

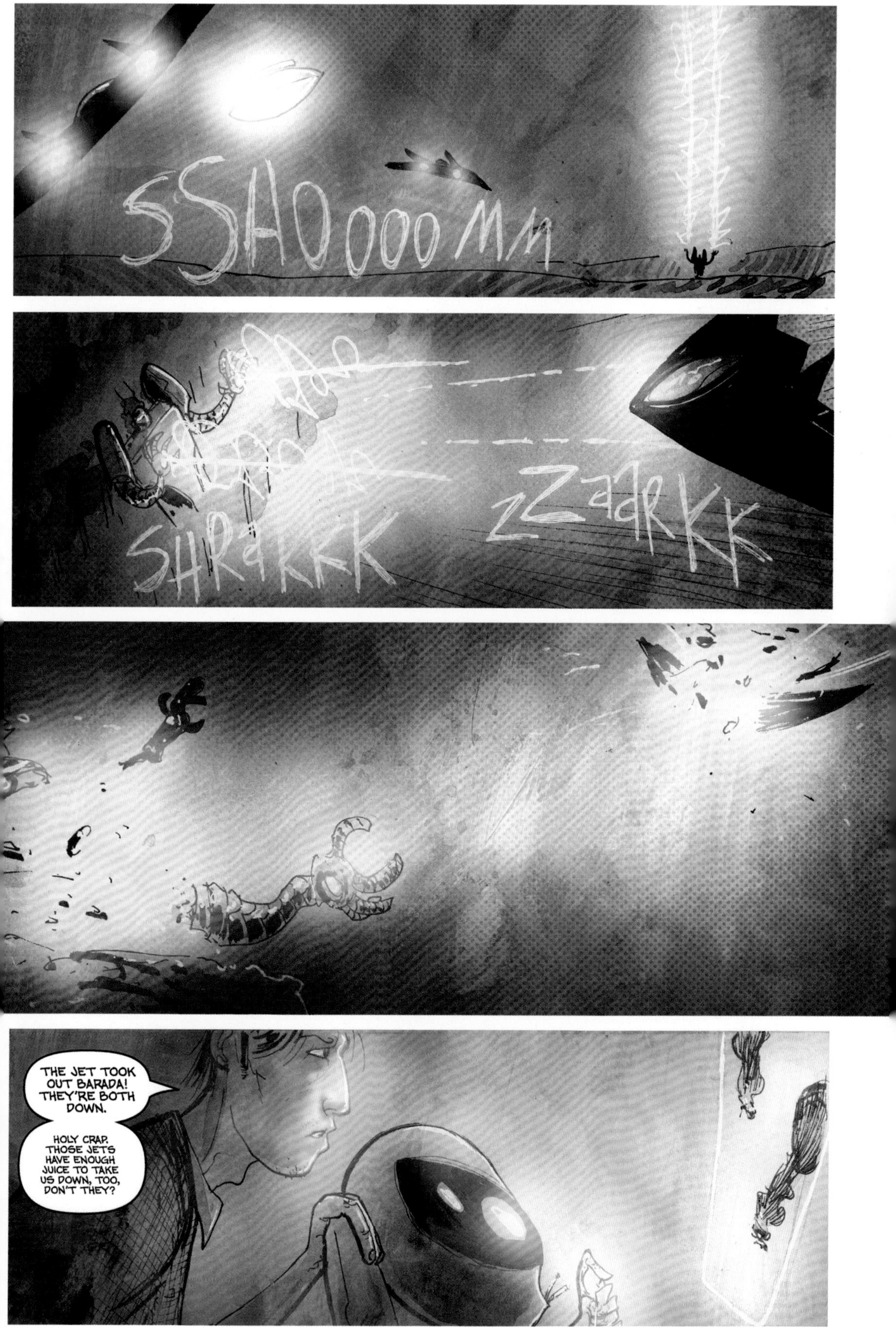
SSHOOOOMM
SHRAKKK
ZZAARKKK
THE JET TOOK OUT BARADA! THEY'RE BOTH DOWN.
HOLY CRAP. THOSE JETS HAVE ENOUGH JUICE TO TAKE US DOWN, TOO, DON'T THEY?

FINALLY. ALWAYS HATED THAT GODDAMNED ROBOT.

STAY ON THEM, BUT DON'T FIRE. MUCH AS HE DESERVES IT, I'D PREFER NOT TO SHOOT DOWN ARCH YET. NOT THAT IT'S LIKELY TO KILL HIM, ANYWAY.

SIR?

THEY'RE LIKELY HEADED BACK TO GROOM. WE'VE GOT THE FORTIFICATIONS TO TAKE THEM ALL DOWN THERE IF NEEDED.

POPE TO BASE. INCOMING. TAKE THE SHIP DOWN BUT MAKE SURE NO ONE CAPS BAUER. HE'S ALL MINE, THE LITTLE CORNPONE PIECE OF CRAP.

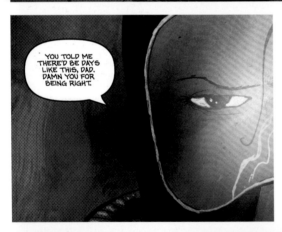

YOU TOLD ME THERE'D BE DAYS LIKE THIS, DAD. DAMN YOU FOR BEING RIGHT.

MR. POPE! WE'VE GOT A PROBLEM! WE HAVE RADAR FUNCTION BACK ON-LINE AND... IT'S PICKING UP SOMETHING. SOMETHING HUGE!

IT'S ARCHIBALD. HE'S ON HIS WAY THERE NOW—

NO, SIR, NOT HIM! IT'S COMING FROM... ABOVE THE BASE, JUST ENTERING OUR ATMOSPHERE! HUGE. TWO HUGE FUCKING BOGEYS!

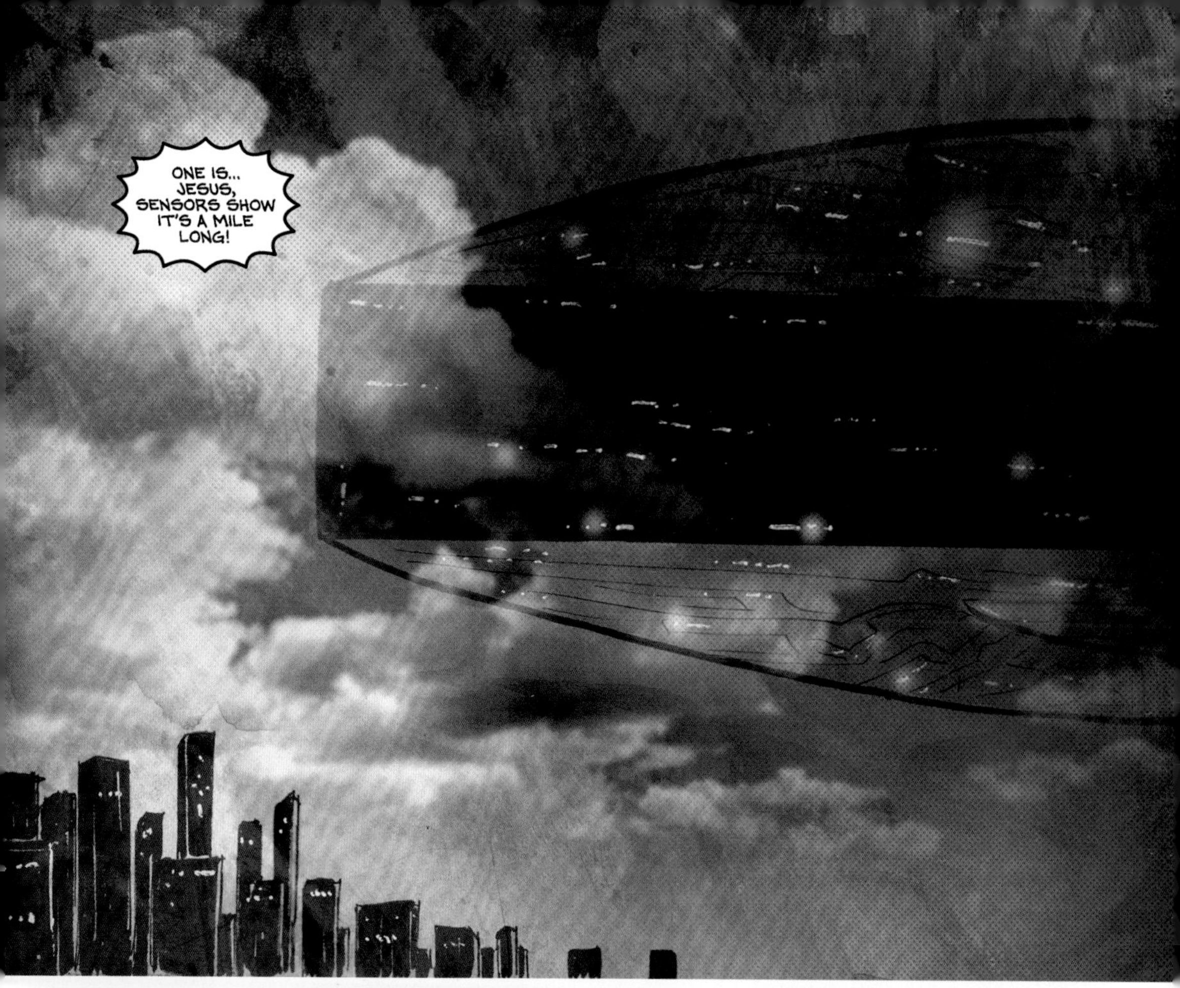
ONE IS... JESUS, SENSORS SHOW IT'S A MILE LONG!

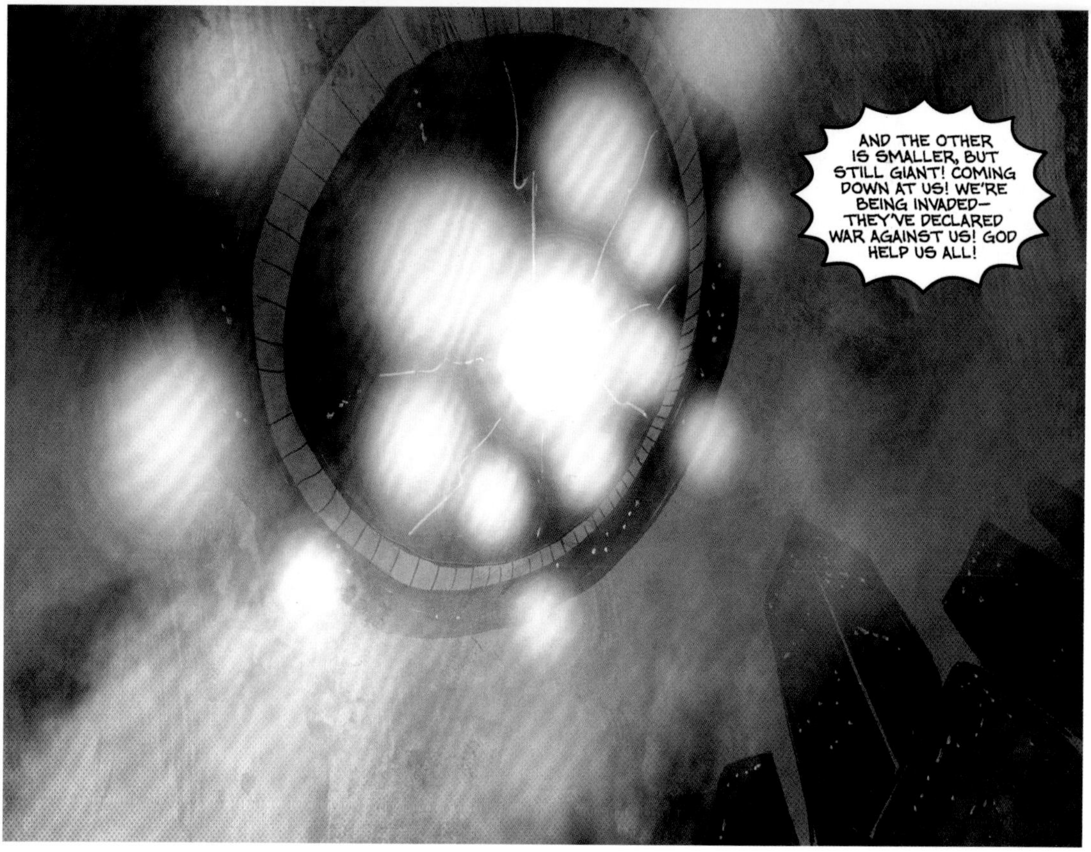
AND THE OTHER IS SMALLER, BUT STILL GIANT! COMING DOWN AT US! WE'RE BEING INVADED— THEY'VE DECLARED WAR AGAINST US! GOD HELP US ALL!

GROOM LAKE, NEW MEXICO.

WOW, WE REALLY DID A NUMBER ON THE PLACE, DIDN'T WE?

WOO-BOY, ARCHIBALD HOME PRETTY DRAFTY NOW.

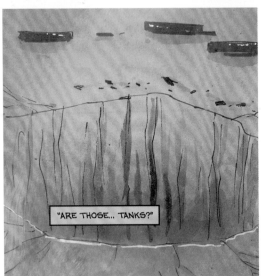

"ARE THOSE... TANKS?"

"NEW HAPPY-TIME WELCOME WAGON!"

OH, MAN, WE BETTER TURN AROUND BEFORE THEY DECIDE TO—

...

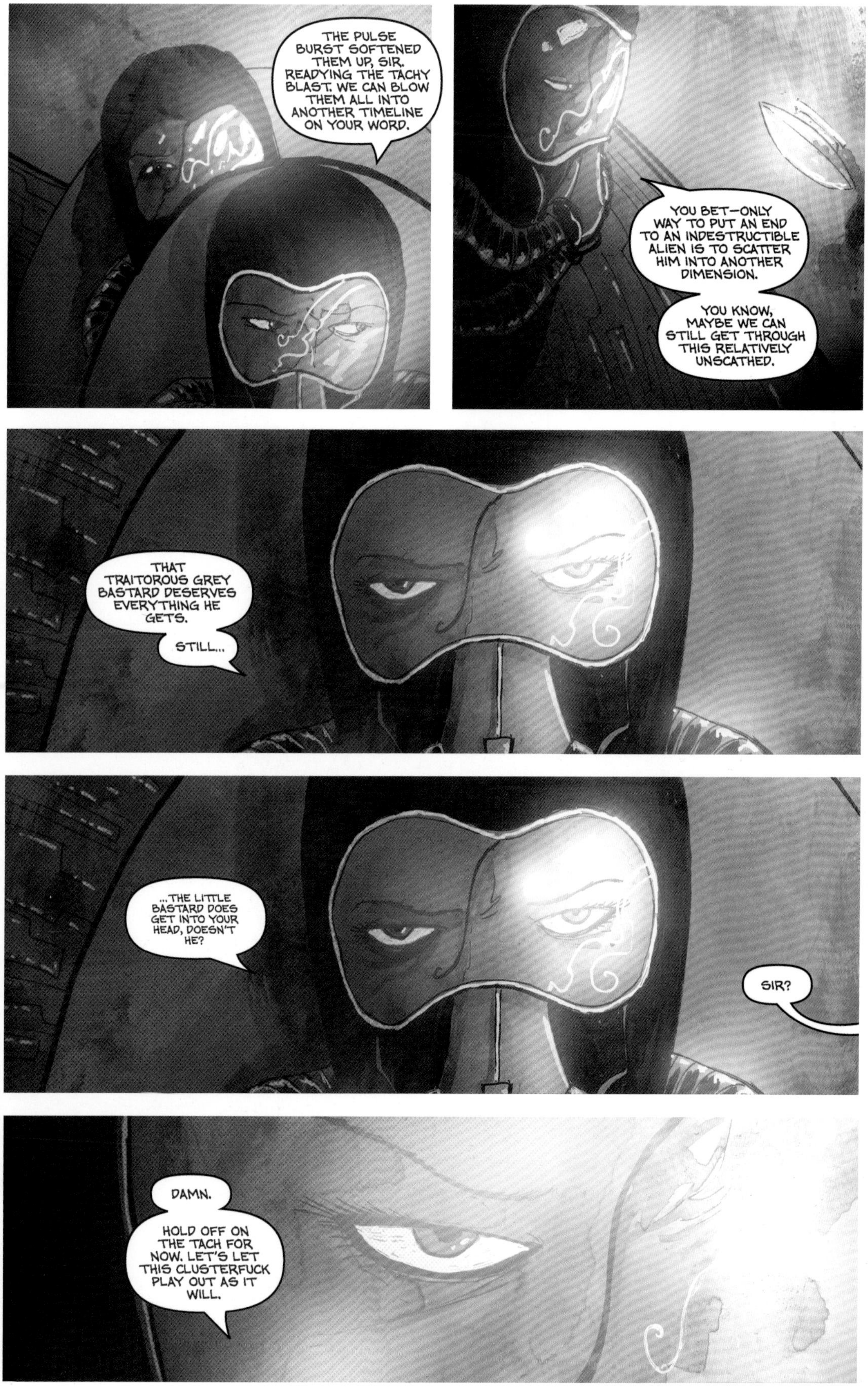
THE PULSE BURST SOFTENED THEM UP, SIR. READYING THE TACHY BLAST. WE CAN BLOW THEM ALL INTO ANOTHER TIMELINE ON YOUR WORD.
YOU BET—ONLY WAY TO PUT AN END TO AN INDESTRUCTIBLE ALIEN IS TO SCATTER HIM INTO ANOTHER DIMENSION.
YOU KNOW, MAYBE WE CAN STILL GET THROUGH THIS RELATIVELY UNSCATHED.
THAT TRAITOROUS GREY BASTARD DESERVES EVERYTHING HE GETS.
STILL...
...THE LITTLE BASTARD DOES GET INTO YOUR HEAD, DOESN'T HE?
SIR?
DAMN.
HOLD OFF ON THE TACH FOR NOW. LET'S LET THIS CLUSTERFUCK PLAY OUT AS IT WILL.

KRUMP WHUMP

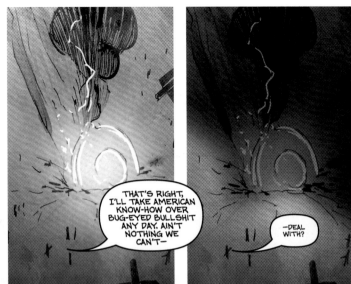

THAT'S RIGHT, I'LL TAKE AMERICAN KNOW-HOW OVER BUG-EYED BULLSHIT ANY DAY. AIN'T NOTHING WE CAN'T—

—DEAL WITH?

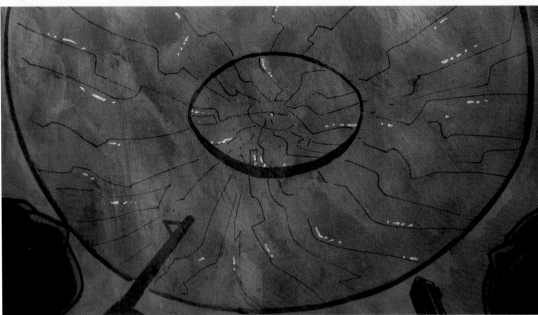

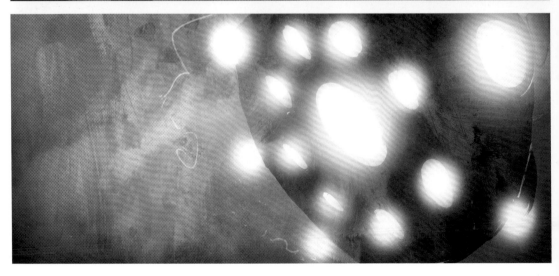

THEY'RE INVADING! SHIIIT!
01000100 01101001 01100101 00100001!*
*Turn.
STOP. STOP. STOP. STOP.
HERE THEY... COME? WAIT...

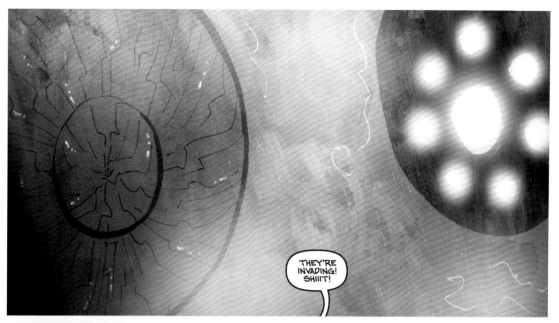

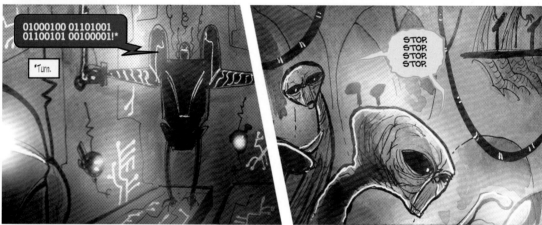

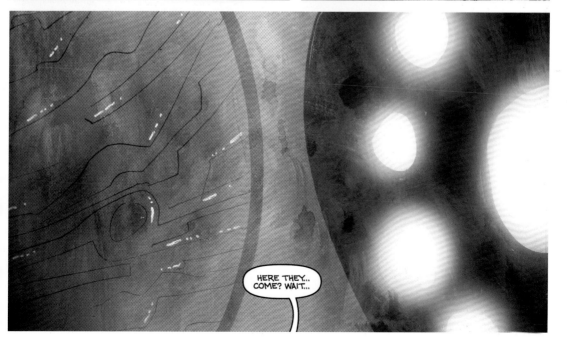

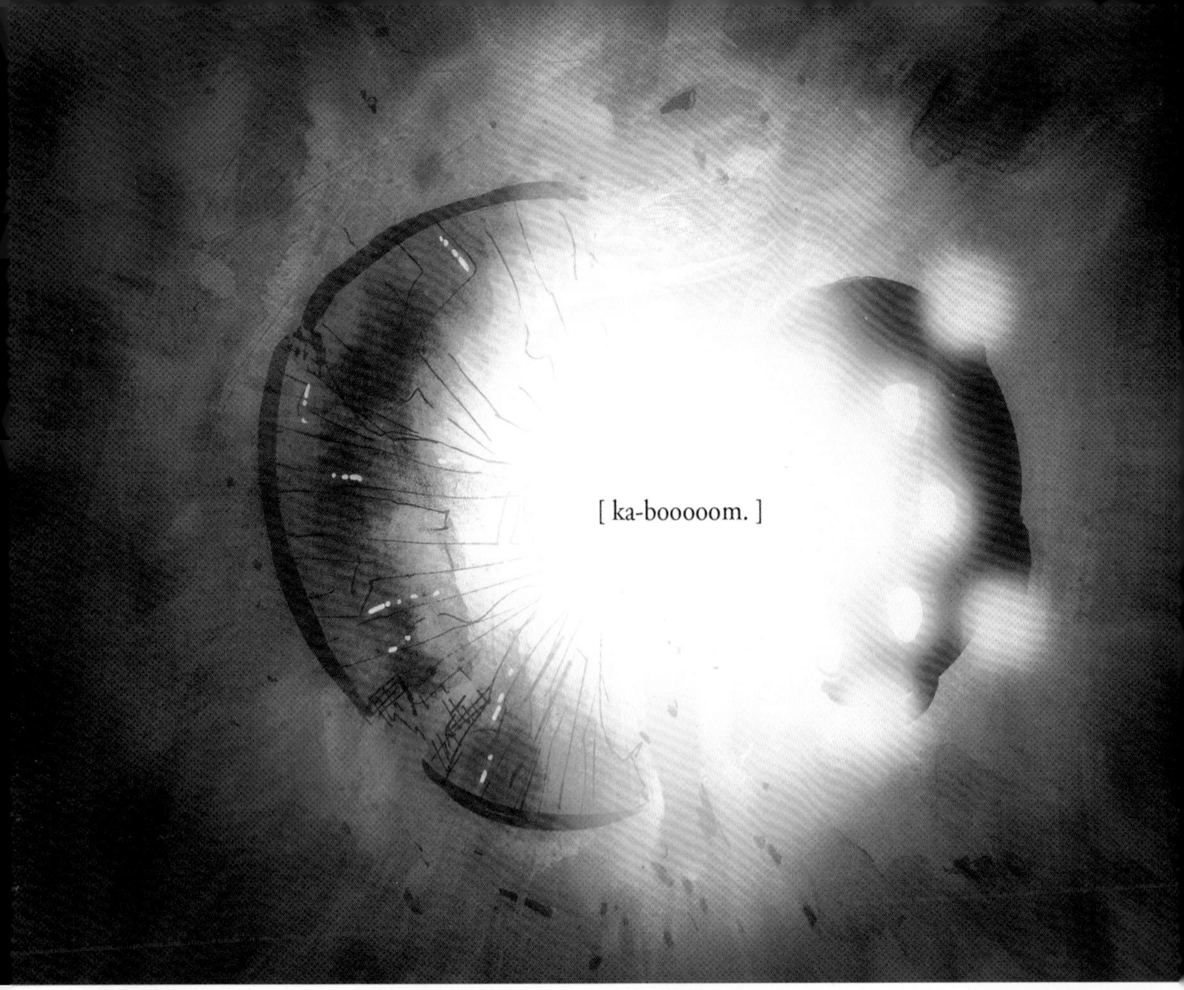
[ka-booooom.]

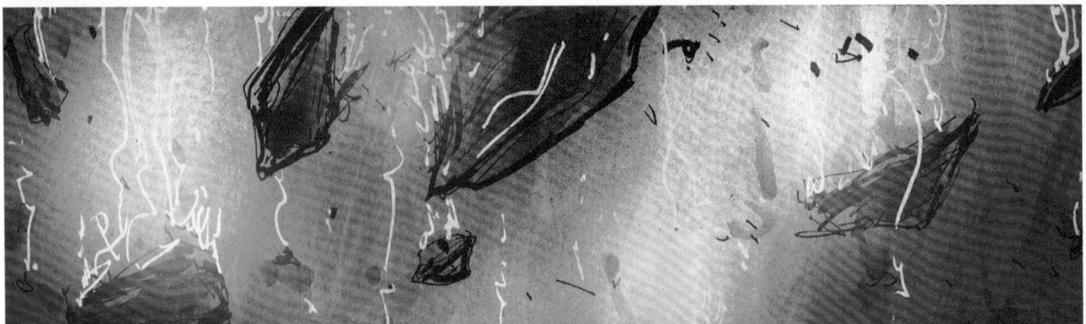

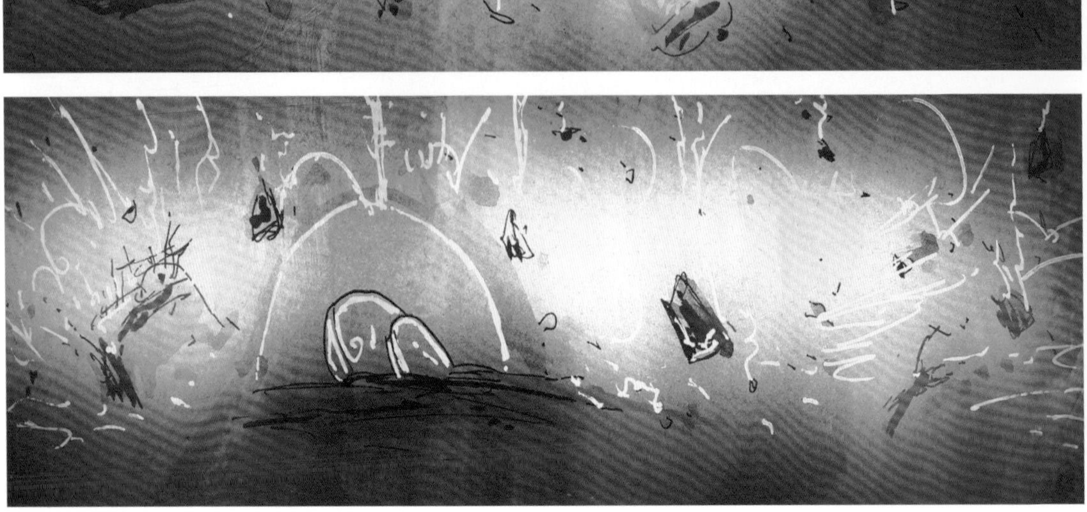

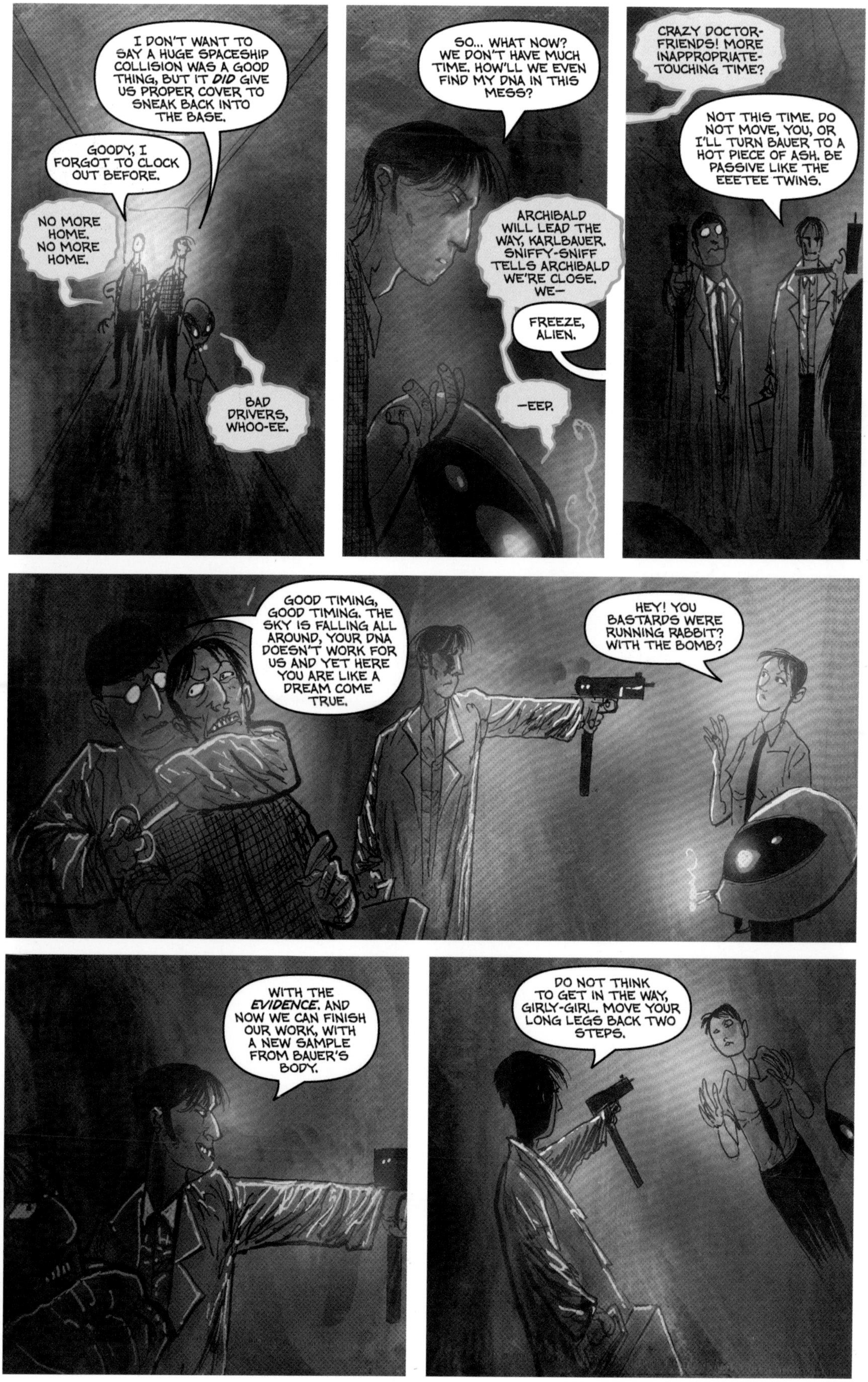
I DON'T WANT TO SAY A HUGE SPACESHIP COLLISION WAS A GOOD THING, BUT IT *DID* GIVE US PROPER COVER TO SNEAK BACK INTO THE BASE.
GOODY, I FORGOT TO CLOCK OUT BEFORE.
NO MORE HOME. NO MORE HOME.
BAD DRIVERS, WHOO-EE.
SO... WHAT NOW? WE DON'T HAVE MUCH TIME. HOW'LL WE EVEN FIND MY DNA IN THIS MESS?
ARCHIBALD WILL LEAD THE WAY, KARLBAUER. SNIFFY-SNIFF TELLS ARCHIBALD WE'RE CLOSE. WE—
FREEZE, ALIEN.
—EEP.
CRAZY DOCTOR-FRIENDS! MORE INAPPROPRIATE-TOUCHING TIME?
NOT THIS TIME. DO NOT MOVE, YOU, OR I'LL TURN BAUER TO A HOT PIECE OF ASH. BE PASSIVE LIKE THE EEETEE TWINS.
GOOD TIMING, GOOD TIMING. THE SKY IS FALLING ALL AROUND, YOUR DNA DOESN'T WORK FOR US AND YET HERE YOU ARE LIKE A DREAM COME TRUE.
HEY! YOU BASTARDS WERE RUNNING RABBIT? WITH THE BOMB?
WITH THE *EVIDENCE*. AND NOW WE CAN FINISH OUR WORK, WITH A NEW SAMPLE FROM BAUER'S BODY.
DO NOT THINK TO GET IN THE WAY, GIRLY-GIRL. MOVE YOUR LONG LEGS BACK TWO STEPS.

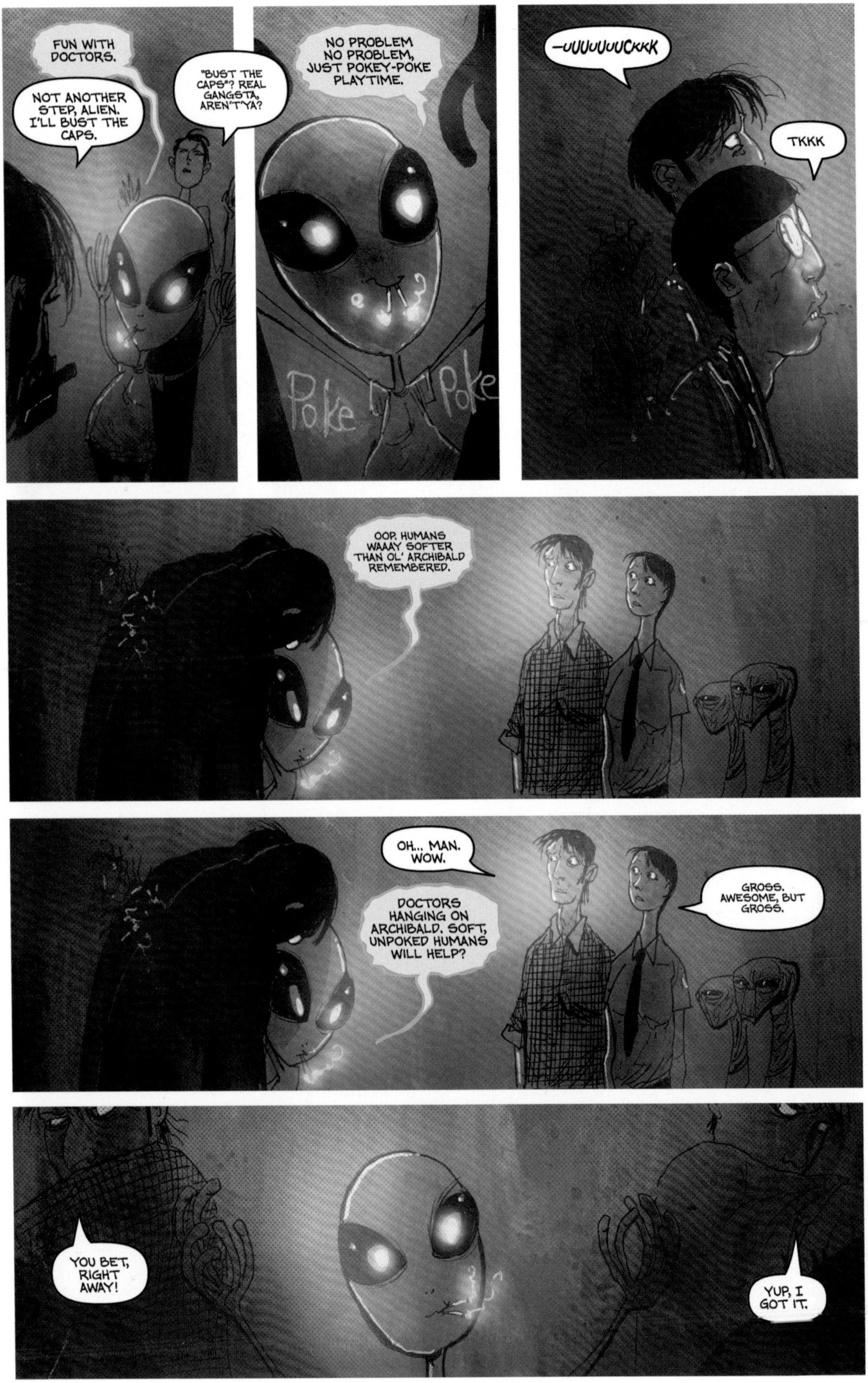
FUN WITH DOCTORS.
NOT ANOTHER STEP, ALIEN. I'LL BUST THE CAPS.
"BUST THE CAPS"? REAL GANGSTA, AREN'T'YA?
NO PROBLEM NO PROBLEM, JUST POKEY-POKE PLAYTIME.
Poke
Poke
—UUUUUUUCKKK
TKKK
OOP. HUMANS WAAAY SOFTER THAN OL' ARCHIBALD REMEMBERED.
OH... MAN. WOW.
DOCTORS HANGING ON ARCHIBALD. SOFT, UNPOKED HUMANS WILL HELP?
GROSS. AWESOME, BUT GROSS.
YOU BET, RIGHT AWAY!
YUP, I GOT IT.

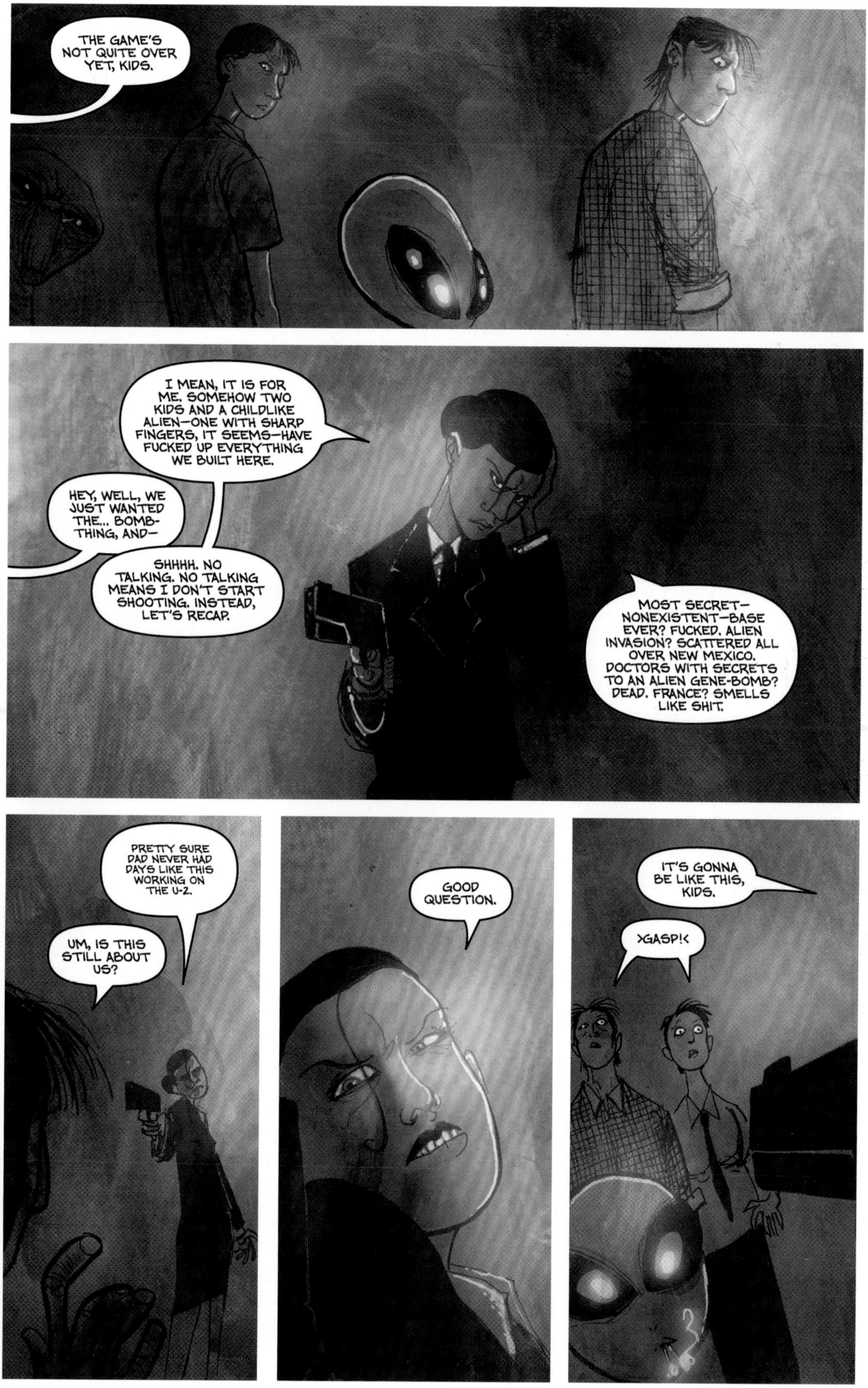
THE GAME'S NOT QUITE OVER YET, KIDS.
I MEAN, IT IS FOR ME. SOMEHOW TWO KIDS AND A CHILDLIKE ALIEN—ONE WITH SHARP FINGERS, IT SEEMS—HAVE FUCKED UP EVERYTHING WE BUILT HERE.
HEY, WELL, WE JUST WANTED THE... BOMB-THING, AND—
SHHHH. NO TALKING. NO TALKING MEANS I DON'T START SHOOTING. INSTEAD, LET'S RECAP.
MOST SECRET—NONEXISTENT—BASE EVER? FUCKED. ALIEN INVASION? SCATTERED ALL OVER NEW MEXICO. DOCTORS WITH SECRETS TO AN ALIEN GENE-BOMB? DEAD. FRANCE? SMELLS LIKE SHIT.
PRETTY SURE DAD NEVER HAD DAYS LIKE THIS WORKING ON THE U-2.
UM, IS THIS STILL ABOUT US?
GOOD QUESTION.
IT'S GONNA BE LIKE THIS, KIDS.
>GASP!<

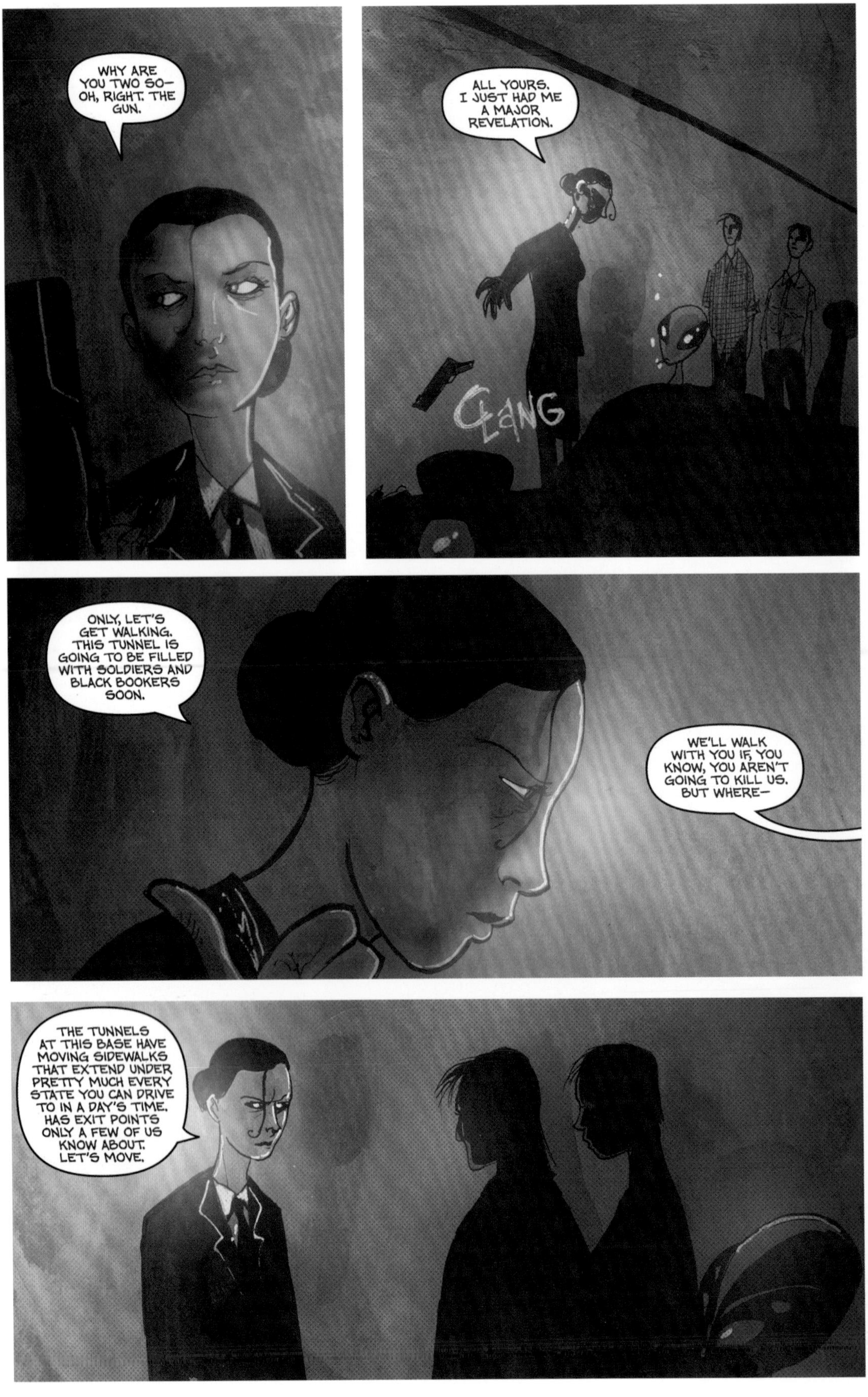
WHY ARE YOU TWO SO— OH, RIGHT. THE GUN.
ALL YOURS. I JUST HAD ME A MAJOR REVELATION.
CLANG
ONLY, LET'S GET WALKING. THIS TUNNEL IS GOING TO BE FILLED WITH SOLDIERS AND BLACK BOOKERS SOON.
WE'LL WALK WITH YOU IF, YOU KNOW, YOU AREN'T GOING TO KILL US. BUT WHERE—
THE TUNNELS AT THIS BASE HAVE MOVING SIDEWALKS THAT EXTEND UNDER PRETTY MUCH EVERY STATE YOU CAN DRIVE TO IN A DAY'S TIME. HAS EXIT POINTS ONLY A FEW OF US KNOW ABOUT. LET'S MOVE.

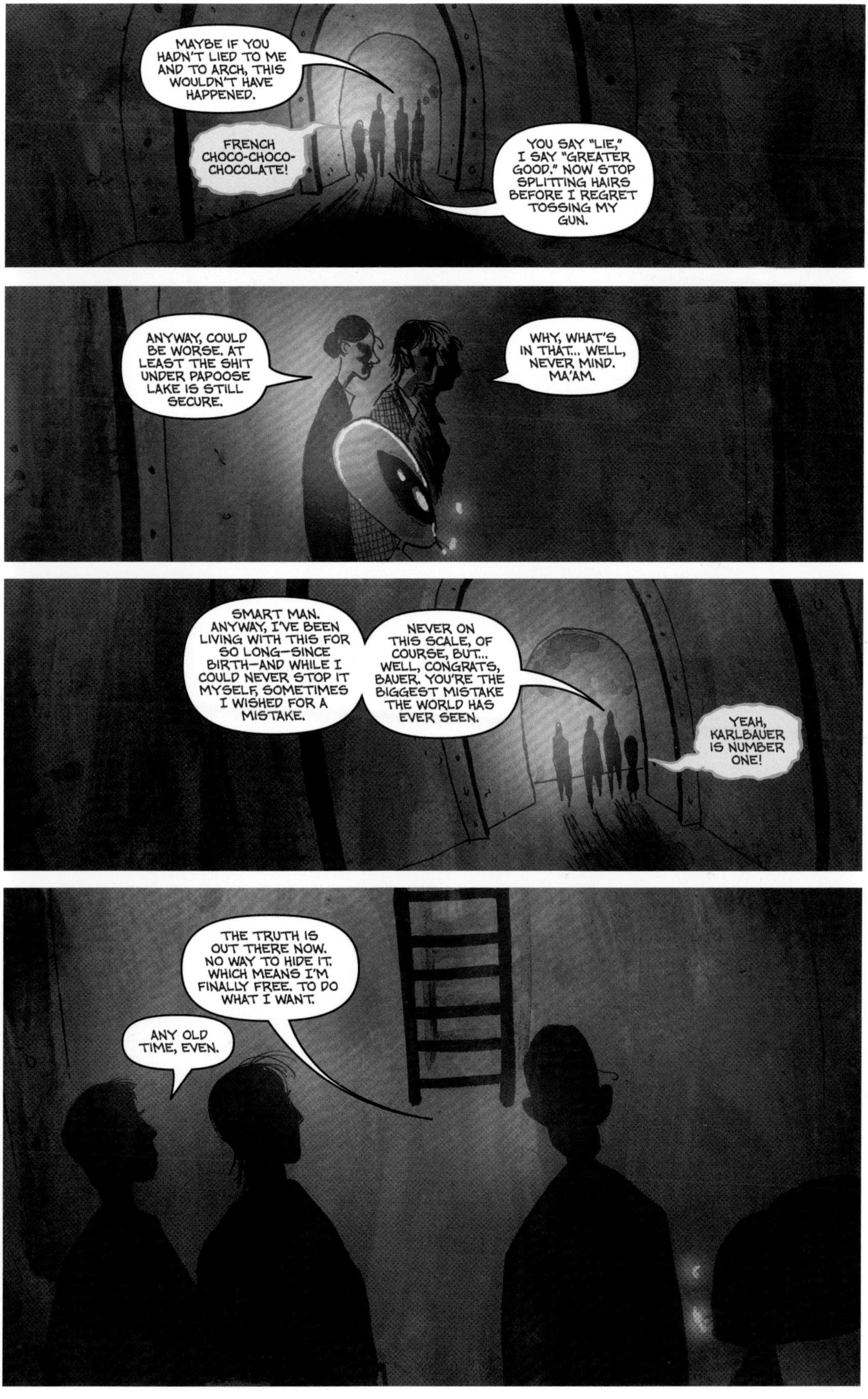
MAYBE IF YOU HADN'T LIED TO ME AND TO ARCH, THIS WOULDN'T HAVE HAPPENED.
FRENCH CHOCO-CHOCO-CHOCOLATE!
YOU SAY "LIE," I SAY "GREATER GOOD." NOW STOP SPLITTING HAIRS BEFORE I REGRET TOSSING MY GUN.
ANYWAY, COULD BE WORSE. AT LEAST THE SHIT UNDER PAPOOSE LAKE IS STILL SECURE.
WHY, WHAT'S IN THAT... WELL, NEVER MIND. MA'AM.
SMART MAN. ANYWAY, I'VE BEEN LIVING WITH THIS FOR SO LONG—SINCE BIRTH—AND WHILE I COULD NEVER STOP IT MYSELF, SOMETIMES I WISHED FOR A MISTAKE.
NEVER ON THIS SCALE, OF COURSE, BUT... WELL, CONGRATS, BAUER. YOU'RE THE BIGGEST MISTAKE THE WORLD HAS EVER SEEN.
YEAH, KARLBAUER IS NUMBER ONE!
THE TRUTH IS OUT THERE NOW. NO WAY TO HIDE IT. WHICH MEANS I'M FINALLY FREE. TO DO WHAT I WANT.
ANY OLD TIME, EVEN.

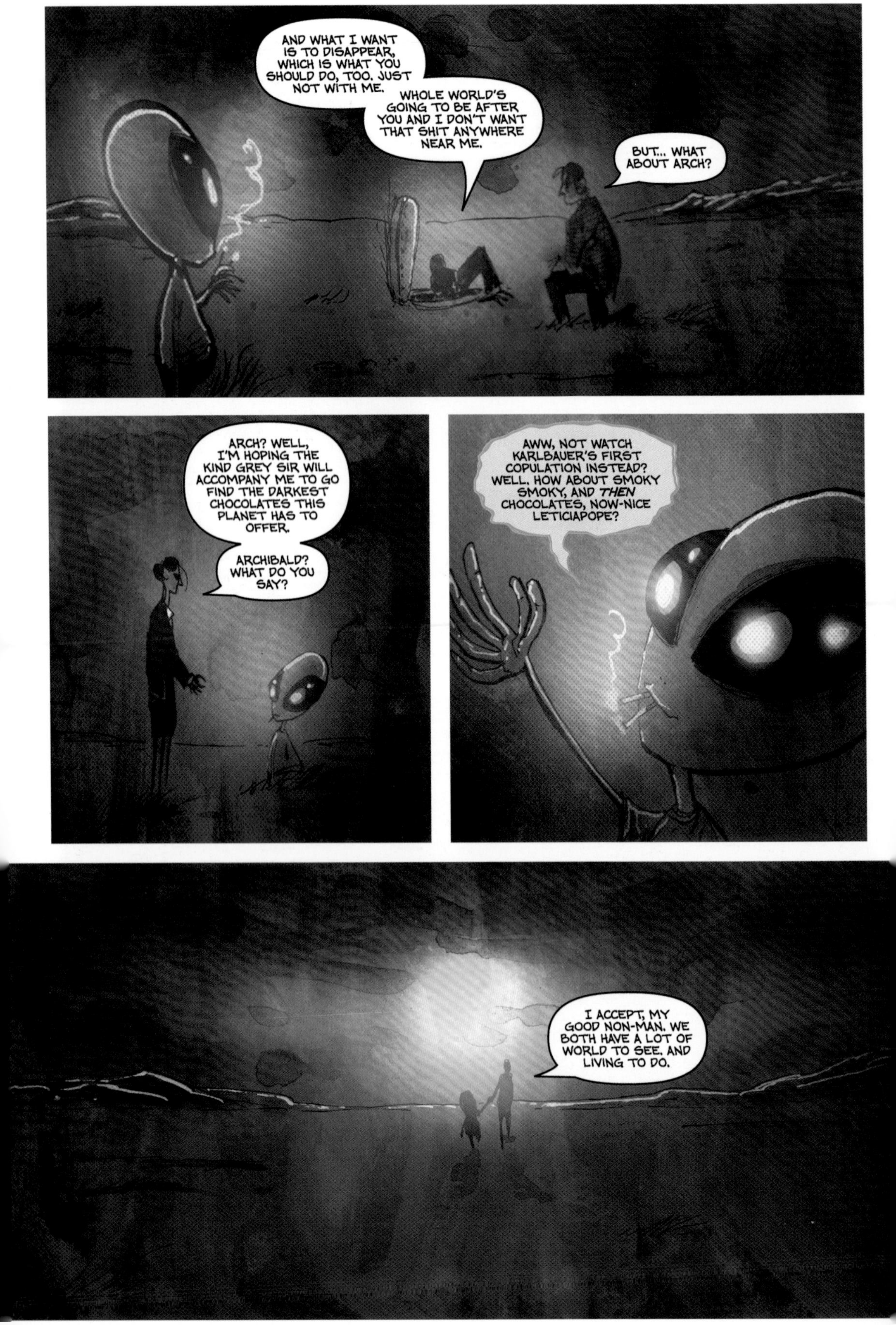
AND WHAT I WANT IS TO DISAPPEAR, WHICH IS WHAT YOU SHOULD DO, TOO. JUST NOT WITH ME.
WHOLE WORLD'S GOING TO BE AFTER YOU AND I DON'T WANT THAT SHIT ANYWHERE NEAR ME.
BUT... WHAT ABOUT ARCH?
ARCH? WELL, I'M HOPING THE KIND GREY SIR WILL ACCOMPANY ME TO GO FIND THE DARKEST CHOCOLATES THIS PLANET HAS TO OFFER.
ARCHIBALD? WHAT DO YOU SAY?
AWW, NOT WATCH KARLBAUER'S FIRST COPULATION INSTEAD? WELL. HOW ABOUT SMOKY SMOKY, AND *THEN* CHOCOLATES, NOW-NICE LETICIAPOPE?
I ACCEPT, MY GOOD NON-MAN. WE BOTH HAVE A LOT OF WORLD TO SEE. AND LIVING TO DO.

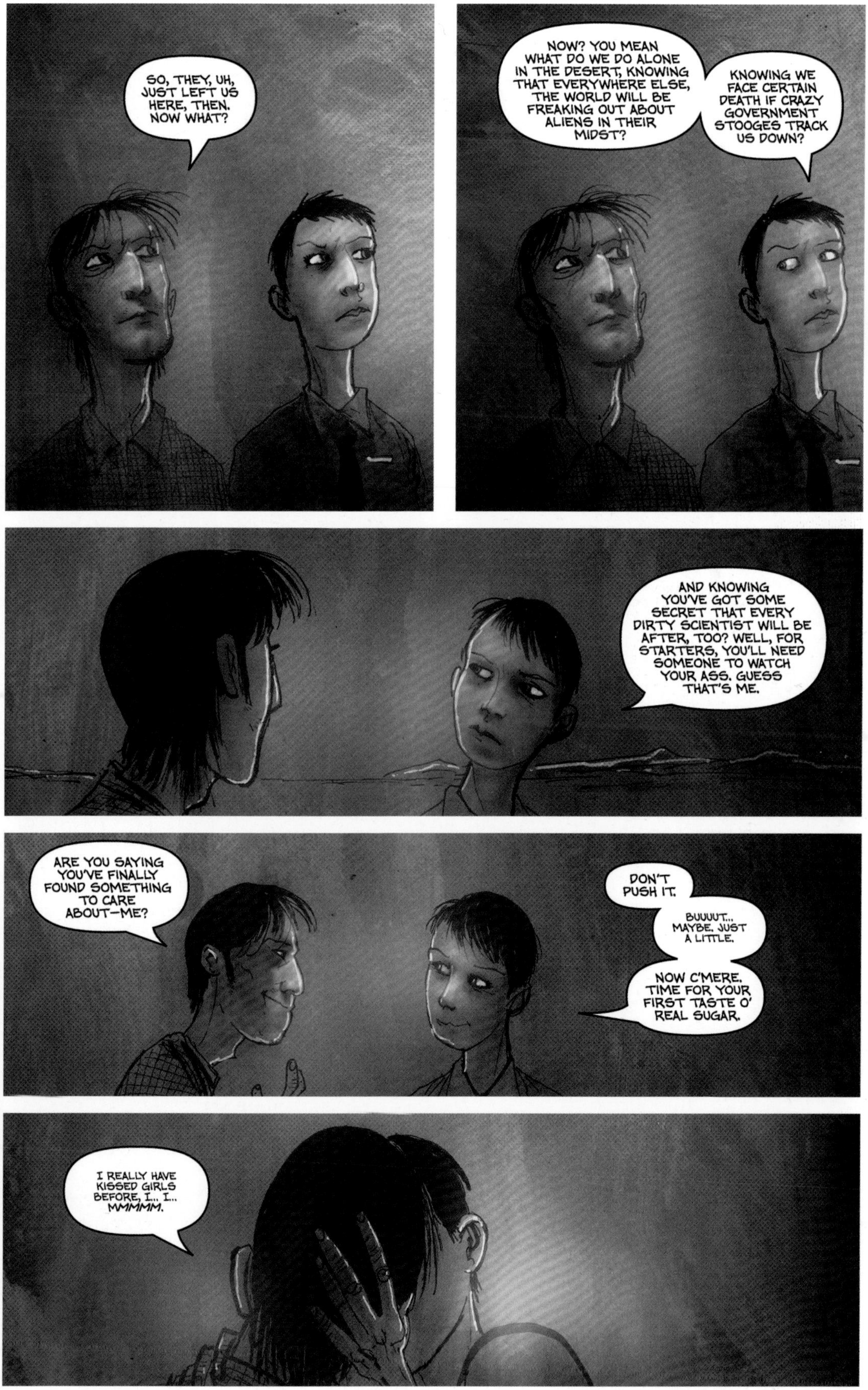
SO, THEY, UH, JUST LEFT US HERE, THEN. NOW WHAT?
NOW? YOU MEAN WHAT DO WE DO ALONE IN THE DESERT, KNOWING THAT EVERYWHERE ELSE, THE WORLD WILL BE FREAKING OUT ABOUT ALIENS IN THEIR MIDST?
KNOWING WE FACE CERTAIN DEATH IF CRAZY GOVERNMENT STOOGES TRACK US DOWN?
AND KNOWING YOU'VE GOT SOME SECRET THAT EVERY DIRTY SCIENTIST WILL BE AFTER, TOO? WELL, FOR STARTERS, YOU'LL NEED SOMEONE TO WATCH YOUR ASS. GUESS THAT'S ME.
ARE YOU SAYING YOU'VE FINALLY FOUND SOMETHING TO CARE ABOUT—ME?
DON'T PUSH IT.
BUUUUT... MAYBE, JUST A LITTLE.
NOW C'MERE. TIME FOR YOUR FIRST TASTE O' REAL SUGAR.
I REALLY HAVE KISSED GIRLS BEFORE, I... I... MMMMM.

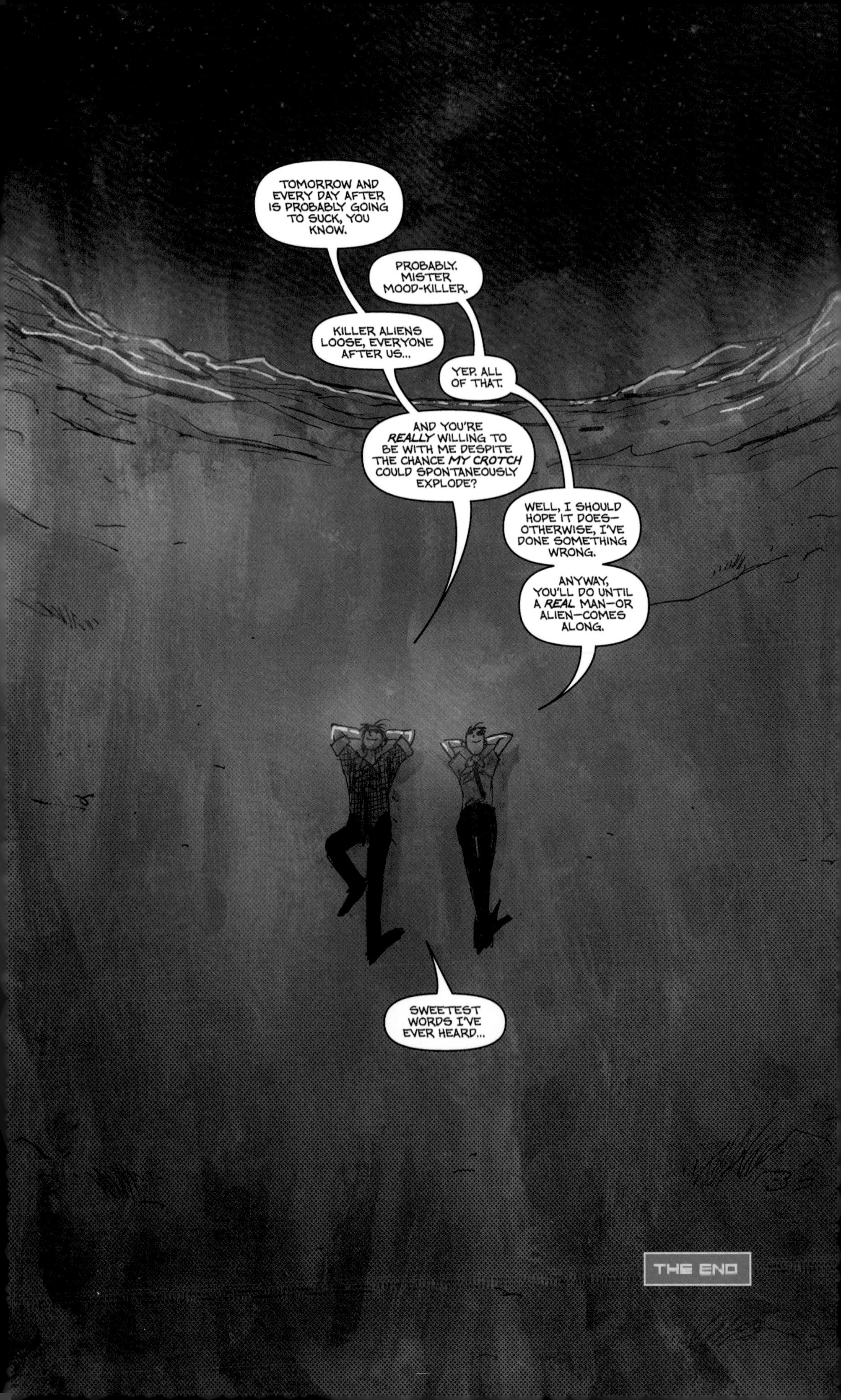
TOMORROW AND EVERY DAY AFTER IS PROBABLY GOING TO SUCK, YOU KNOW.
PROBABLY. MISTER MOOD-KILLER.
KILLER ALIENS LOOSE, EVERYONE AFTER US...
YEP. ALL OF THAT.
AND YOU'RE *REALLY* WILLING TO BE WITH ME DESPITE THE CHANCE *MY CROTCH* COULD SPONTANEOUSLY EXPLODE?
WELL, I SHOULD HOPE IT DOES—OTHERWISE, I'VE DONE SOMETHING WRONG.
ANYWAY, YOU'LL DO UNTIL A *REAL* MAN—OR ALIEN—COMES ALONG.
SWEETEST WORDS I'VE EVER HEARD...
THE END

"Man fears what he does not understand"

International UFO Bureau
In Cooperation With Canadian UFO Report Magazine
INTERNATIONAL HEADQUARTERS
P.O. Box 1281 • OKLAHOMA CITY, OKLAHOMA 73103

Sighting
Form

1. NAME   PLACE OF EMPLOYMENT
    ADDRESS   OCCUPATION
                                            SPECIAL TRAINING
    TELEPHONE   MILITARY SERVICE

2. DATE OF OBSERVATION   TIME   AM   PM

3. LOCALITY OF OBSERVATION

4. HOW LONG DID YOU SEE THE OBJECT?   HOURS   SECONDS

5. PLEASE DESCRIBE WEATHER CONDITIONS AND THE TYPE OF SKY; I.E.:
    BRIGHT DAYLIGHT, NIGHTTIME, DUSK, ETC.

6. POSITION OF THE SUN OR MOON IN RELATION TO THE OBJECT AND TO YOU.

7. IF SEEN AT NIGHT, TWILIGHT, OR DAWN, WERE THE STARS OR MOON VISIBLE?

8. WERE THERE MORE THAN ONE OBJECT?   IF SO, PLEASE TELL HOW MANY, AND DRAW A
    SKETCH OF WHAT YOU SAW, INDICATING DIRECTION OR MOVEMENT, IF ANY.

9. PLEASE DESCRIBE THE OBJECT(S) IN DETAIL. FOR INSTANCE, DID IT (THEY) APPEAR
    SOLID, OR ONLY AS A SOURCE OF LIGHT; WAS IT REVOLVING, ETC.? PLEASE USE
    ADDITIONAL SHEETS OF PAPER, IF NECESSARY.

10. WAS THE OBJECT(S) BRIGHTER THAN THE BACKGROUND OF THE SKY?

11. IF SO, COMPARE THE BRIGHTNESS WITH THE SUN, MOOON, HEADLIGHTS, ETC.

12. DID THE OBJECT(S) -- (PLEASE ELABORATE, IF YOU CAN GIVE DETAILS)

    A. APPEAR TO STAND STILL AT ANY TIME?
    B. SUDDENLY SPEED UP AND RUSH AWAY AT ANY TIME?
    C. BREAK UP INTO PARTS OR EXPLODE?
    D. GIVE OFF SMOKE?
    E. LEAVE ANY VISIBLE TRAIL?
    F. DROP ANYTHING?
    G. CHANGE BRIGHTNESS?
    H. CHANGE SHAPE?
    I. CHANGE COLOR?

13. DID THE OBJECT(S) AT ANY TIME PASS IN FRONT OF, OR BEHIND OF, ANYTHING? IF SO,
    PLEASE ELABORATE GIVING DISTANCE, SIZE, ETC., IF POSSIBLE.

14. WAS THERE ANY WIND?   IF SO, PLEASE GIVE DIRECTION AND SPEED.

15. DID YOU OBSERVE THE OBJECT(S) THROUGH AN OPTICAL INSTRUMENT OR OTHER AID,
    WINDSHIELD, STORM WINDOW, SCREENING, ETC.?   WHAT?

16. DID THE OBJECT(S) HAVE ANY SOUND?   WHAT KIND?   HOW LOUD?

17. PLEASE TELL IF THE OBJECT(S) WAS (WERE) --

    A. FUZZY OR BLURRED
    B. LIKE A BRIGHT STAR
    C. SHARPLY OUTLINED

18.   WAS THE OBJECT --

        A. SELF-LUMINOUS?   NOTICE
        B. DULL FINISH?   PLEASE DRAW, TO THE BEST OF YOUR ABILITY,
        C. REFLECTING?   A SKETCH OF THE OBJECT(S), INCLUDING ALL
        D. TRANSPARENT?   DETAILS. YOU MAY USE EXTRA SHEET.

19.   DID THE OBJECT(S) RISE OR FALL WHILE IN FLIGHT?

20.   TELL THE APPARENT SIZE OF THE OBJECT(S) WHEN COMPARED WITH THE FOLLOWING HELD AT
        ARM'S LENGTH:

        A. PINHEAD   D. NICKEL   G. ORANGE
        B. PEA   E. HALF DOLLAR   H. GRAPEFRUIT
        C. DIME   F. SILVER DOLLAR   I. LARGER
        OR, IF EASIER, GIVE APPARENT SIZE IN INCHES ON A RULER HELD AT ARM'S LENGTH.

21.   HOW DID YOU HAPPEN TO NOTICE THE OBJECT(S)?

22.   WHERE WERE YOU AND WHAT WERE YOU DOING AT THE TIME?

23.   HOW DID THE OBJECT(S) DISAPPEAR FROM VIEW?

24.   COMPARE THE SPEED OF THE OBJECT(S) WITH A PISTON OR A JET AIRCRAFT AT THE SAME
        APPARENT ALTITUDE.

25.   WERE THERE ANY CONVENTIONAL AIRCRAFT IN THE LOCATION AT THE TIME OR IMMEDIATELY
        AFTERWARDS? IF SO, PLEASE ELABORATE.

26.   PLEASE ESTIMATE THE DISTANCE OF THE OBJECT(S).

27.   WHAT WAS THE ELEVATION OF THE OBJECT(S) IN THE SKY?

28.   NAMES AND ADDRESSES OF OTHER WITNESSES, IF ANY.

29.   PLEASE DRAW A MAP OF THE LOCATION OF THE OBSERVATION SHOWING NORTH; YOUR
        POSITION; THE DIRECTION FROM WHICH THE OBJECT(S) APPEARED AND DISAPPEARED FROM
        VIEW; THE DIRECTION OF ITS COURSE OVER THE AREA; ROADS, TOWNS, VILLAGES,
        RAILROADS, AND OTHER LANDMARKS WITHIN A MILE. PLEASE USE EXTRA SHEET FOR MAP AND
        ATTACH TO FORM.

30.   IS THERE AN AIRPORT, MILITARY, GOVERNMENTAL OR RESEARCH INSTALLATION IN THE AREA?

31.   HAVE YOU SEEN OTHER OBJECTS OF AN UNIDENTIFIED NATURE? IF SO, PLEASE DESCRIBE
        THESE OBSERVATIONS, USING A SEPARATE SHEET OF PAPER.

32.   PLEASE ENCLOSE PHOTOGRAPHS, MOTION PICTURES, NEWS CLIPPINGS, NOTES OF RADIO OR
        TELEVISION PROGRAMS (INCLUDING TIME, STATION, AND DATE, IF POSSIBLE) REGARDING
        THIS OR SIMILAR OBSERVATIONS, OR ANY OTHER BACKGROUND MATERIAL. WE WILL RETURN
        THE MATERIAL TO YOU.

33.   WERE YOU INTERROGATED BY AIR FORCE INVESTIGATORS? BY ANY FEDERAL, STATE, COUNTY,
        OR LOCAL OFFICIALS? IF SO, PLEASE STATE THE NAME AND RANK OF THE AGENT, HIS
        OFFICE, AND DETAILS AS TO WHEN AND WHERE THE QUESTIONS TOOK PLACE.
        WERE YOU ASKED OR TOLD NOT TO REVEAL OR DISCUSS THE INCIDENT? IF SO, WERE THE
        REASONS OR OFFICIAL EXPLANATION MENTIONED? IF YES, PLEASE ELABORATE CAREFULLY.

34.   WE WOULD LIKE PERMISSION TO QUOTE YOUR NAME IN CONNECTION WITH THIS INCIDENT.
        THIS ACTION WILL ENCOURAGE RESPONSIBLE CITIZENS TO REPORT THEIR OBSERVATIONS TO
        THE IUFB. HOWEVER, IF YOU DECLINE, WE WILL KEEP YOUR NAME CONFIDENTIAL. PLEASE
        NOTE YOUR CHOICE BY CHECKING THE FINAL LINE. IN ANY CASE, PLEASE FILL IN ALL
        PARTS OF THE FORM, FOR OUR CONFIDENTIAL FILES. THANK YOU FOR YOUR COOPERATION.

        YOU MAY USE MY NAME   PLEASE KEEP MY NAME CONFIDENTIAL

35.   DATE OF FILLING OUT THIS REPORT: SIGNATURE:

ART GALLERY
by Ben Templesmith

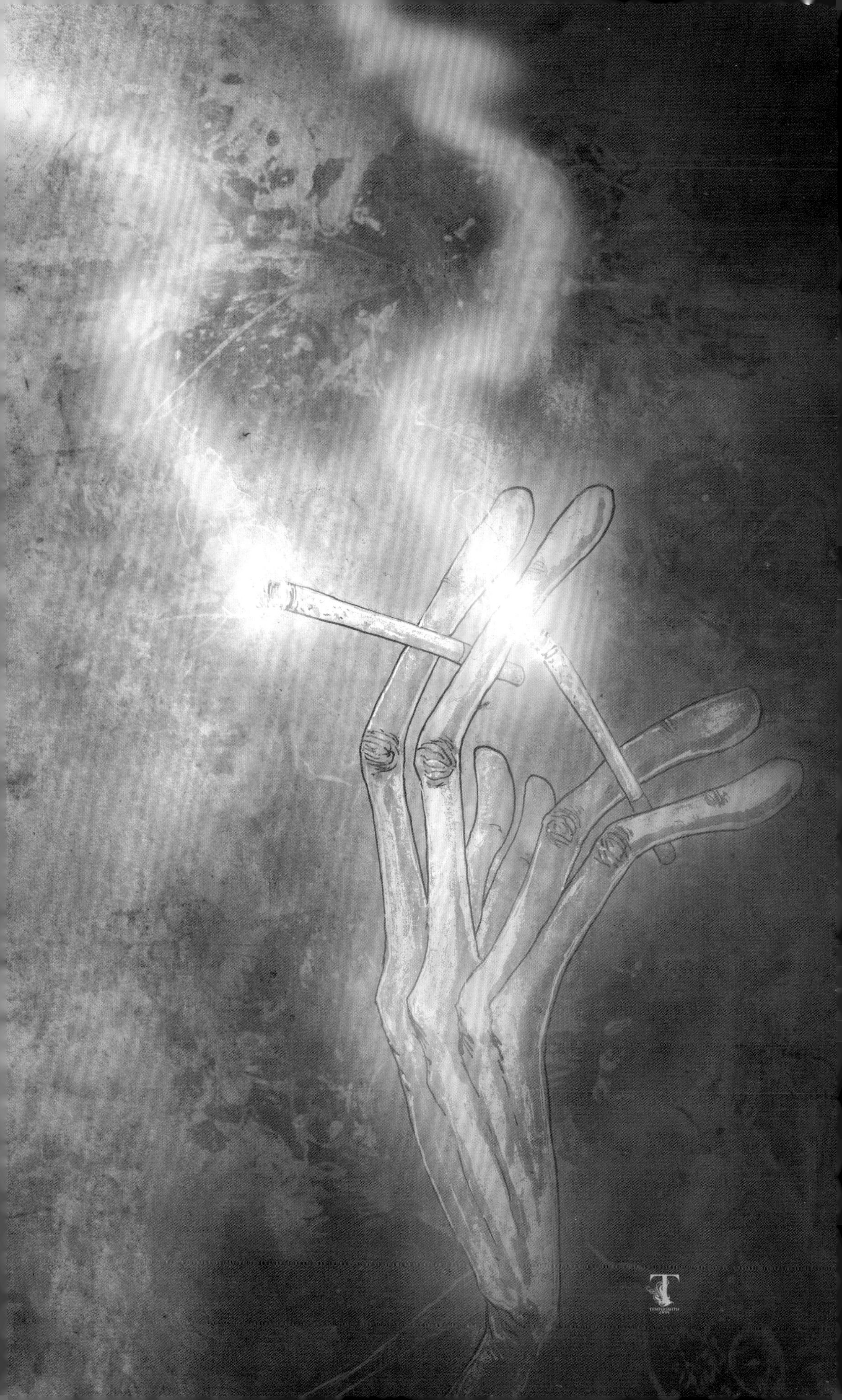

TEMPLESMITH

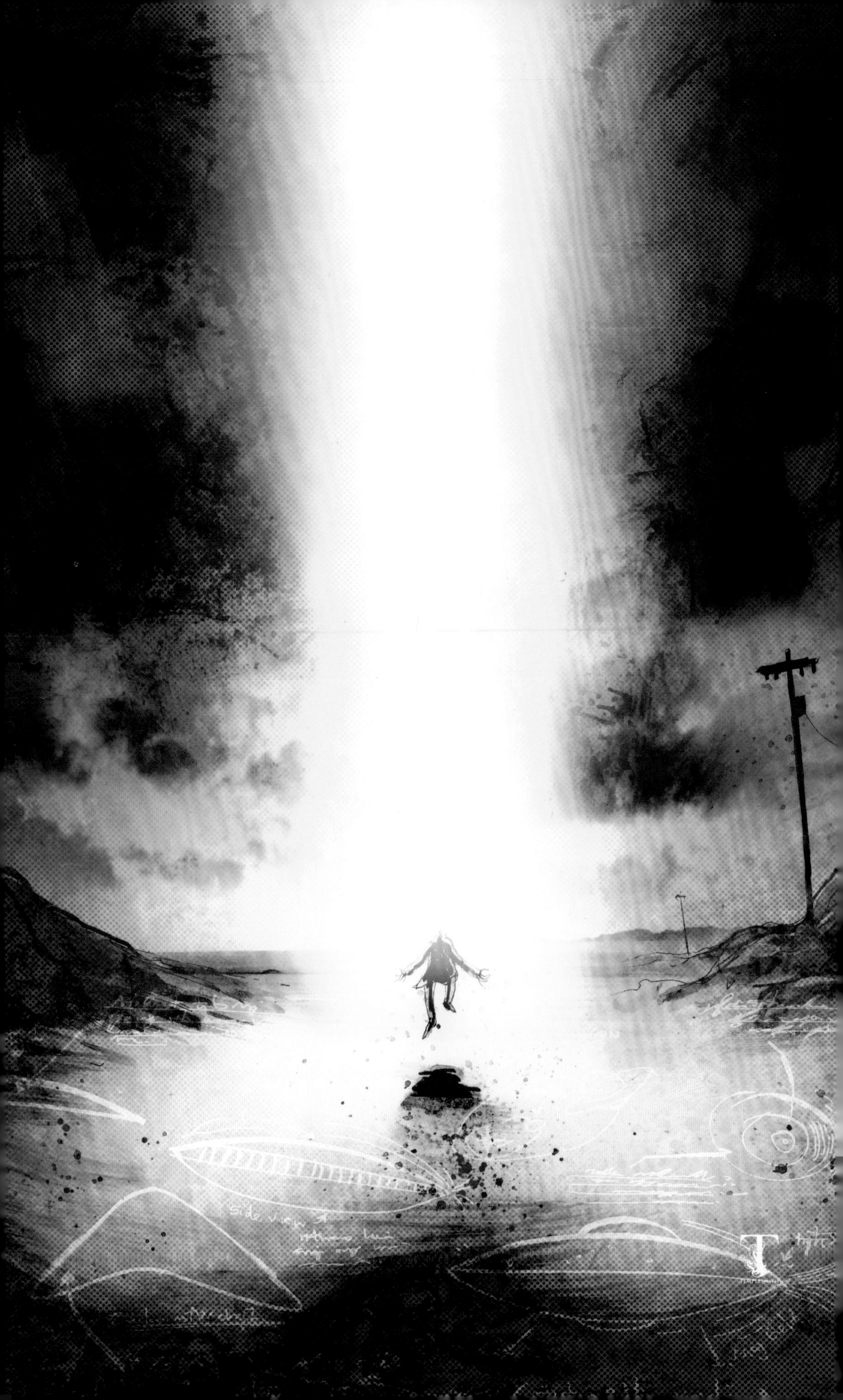

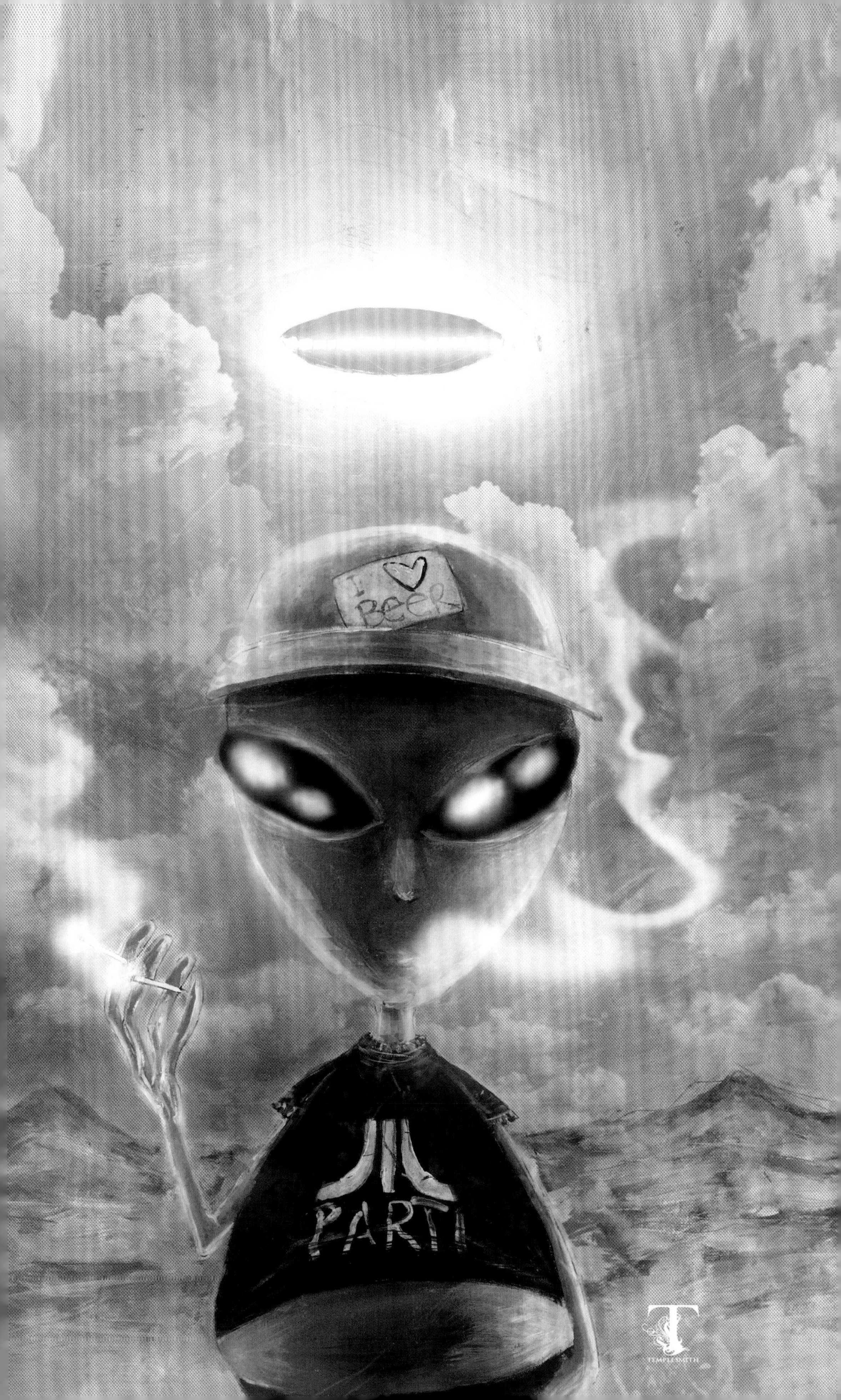
I ♥ BEER
PARTI

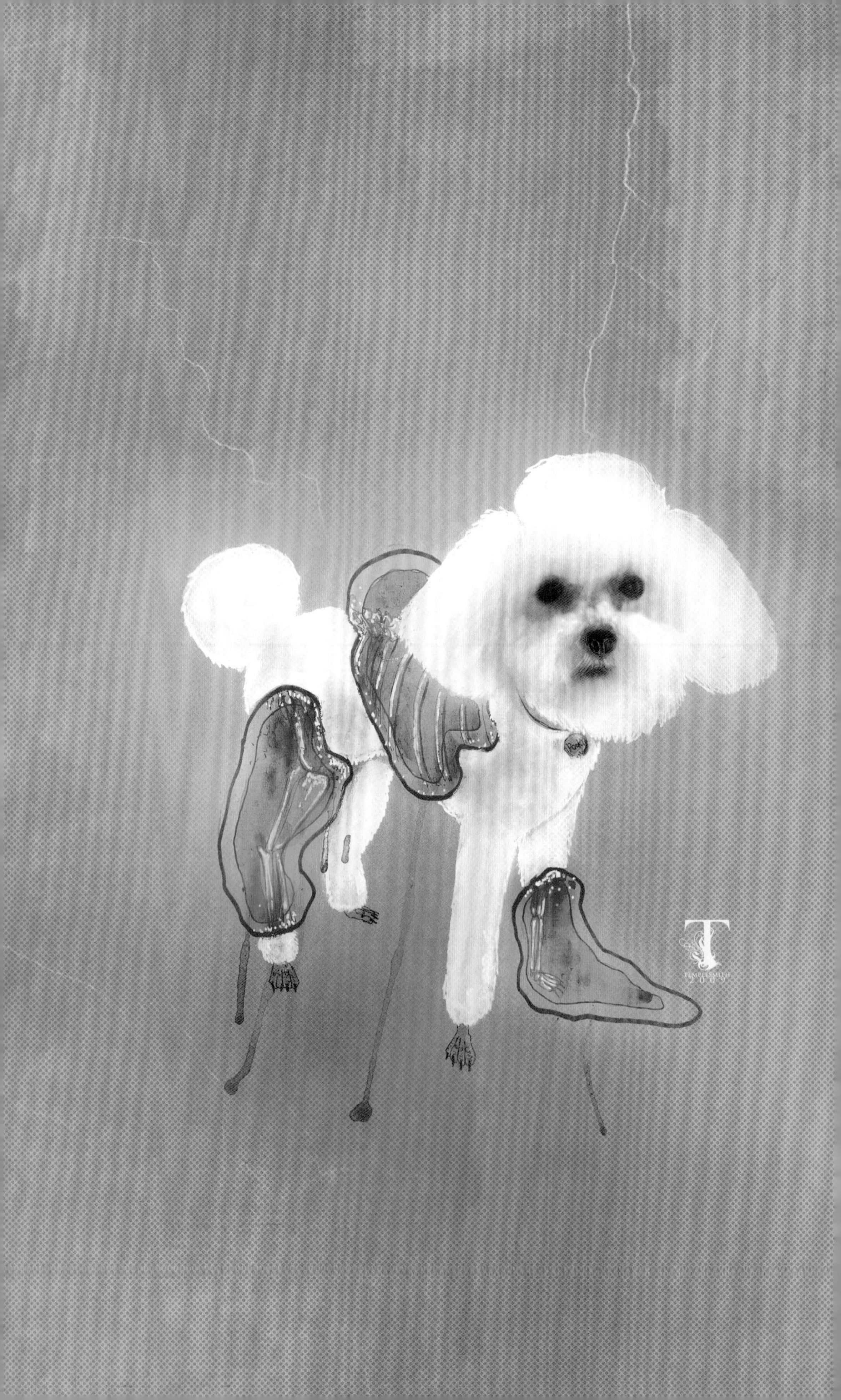
TEMPLESMITH
2009

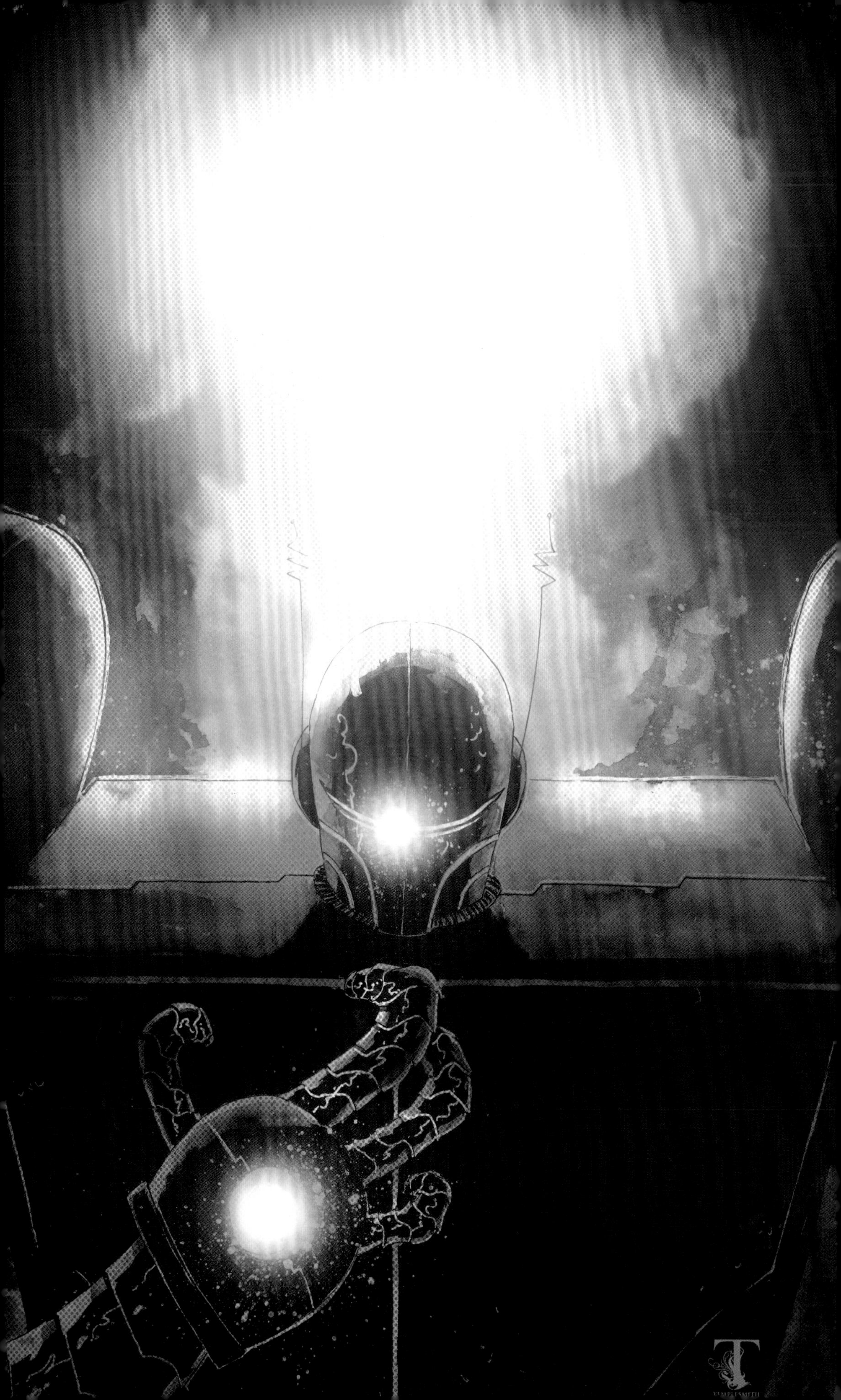

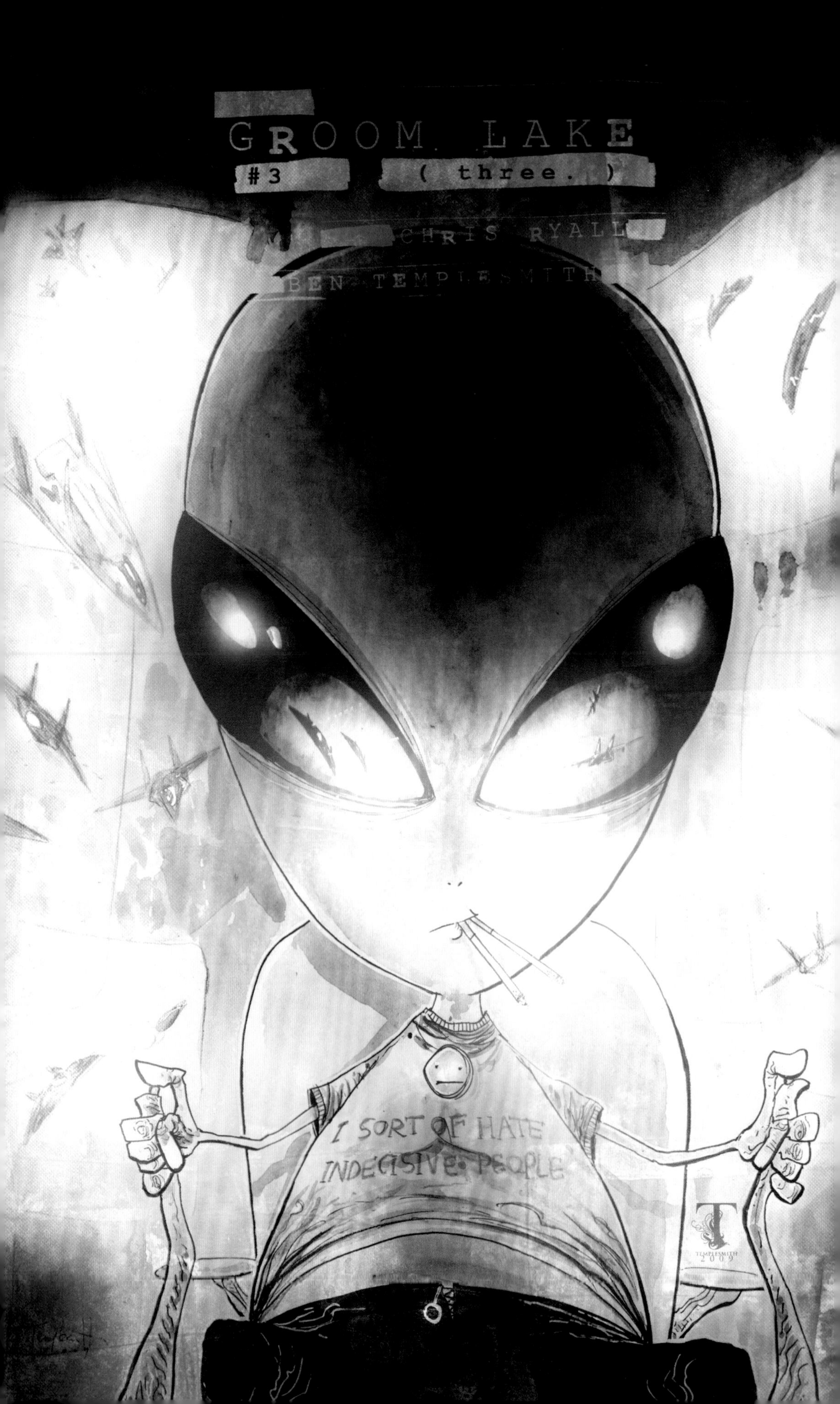
GROOM LAKE
#3
(three.)
CHRIS RYALL
BEN TEMPLESMITH
I SORT OF HATE INDECISIVE PEOPLE
TEMPLESMITH 2009

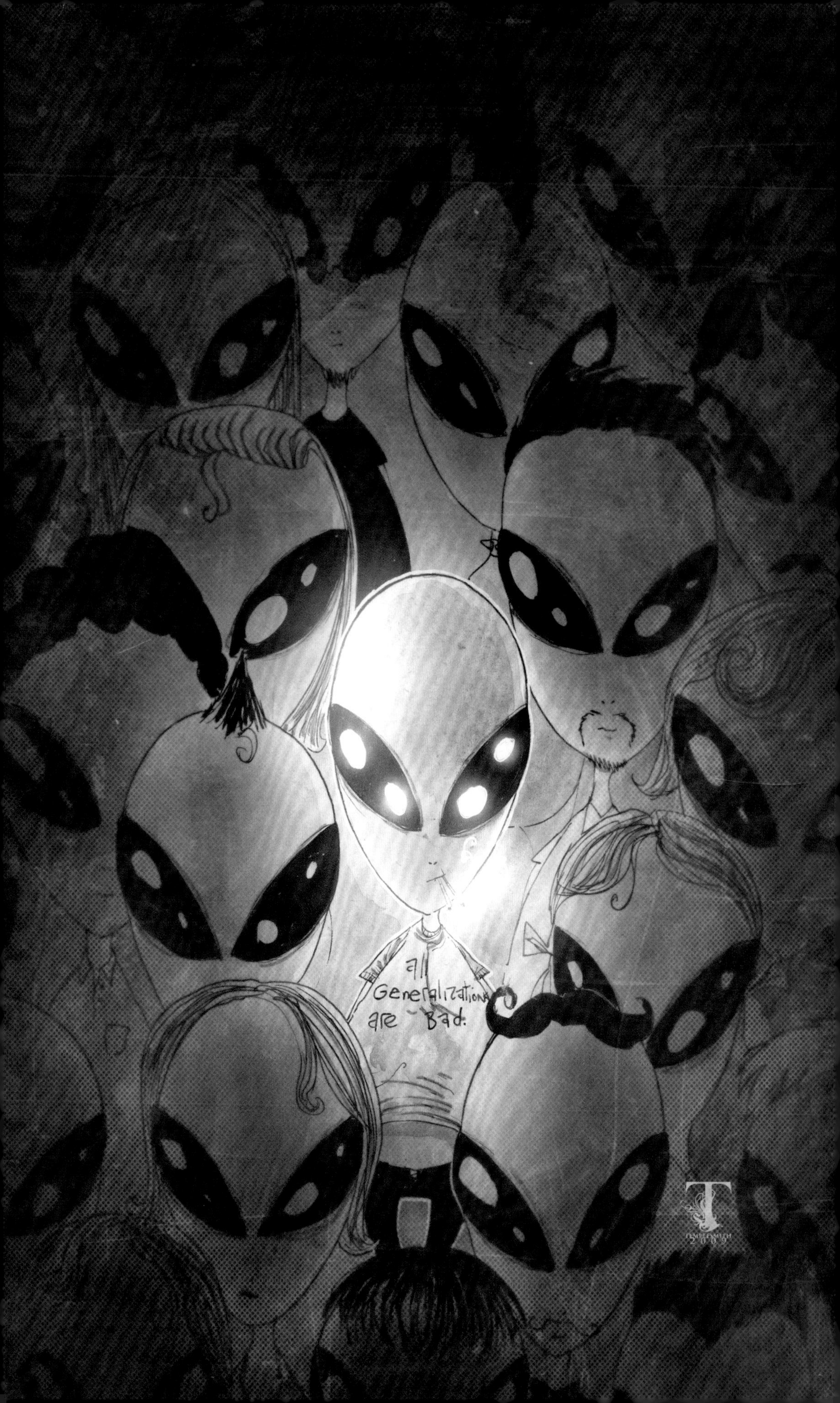
all Generalizations are Bad.

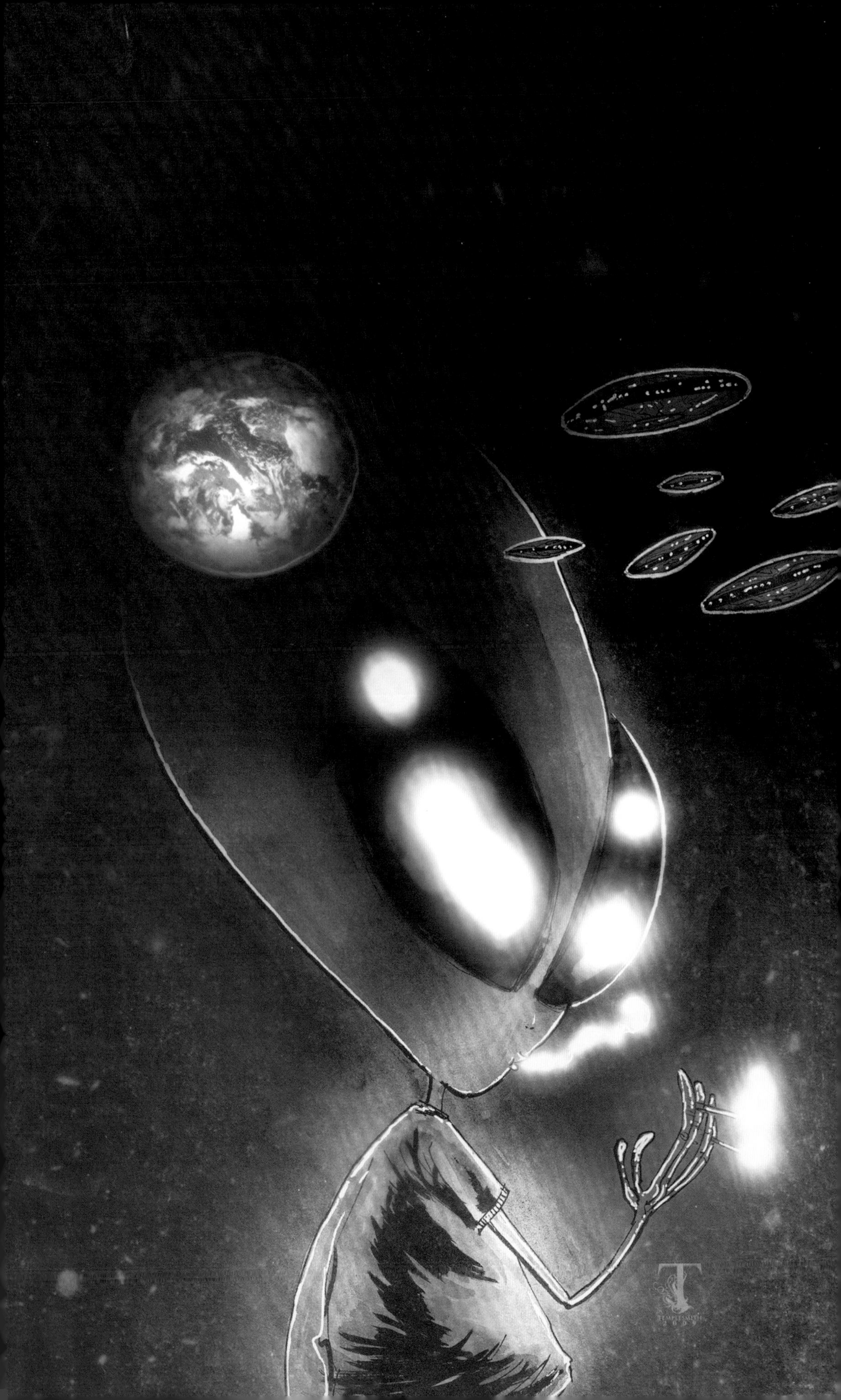

PIN-UP GALLERY

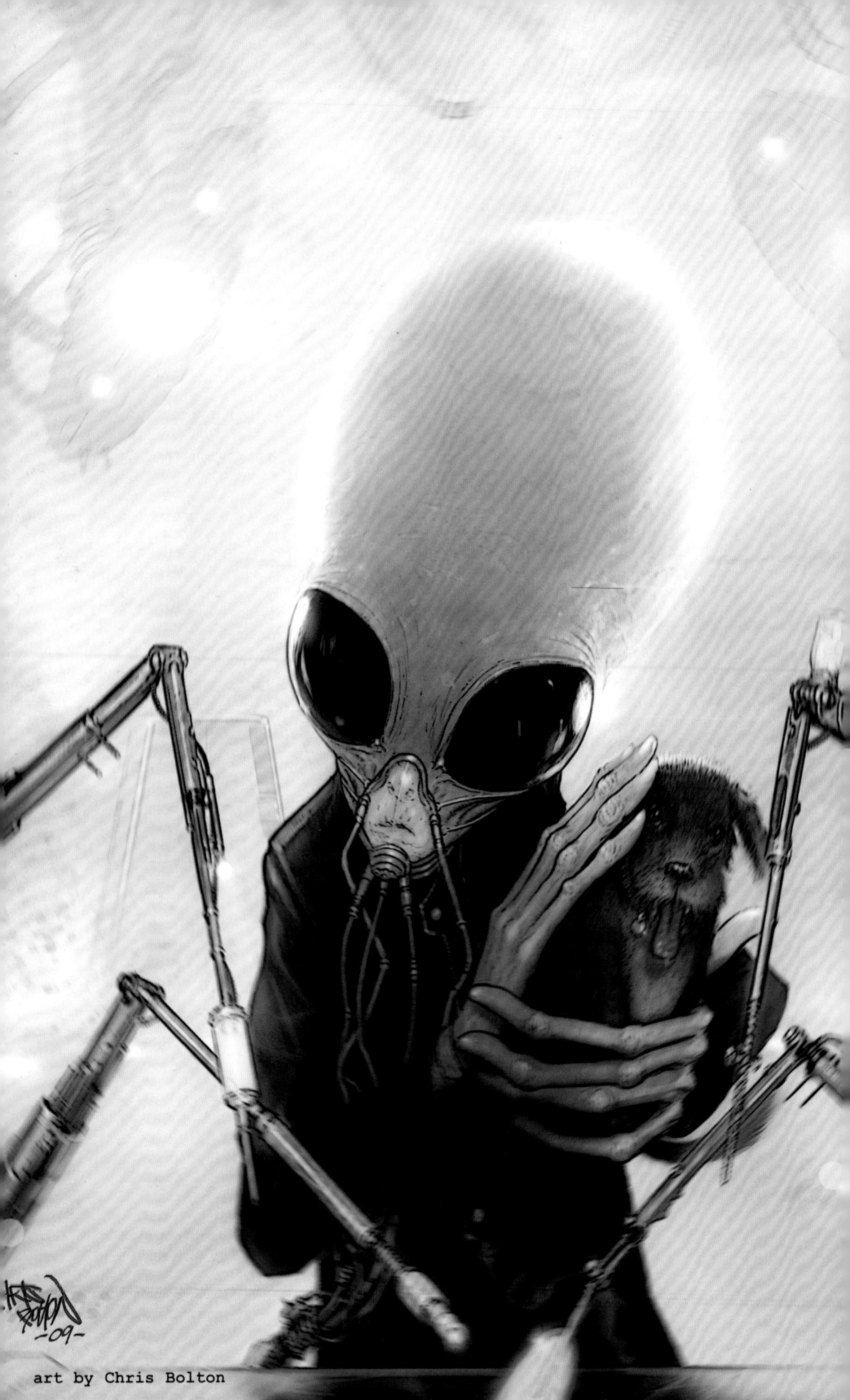

art by Chris Bolton

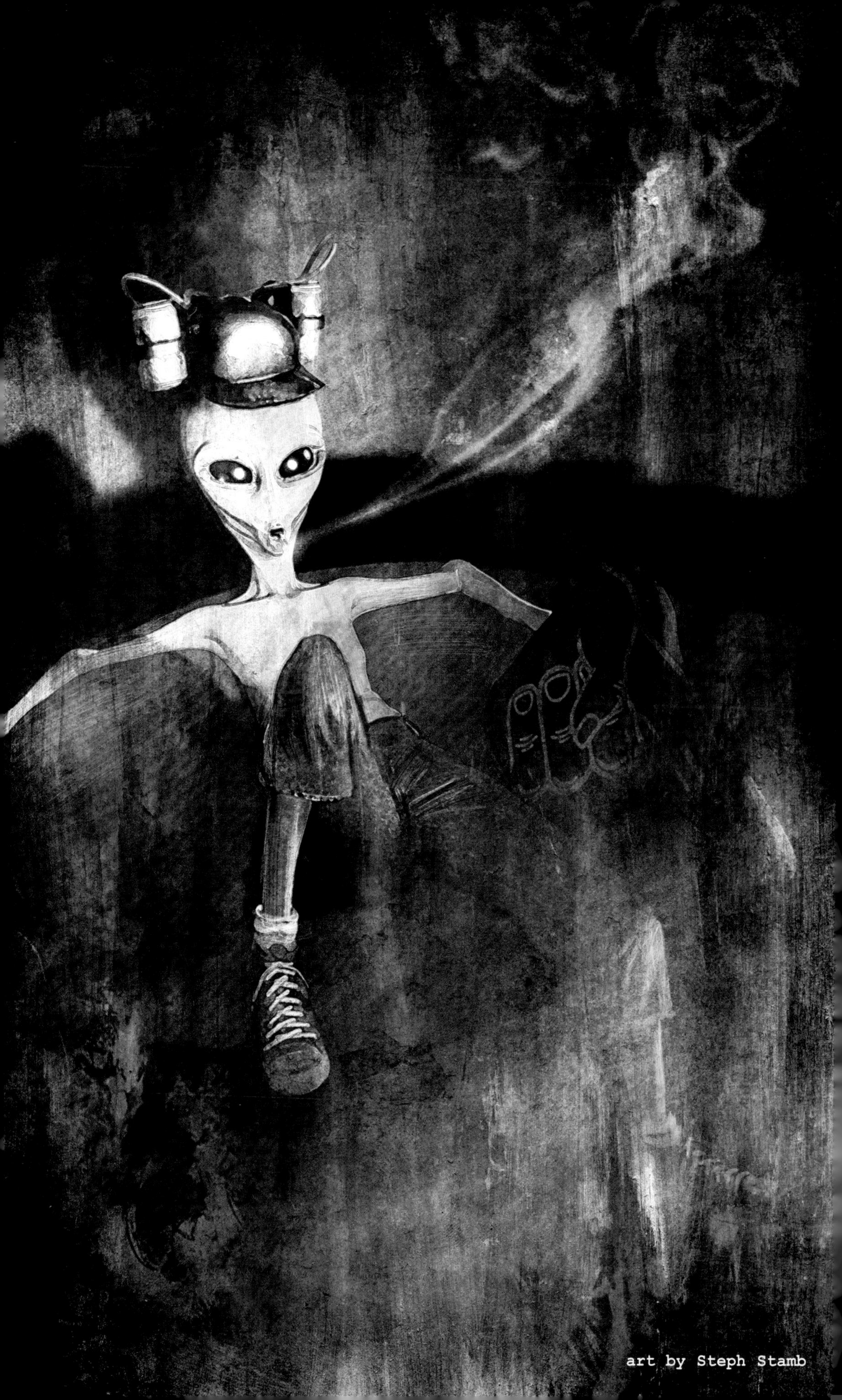
art by Steph Stamb

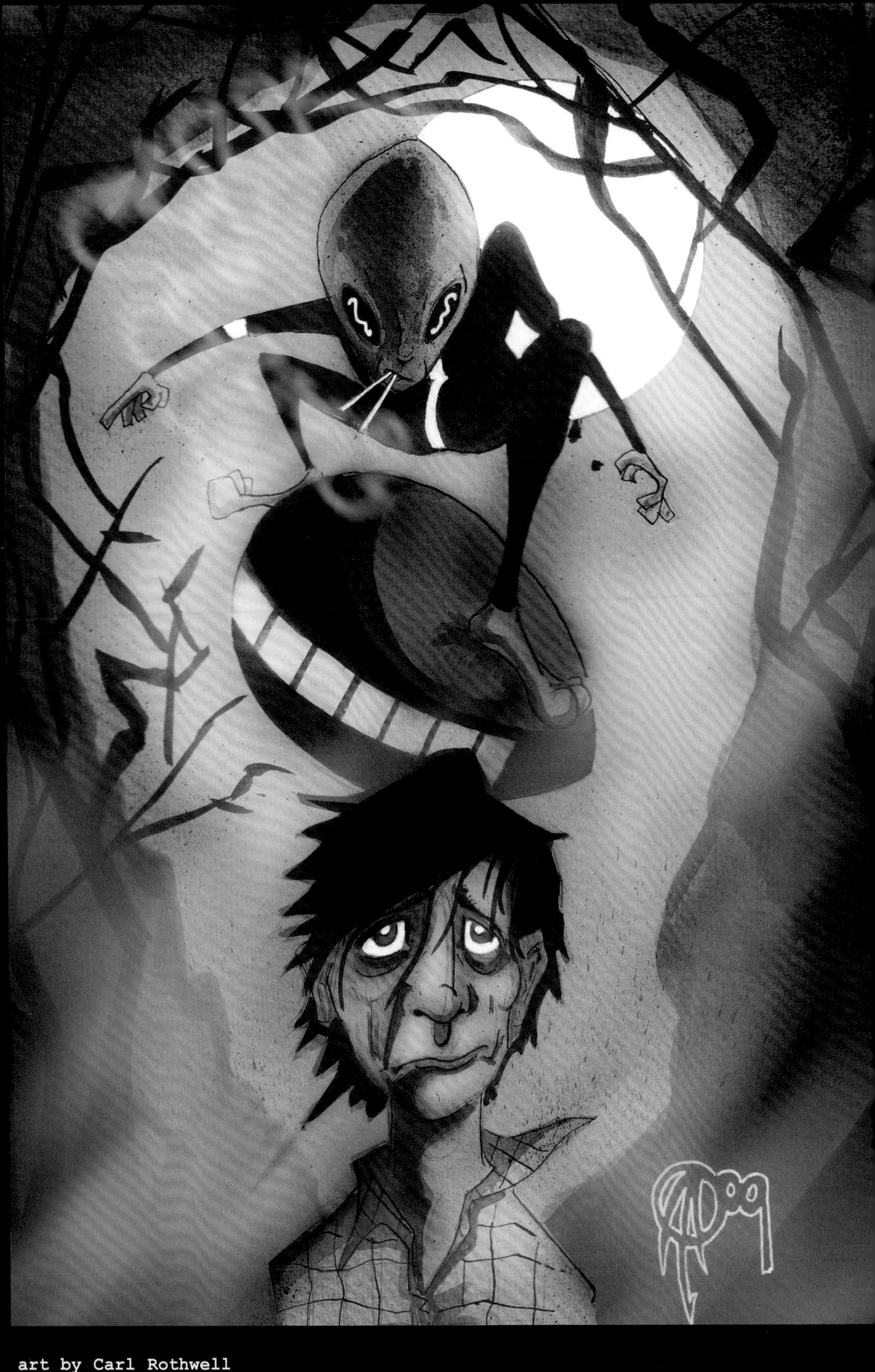

art by Carl Rothwell

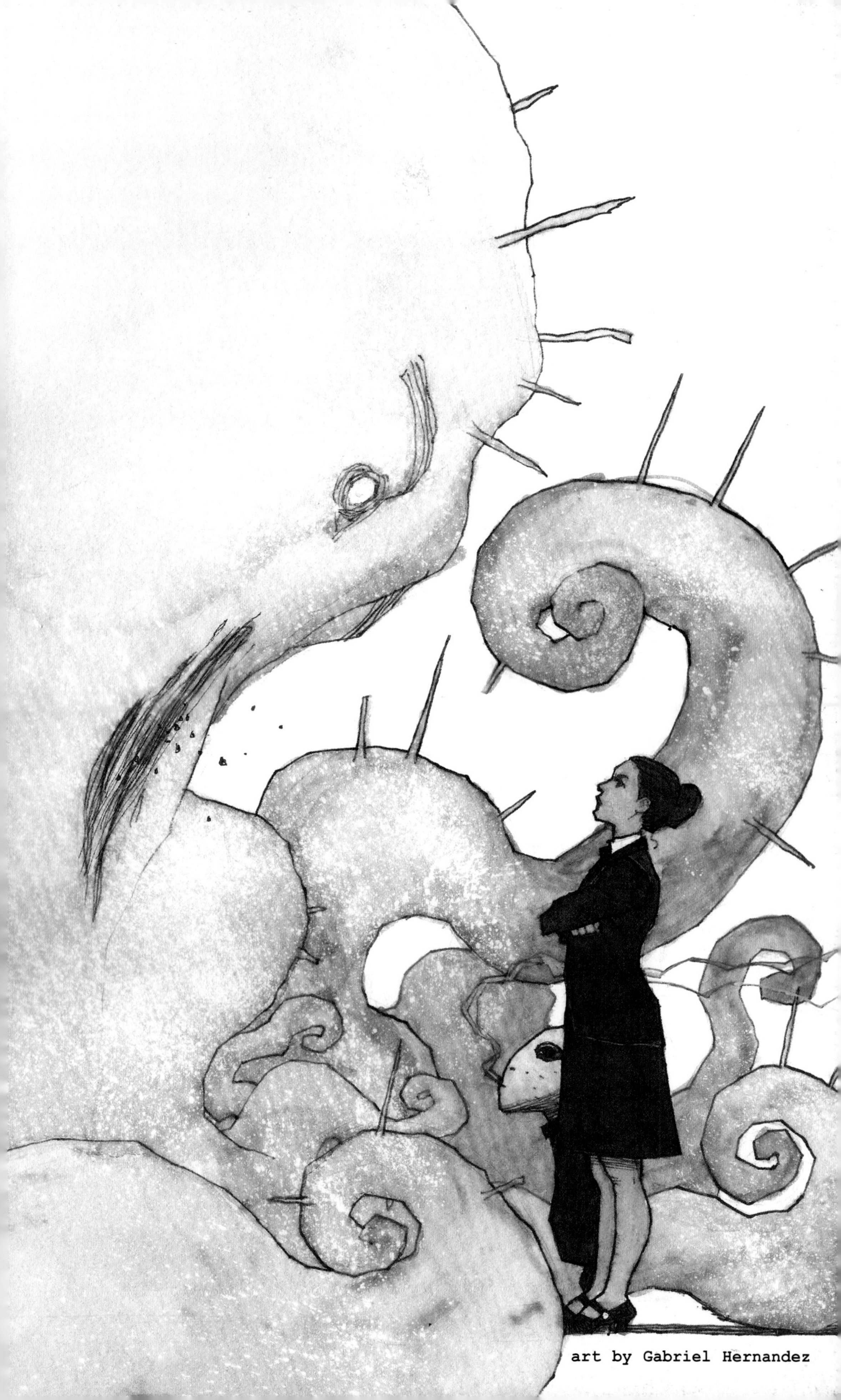

art by Gabriel Hernandez

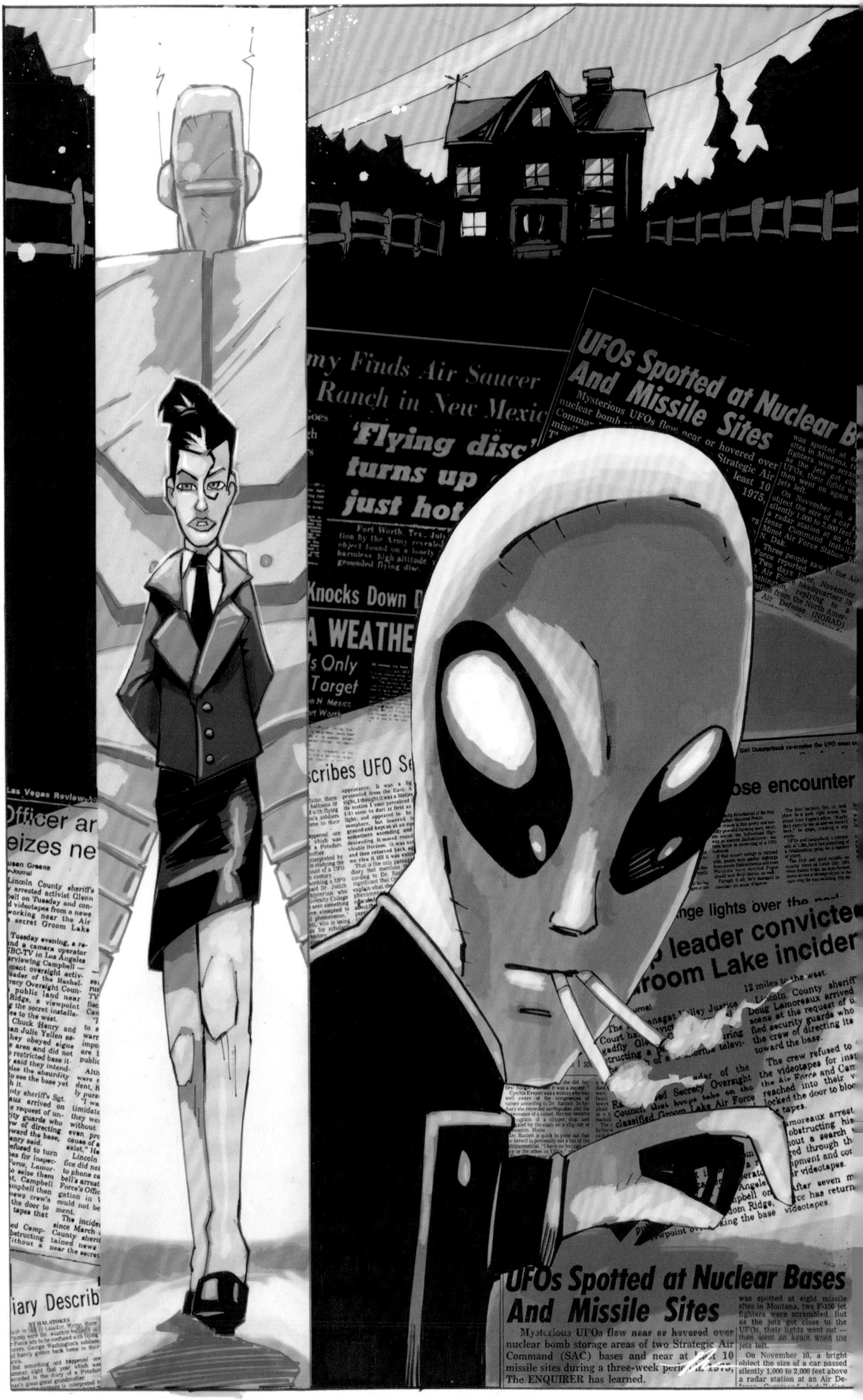
UFOs Spotted at Nuclear B
And Missile Sites
my Finds Air Saucer
Ranch in New Mexic
'Flying disc'
turns up
just hot
Knocks Down D
A WEATHE
's Only
Target
scribes UFO Se
ose encounter
nge lights over the
leader convicte
room Lake incider
Officer ar
eizes ne
iary Describ
UFOs Spotted at Nuclear Bases
And Missile Sites
Mysterious UFOs flew near or hovered over nuclear bomb storage areas of two Strategic Air Command (SAC) bases and near at least 10 missile sites during a three-week period in 1975, The ENQUIRER has learned.

art by Pat Parnell

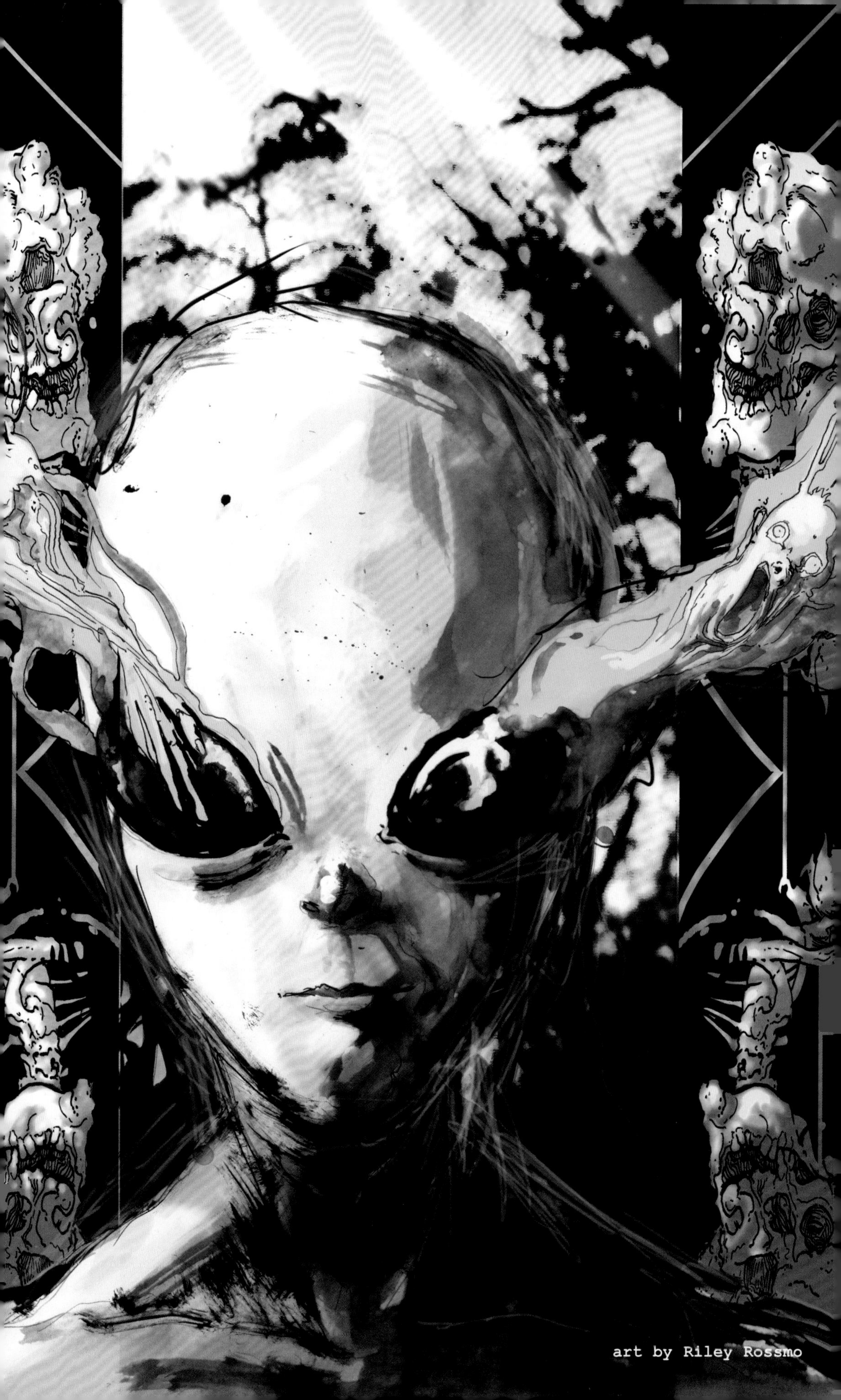

art by Riley Rossmo

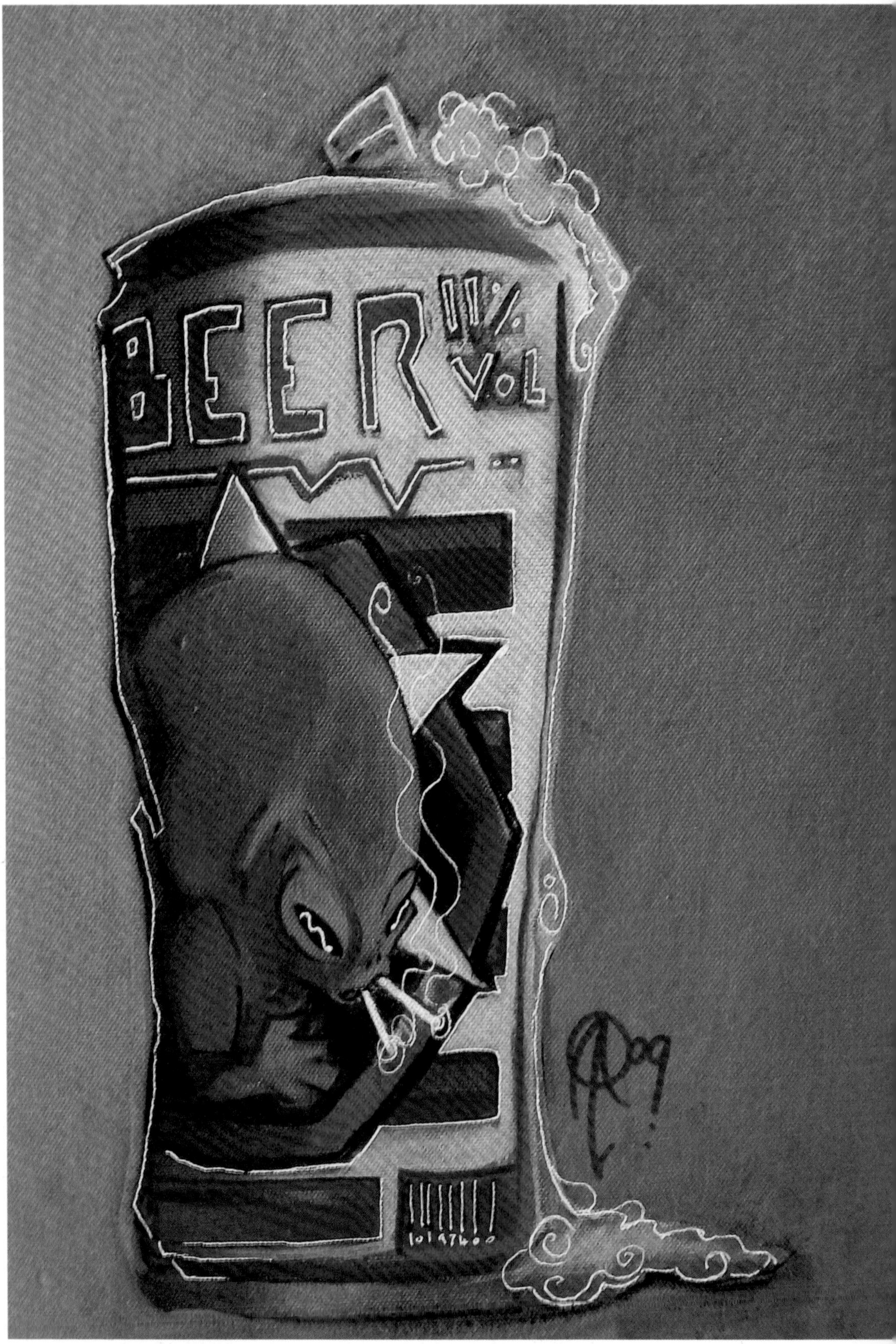
BEER
11% VOL

art by Carl Rothwell

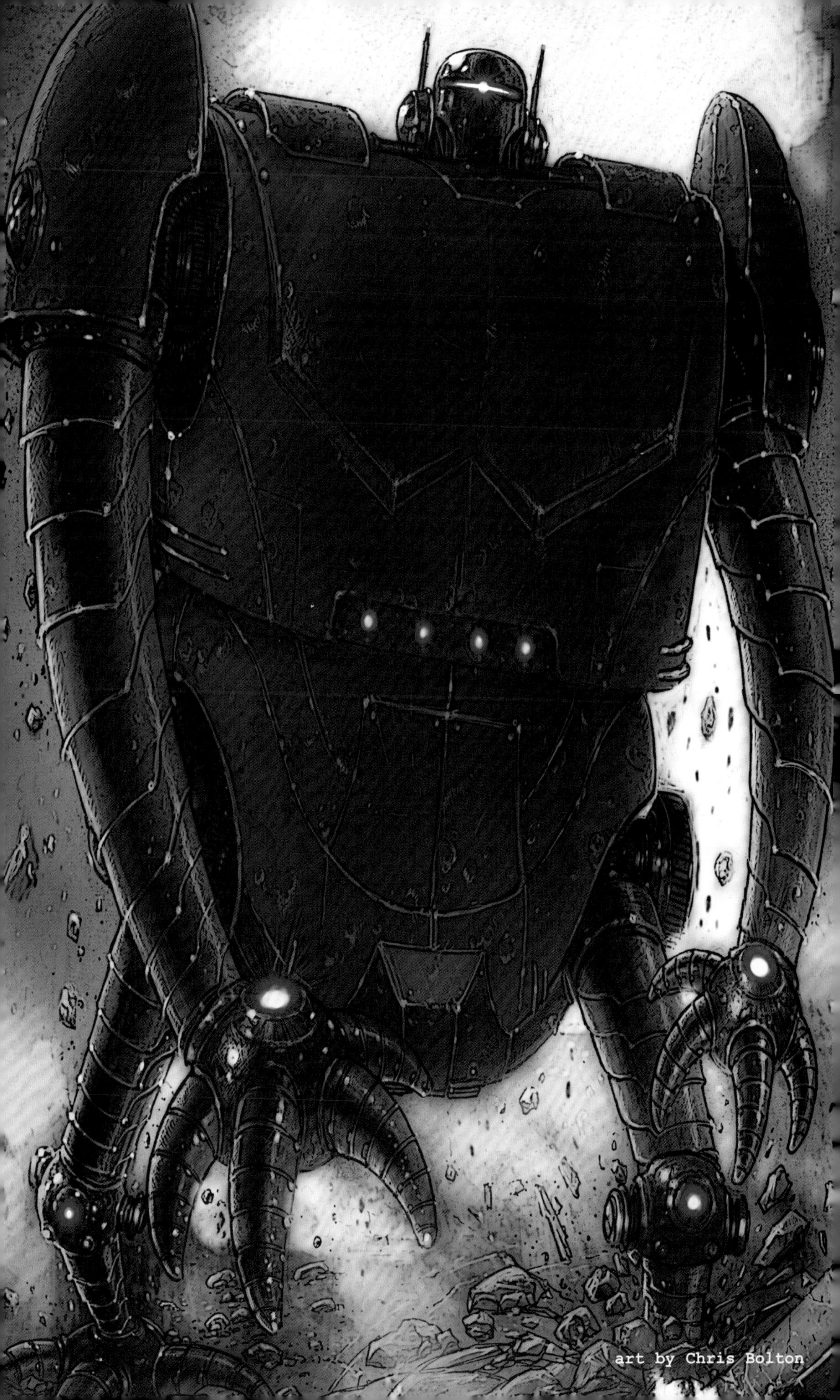

art by Chris Bolton

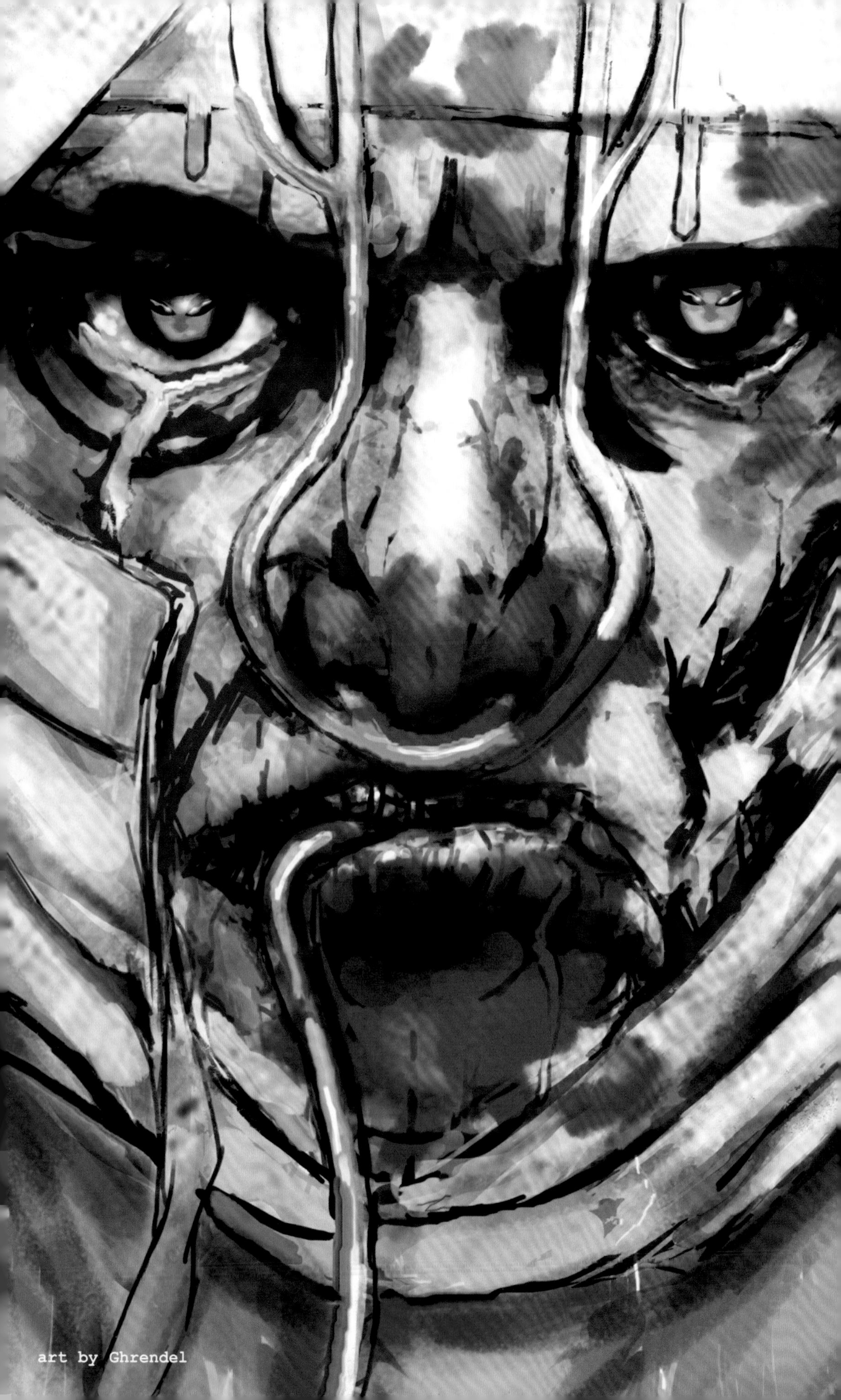
art by Ghrendel

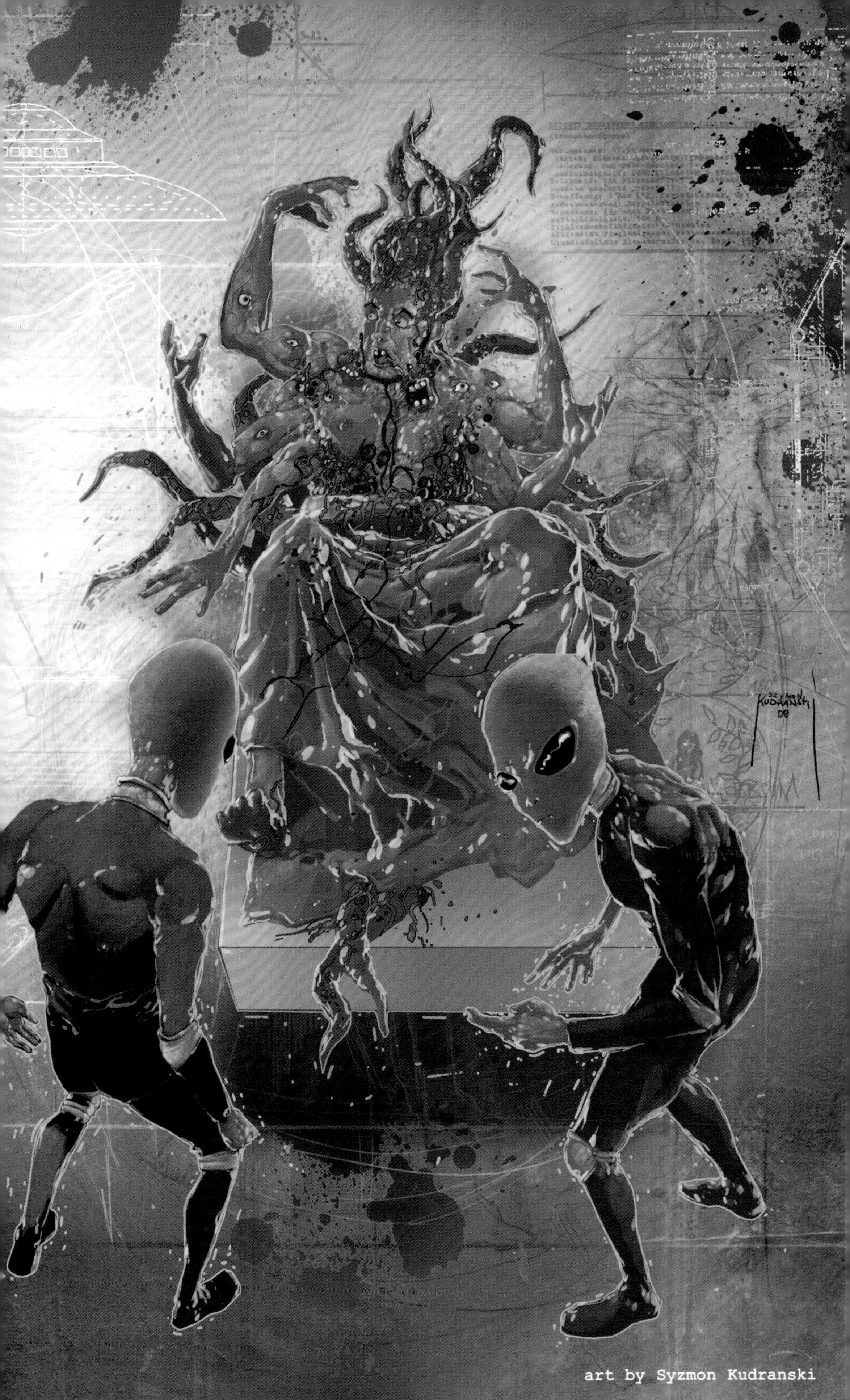

art by Syzmon Kudranski

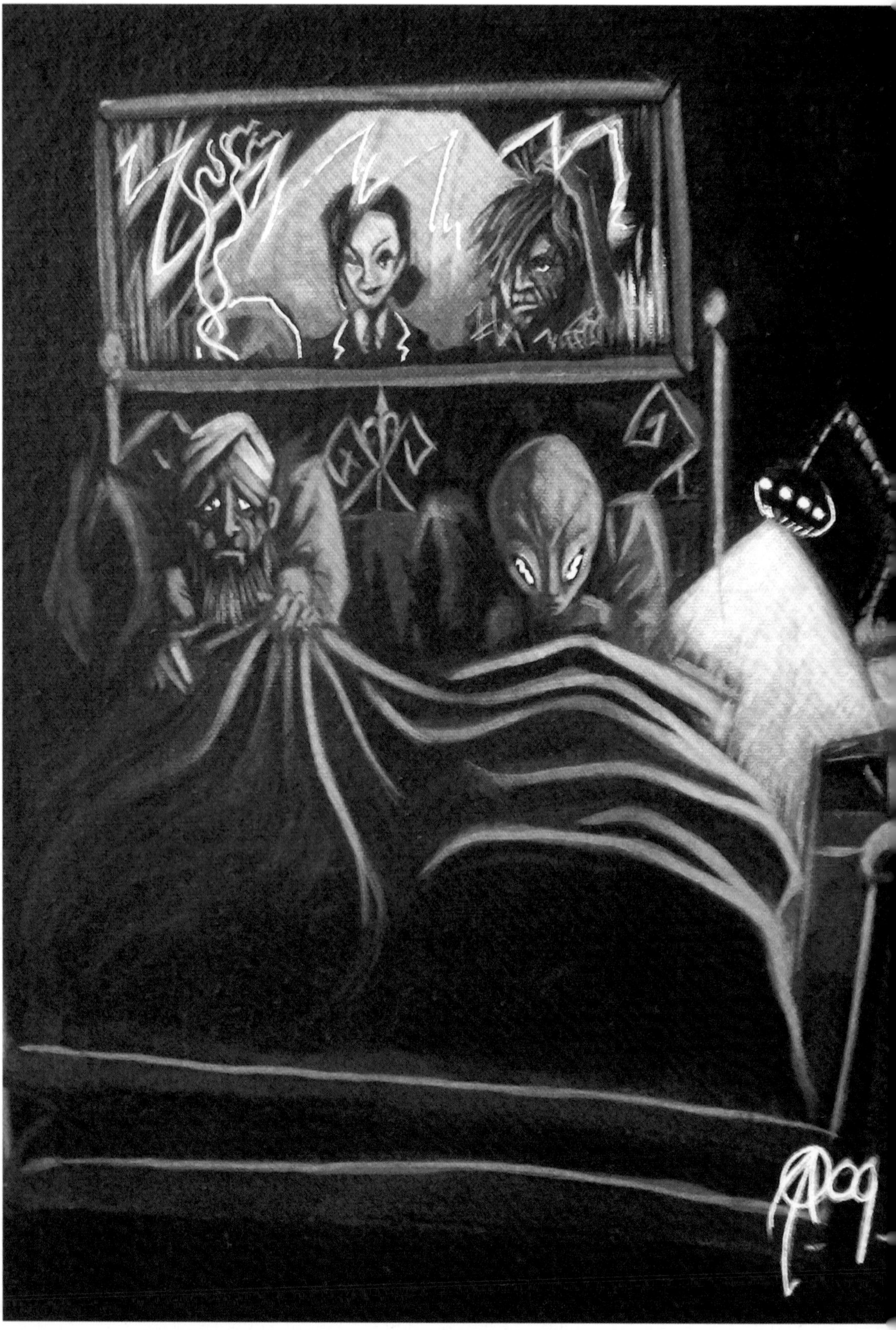

art by Carl Rothwell

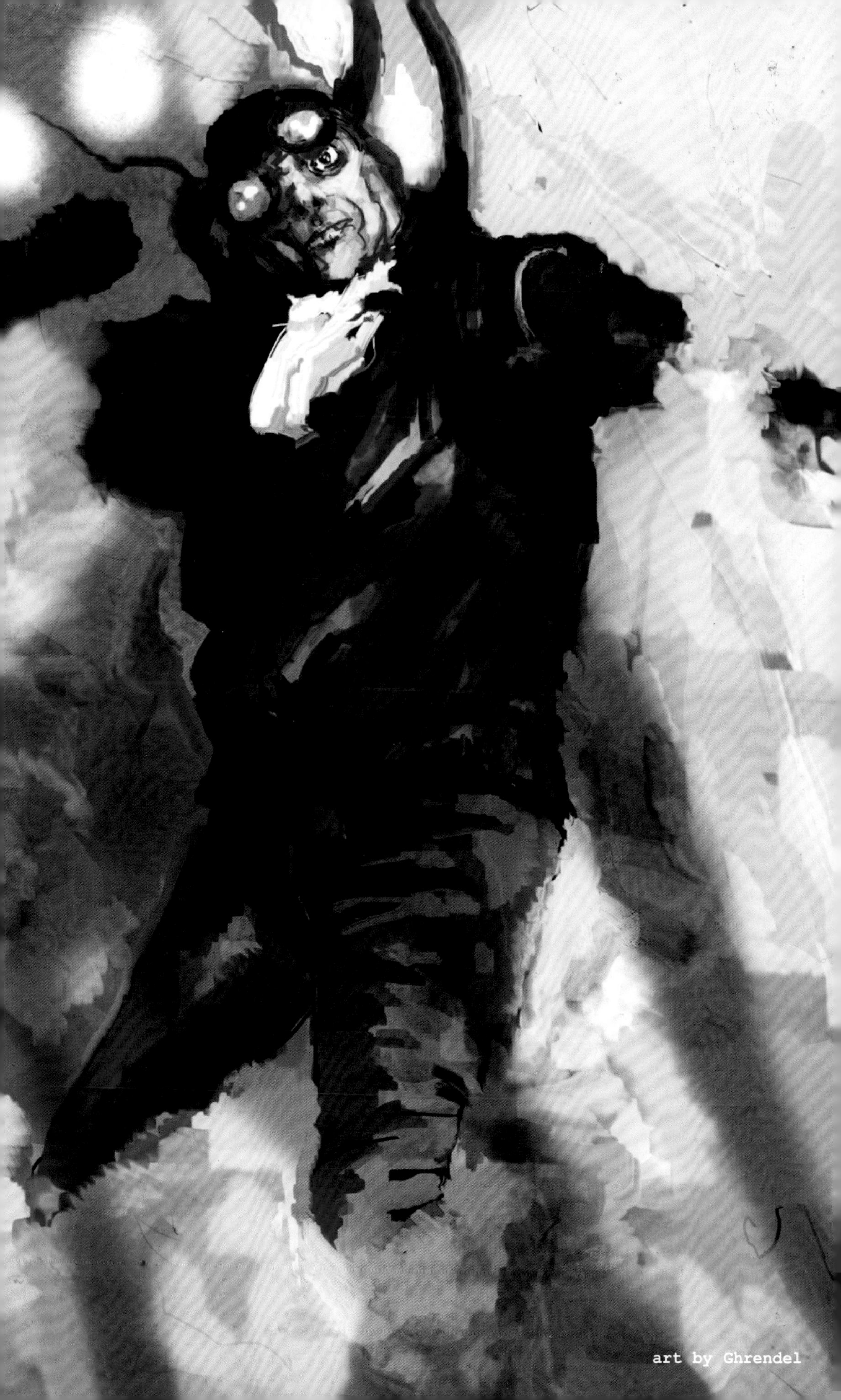

art by Ghrendel

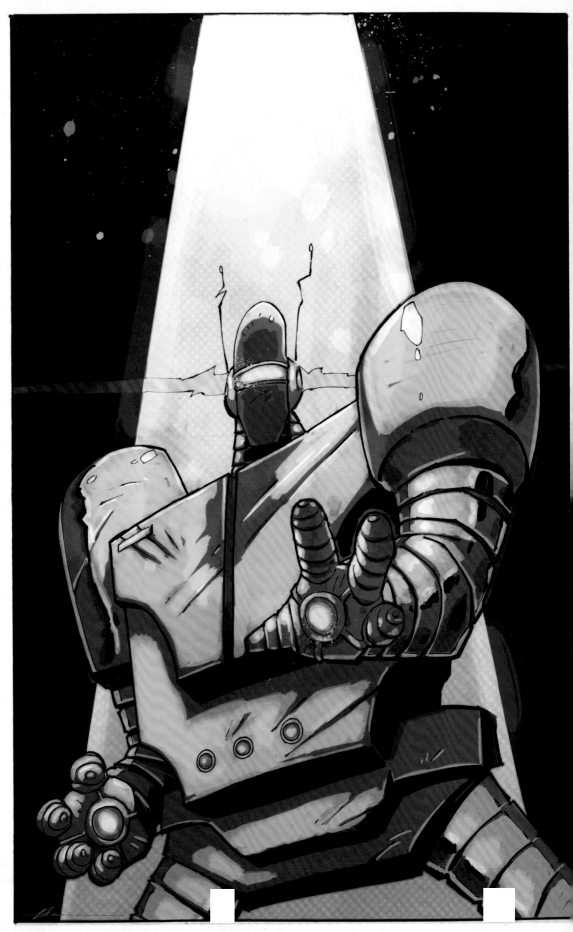

art by Pat Parnell

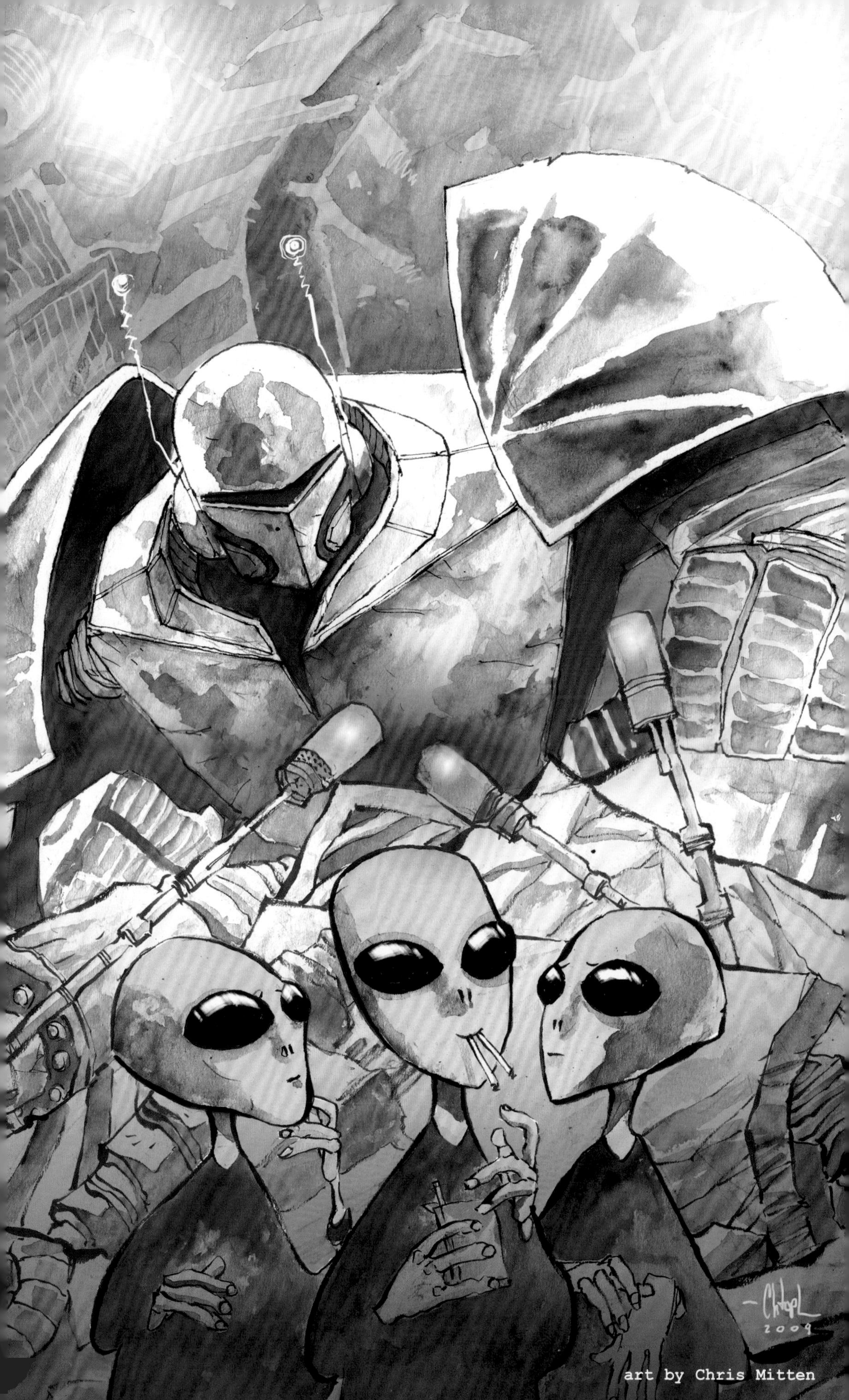

art by Chris Mitten

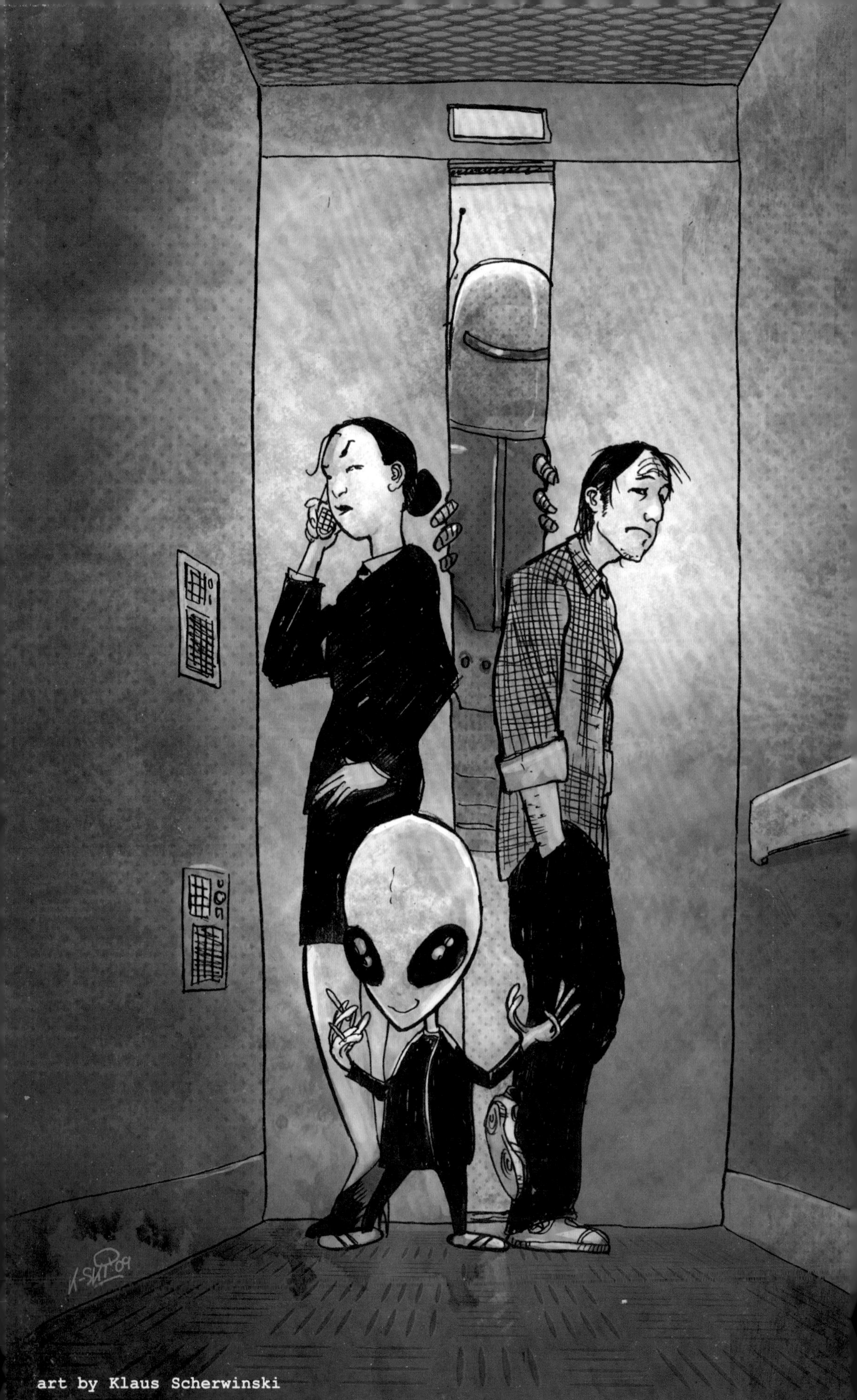
K-SKI '09

art by Klaus Scherwinski